Cooling Red Hot Relationships

Cooling Red Hot Relationships

New Ways Couples Can Defuse Anger and Keep the Passion

Shari L. Kirkland, Ph.D.
and Lorel L. Lindstrom, Ph.D.

New Horizon Press
Far Hills, NJ

Requests for permission should be addressed to:
New Horizon Press
P.O. Box 669
Far Hills, NJ 07931

Kirkland, Shari L., and Lindstrom, Lorel L.
    Cooling Red Hot Relationships: New Ways Couples Can Defuse Anger and Keep the Passion

Interior Design: Susan Sanderson
Jacket Design: Wendy Bass

Library of Congress Catalog Card Number: 2003115372

ISBN: 0-88282-245-4

New Horizon Press

Manufactured in the U.S.A.

2007 2006 2005 2004 / 5 4 3 2 1

Author's Note

This book is based on our research, a thorough study of the available literature and experience counseling patients, as well as our clients' own real life experiences. Fictitious identities and names have been given to all characters in this book in order to protect individual privacy and some characters are composites.

Contents

Part 2: Solutions

Foreword

Cross-cultural research indicates that all over the world people identify anger as the one emotion that does the most damage to interpersonal relations. Also, anger is the emotion least likely to elicit empathy and understanding from others. The message is really clear, when you get angry, people do not feel sorry for you and they keep their distance. Our research on anger indicates that anger, and anger disorders, are studied less than other distressing emotions such as anxiety or depression. So mental health professionals know less about anger than they do about other emotional problems. Therefore, they understand anger less and have fewer options available to treat anger problems.

This does not mean that anger is not a frequent problem for people. Whenever I conduct continuing education workshops for mental health professionals on anger, I have the audience become aware of just how common anger problems are in marriages and families. I ask them to think of the last family or marital therapy session they have had, and to raise their hands if anger was the most important emotional problem discussed in that session. Consistently, over ninety percent of the audience raises their hands. This suggests that most family problems that end up in therapists' offices revolve around anger.

Lorel Lindstrom and Shari Kirkland have provided a helpful book to address this real need. They clearly explained how anger problems differ from other emotional disorders. During anger episodes, people tend to focus on how the world or others "should" have behaved differently. Usually angry people hold on to these beliefs so strongly that they forget to evaluate the effect their anger has on them, the problem they wish to solve, or their interpersonal relationships. This aspect of anger leads people to stay angry. I always say that people who are angry do not come for therapy. They come for supervision. The know the problem resides in the person who is the target of their anger. They have tried many things to change that person and failed. Now they ask the therapist for advice on how to change the other person, not to change their anger. People will not change a problem they do not think they have. Lindstrom and Kirkland point out the destructive nature of anger on relationships and if you attend carefully to chapter two of this book, you may become aware of how your anger hurts your relationship and start focusing on changing the only thing you can change—yourself.

Lindstrom and Kirkland explain the role of people's thinking and expectations in causing their anger. According to the principles of rational Emotive Behavior Therapy, upon which this book is based, most anger results from absolutistic thinking that the people or the world must be the way you want it to be. Anger is a primitive emotion that first appears in infancy. Like infants, angry adults want what they want NOW and cannot imagine the world failing to comply with their demands. Many people do not get this concept because they cannot believe that a grown person would be so stupid as to think that the world has to be the way she or he wants it to be, rather than the way it is. Well, the next time you get angry, listen to yourself. Do you say things like, "I can't believe that so and so did that?" Or, after your spouse or mate has done the same thing that has angered you for years, do you say, "How could he or she have done that?" Well, the answer is, easily. They have been doing it for years. And if you acknowledged that they act the way they do, you would have expected them to behave as he or she did rather than how you wanted them to behave.

Lindstrom and Kirkland not only point out how this type of irrational thinking operates, but they identify numerous strategies to get you to change. The good news is that treatment of anger works. You do not have to be stuck in a hostile relationship. Read this book and learn how changing your thinking and your behavior does overcome your anger and leave you open to a more rewarding relationship.

—Raymond DiGiuseppe

(Dr. DiGiuseppe received his Ph.D. from Hofstra University and completed his Post Doctoral Fellowship at the Institute for Rational Emotive Therapy with Dr. Albert Ellis. The author of over sixty journal articles and co-author of five books, Dr. DiGiuseppe currently is a Professor of Psychology at St. John's University and Director of Professional Education at the Institute for Rational Emotive Therapy.)

Preface to the
Revised and Expanded Edition

Since we wrote our first book on dealing with anger in relationships in 1998, several significant changes have occurred in our country and in the world. For Americans, the attack on the World Trade Center and other United States facilities in 2001, the continuing menace of terrorism, the war in Iraq and serious problems with the economy as well as an escalating unemployment rate are all powerful factors which impact our lives and intimate relationships. While each of these factors is very grim in its own right, the combined effect of all of them places enormous additional stress on couples. In view of the additional challenges that these issues pose and the danger they at times create within close relationships, we felt these issues important to address.

We hope that you will find our new book of special usefulness if today's tensions are making your intimate relationship more volatile. It is our firm conviction that for couples to live well and thrive emotionally, we must think and behave in ways that are rational and compassionate even in chaotic times. We then give our relationship the best chance at defeating all of the other negative forces affecting our lives.

Acknowledgments

Thanks to my parents, Dan and Sumatra, my first and most significant teachers. Their belief in my ability, and active pursuit of their own aspirations laid the foundation for my achievement. Thanks to my sister, Diane, who taught me to have the courage to dream, and to my brother, Mark, who taught me about the discipline necessary to bring those dreams to fruition. Mostly, thanks to Infinite Intelligence, without which nothing would be possible.

Shari L. Kirkland, Ph.D.

This book is the fruit of the inspiration given to me by Jim Lathrop, who taught me how to be a therapist, and Ray DiGiuseppe and Albert Ellis, who provided me with the tools to help people. I wish to thank Karen Tabbah for her insights and help while proofreading the manuscript, and Joan Dunphy for believing in us. Finally, I thank my wife, Martha, for being there for me in the caring and supportive manner that is so typical of her.

Lorel L. Lindstrom, Ph.D.

Prologue

You are both in charge of your relationship and the emotions you feel within the context of that relationship. What counselors do is really secondary therapy. We talk to you both, reason with you both, demonstrate ideas to you both, just as a good teacher or coach does for her pupils. But you are the ones who make the final decision to listen, try out the advice, and practice what is suggested. You are the ones who are the primary therapists. You are the ones in control. Everything else is secondary; it's input to be accepted or rejected by you both, analyzed by you both, and acted upon by you both. If you and your partner decide that what the teacher, coach or therapist suggests is reasonable and believable, and these are skills and knowledge that you both want to acquire, then you will accept, believe, and practice them. You will do the homework.

With enough work and practice on both your parts, you can eventually become your own therapists, in large part. Each of you will know what it is that you're doing wrong, and what to do to correct it.

Our goal, then, is to help both of you become your own therapist, to fix your emotional swings when you're upset. If you can fix yourself first, then you are taking the first step to fixing the relationship that is troubled by these emotional swings. It's very difficult to work on improving any relationship unless each of you is in emotional control of yourself first. Once you know that it is the thinking that is destroying your relationship, you can fix it, feel better, function better, and forge the kind of relationship you want and deserve. Each of you must accept responsibility for your own thinking, and change it. This is something only you can do and by doing so, you put yourself in control of your emotional life and the relationship you want to build together.

Reach inside, not outside of yourself to find the solution to your relationship problems. Remember, those solutions are found in your thoughts. Your thoughts and beliefs are the cause of your feelings, good or bad, and they control your behavior.

Part 1

Problems

Chapter 1

If the Shoe Fits:
Common Characteristics of
Partners in Angry Relationships

Relationship problems between lovers are the number one complaints in psychological clinics throughout the country: "She never wants to have sex anymore"; "He acts like I don't exist"; "We don't communicate; it's like talking to a wall." While people complain about many different problems with their significant others—problems with sexual intimacy, communication, lack of consideration— more often than not, these problems are merely symptoms of the real problem, which is, anger.

Besides the obvious rage, anger takes many different forms, and if anger is not addressed directly, it cannot be mastered. It's like prescribing painkillers for someone with a broken leg. Sure, she'll temporarily be more comfortable, but if the real problem isn't addressed, if the broken bone is not set, problems with the leg will persist.

Before moving on to an analysis of anger in relationships, it is important to note that there are no quick fixes in good self-therapy. Mostly, it is the result of a lot of work and practice. Even though we will address the role of socialization and early experience with anger, you and your partner are not doomed by your pasts; you always have the capacity to change your thinking and behavior. Your present problem is the result of your present philosophies or viewpoints of life—not past childhood traumas or fouled up parents. People are going to feel the way they think and as a result, react to situations based on these feelings.

Is Anger at the Core of Your Relationship?

What is this thing called anger? What is it really about and when is it a real relationship problem or just a passing feeling?

Anger becomes an issue in our relationships when we want our partners or our relationships to change and we alone are unable to make that change happen. It's the feeling that comes about when we are confronted with the realization that there is a difference between what we want to control versus what we really can control. Angry people tend to feel as though they are out of control. They have too little control over themselves and never enough control over others. This need for control is at the core of anger so that angry people tend to share certain common characteristics that give rise to angry responses.

A need for control coupled with irrational thinking often manifests itself within an individual as impatience, judgmental attitudes, demanding behavior, perfectionism, possessiveness or a sense of humor. The important thing to recognize at this time is that because they share common characteristics, angry people also tend to complain about the same kinds of relationship problems. These individual characteristics manifest themselves within intimate relationships most frequently as jealousy, possessiveness, ineffective communication, punitive behavior and passive-aggression.

It is perfectly normal to see some of these behaviors in relationships from time to time. Even the most loving couples need time away from their partners, experience moments of discontent, think nasty thoughts about their partners and even argue. However, if these behaviors are more than occasional isolated events, that is, if these are consistent patterns that characterize your relationship, chances are you and, therefore, your relationship have a problem with anger. Any one of the following characteristics is enough to destroy a relationship. How many characterize yours?

Impatience and Low Frustration Tolerance

As practicing psychologists for the nation's largest HMO, we've treated thousands of couples. The first feature we've found in most angry partners is impatience. Angry people want things done right now, in fact, yesterday if at all possible. They usually feel that they can't tolerate any delay in getting things accomplished or solved. When a serious problem or conflict has to be resolved, adding the pressure of having to fix it immediately adds an enormous stress. This tends to escalate the situation at hand, thereby increasing the emotional disturbance they already feel.

The inability to wait or delay gratification is really a fraction of a larger problem, called *low frustration tolerance*. Most people have some type of low frustration tolerance. Usually, low tolerance for any type of frustration is most prevalent in situations involving physical discomfort, personal achievement or, most frustrating of all, relationship issues. Oftentimes the situation concerns the amount of effort that one partner thinks he should exert to get a certain result. Generally, people have some kind of idea about how much of anything they can tolerate at any given time. Sometimes they're aware of setting limits on this internal gauge, but often they aren't.

One couple we counseled that was faced with this problem was Heather and Jim. "I just hate my husband a lot of the time," Heather said tearfully. "He thinks I can't do anything as well or as fast as he can and never gives me credit for being able to do things by myself. I got so mad today when he was peeking over my shoulder that I told him 'back off, I can do it on my own.' Jim's just got to stop checking up on me and give me a chance to do some things on my own. If I make a mistake, I'll learn from it. I just can't take it any-more."

We had two problems to deal with here: Heather's feelings of anger and Jim's impatience. Heather needed to develop more con-structive means of handling her anger. We also had to help Jim to see that he needed to work on his impatience first and then that would give him, and us, a little more flexibility to creatively problem solve how he was going to deal with his impatience with his wife.

This same phenomenon, where the added pressure of urgent time constraints adds enormously to the stress and anger involved, also occurs in other areas. The term *discomfort anxiety* refers to the amount of stress a person tells himself that he can endure. An important manifestation of discomfort anxiety occurs when a person encounters unfair treatment or unjust behavior from someone else, especially a person with whom he has an inti-mate relationship. Not only does the partner have to deal with the issue of the unfair treatment itself, but on top of this, he tells him-self: *I've got to solve this problem right away. I can't wait another minute to deal with it. I've got to straighten my spouse out now!* The discomfort comes from the fact that he can't stand having to wait to solve the problem or get back to his partner about it later. Somehow, it must be dealt with immediately. When the irrationally angry partner makes this demand of himself, he places two expec-tations on himself: he has to get the problem, if not the relation-ship, fixed, and he has to do it immediately. This sort of urgency imposes even more pressure on a relationship that is already being strained by the original problem.

Couples place demands related to this discomfort anxiety on themselves all the time when they get upset: *I just can't stand the way my husband treats me; It's awful; I couldn't possibly sit down and do all the work on this house that would be required to satisfy her. It's just too much; I need to get this argument with my girlfriend settled right now. I can't wait another instant to figure it out!* In addition to adding to emotional distress and anger, this kind of difficulty in dealing with frustration can also potentially lead to addictive behaviors.

The limits we set are affected by many things: an arbitrary cutoff in our minds, our immediate physical status or comfort level and our beliefs about how the world should be. Some are momentous and others trivial. For example, Joe came to us one day stating, "My wife, Tracy, hasn't fed our cats for the last four days; I'm sick of being the one to wake up early and do it!" This is an instance of putting an arbitrary limit on a given behavior. Joe made up his mind that four days of neglect was the limit he could stand of his wife not feeding the cats. He could just as well have put a limit of one or ten or one hundred. Of course, Joe's real problem with Tracy may have nothing to do with the way she feeds the cats. Other dynamics may be at work.

In the immediate trigger situation, often the limiter is vaguely set on a momentary basis: "You must have put up the thermostat. I just can't stand the heat in this room right now. I've got to get out," is a very different statement from "I really don't like the house being this warm." The first statement may be inaccurate. His partner may not have adjusted the heat and he can stand it. The second statement is much more accurate. You truly don't like it but are tolerating it nevertheless.

Often people have general ideas, also, of how kindly the world must treat them, and how much wealth, recognition or prestige they deserve. For example, a person may see a man and an attractive young woman driving down the street in a Mercedes and tell himself, *Wow, those two really have it easy. I wish I had it as good as they do. I deserve to be that lucky too. I wish I had his cushy job and a gorgeous girl sitting next to me.* What he does not know is that the guy driving the Mercedes may be a cardiovascular surgeon, who spent the last twenty-five years of his life training to do his job, at which he works eighteen hours a day, with only four days off in the last two years.

It is another situation entirely if a partner in a relationship looks at the guy driving the red sports car and says to himself, *If I didn't have to support that spoiled brat and buy her everything she wants, I could afford that Mercedes,* and steps down hard on his own gas pedal. The person with low frustration tolerance tends not only to underestimate how much effort the other person had to put into getting where he is or to be inaccurate about his wife's demands interfering with his getting what he wants. He feels he is owed what others have gained as well. The point is, angry people tend to jump to conclusions without bothering to correctly assess the situation. They mistake their hypotheses for facts and act as if their theories are the same as reality.

The most common type of low frustration tolerance that people in close unsatisfying relationships often exhibit is impatience. Angry people often want to get things resolved or settled immediately. They put enormous pressures on themselves and others to get them fixed. This is especially true in interpersonal relationships. Experiencing impatience sets the angry partner up to fight or stage a scene because of his or her heightened emotional state and hyper-reactivity. If you're an angry partner, ask yourself next time, *Do I really need to solve this right away?* Generally, the answer will be no. Ninety-nine out of one hundred situations don't need to be resolved right away. Sure, there are emergency situations in which we have to act immediately, such as a child running out in front of a speeding car, but generally we have some time in which to react, think and act.

Judgmental Attitudes

Another feature that angry people in relationships share is judgmental attitudes. Angry people tend to be extremely hard on themselves and on other people, especially those with whom they are intimately involved. They are constantly grading, judging and ranking themselves and their significant others on some internal perfectionist scale that is invariably difficult to score well on. As if this judging wasn't bad enough, they tend to despair, feel hopeless and reject themselves when they fail to measure up. This failure to measure up can lead to self-esteem problems. The angry person's self-esteem becomes fragile, because it is dependent on self-judgments that are based on a very demanding self-rating scale. Although angry people apply this scale to their partners as well, they reserve the harshest judgments and tests for themselves.

Usually these judgments revolve around some kind of action that has occurred, or will occur, in either the angry person himself or in his significant other. One of the mistakes that angry people frequently make is to confuse the action with the person. Instead of judging simply the act in question as bad or wrong, he or she judges the whole person to be bad.

Pete came to our office last month, complaining bitterly about his girlfriend. "She talks back to me all the time and really aggravates me. She has really turned into a bitch and I feel like breaking up with her. That would teach her!" Pete forgets that the person is not the same as the action. Even if his girlfriend is acting out in a way that infuriates him, that hardly qualifies her for the label of bitch.

If angry people could just focus on the undesirable action, instead of the person involved, they would resolve not only many of their conflicts but their own conflicted feelings as well. Instead, they generalize that a particular incident is indicative of the whole person and jump to some overall rating of that person's character. In an angry person's eyes, it's very easy to be a bitch, because many angry people have very refined senses of what's just and fair. They are exquisitely sensitive to slights, no matter how small. Consequently, it is very easy to fail on this fairness scale. One of the things an irrationally angry person tends to forget is that the world can indeed seem to be unfair. In reality, the world is neither fair nor unfair—it just is. Fairness ratings are imposed by humans; the world itself is oblivious to notions of equality and justice. The truth is, the world runs on the basis of physical laws and principles, not on the basis of fairness. As a matter of fact, why should the world be fair? Fairness is a human concept, not an inherent law of the universe.

Once people in close relationships start forming opinions on particular actions, instead of placing labels on their partners based on isolated incidents, they free themselves from the trap of evaluating the other person's whole character on the basis of a single act. As the angry partner starts to see that humans are fallible and imperfect creatures just trying to get along as best as they can in the world, they begin to see that for the most part there are no saints or sinners, no good or bad people, just people with a wide range of characteristics, some of which are good, some bad. Some people have more good characteristics than others but their essential worth as human beings remains the same. In fact, each of us is born with an equal amount of human worth, no matter what our sex, social status or ethnic heritage. People don't exist in hierarchies of human worth; they exist on a platform of togetherness. The way out of the judgmental and self-esteem trap is first to start accepting ourselves unconditionally, rather than judging ourselves. We should do this for two reasons: because we exist and because we decide that each of us is valuable. Otherwise, we place ourselves in that self- esteem/self-judgment trap.

We can judge our behaviors all we want and strive to improve faulty traits, while stubbornly refusing not to judge ourselves. Once we've rationally refrained from judging ourselves, it is easier to stop judging the person we are involved with, because the same principles apply to others as apply to ourselves. When we stop generalizing, we are taking a step toward dissolving angry relationships and building satisfying ones.

Related to the tendencies to judge right from wrong is an intractable perspective about unfairness. Angry people are often unaware of the irrationality within their viewpoints. Yet their beliefs and viewpoints are once again critical to the situation. Usually, some kind of *catastrophizing* goes into a judgment. That viewpoint is often seriously out of whack. Visualize, for example, a farmhouse. How do you see it? Are you looking at it from the front yard, from the rear garden, from the side of the house, from the sky looking down at it or from a great distance away? The point is that you're looking at it from one perspective and not as a whole. Whenever you are involved in a discussion with your partner and you find yourself getting upset, stop for a few minutes and examine your viewpoint or thoughts on the topic and try to figure out what your perspective is, and what angle you are missing.

We often ask angry couples who are bitterly complaining not only about each other but usually also about the unfairness in the world, "You're a pretty bright person, right? What about all the stupid people out there in the world? You're much smarter than they are, yet we don't hear you whining and complaining about how unfair that is." Often, this humorous aside gets them to see some light! Our task is to help people see that unfairness does exist in the world and that we all had better accept it and learn to cope with it as best we can, getting as much pleasure and happiness as possible. You alone are responsible for your own happiness.

When people are involved in relationships in which they are treated unfairly, they can be passive and do nothing about it. This behavior implies acceptance of the treatment, with no objections to it. The unfair treatment will likely continue because there is no feedback loop, and the ulcers and migraines of both parties just continue to get worse. Or, the person treated unfairly can vent the anger freely, go into a rage and let the other person know the extent of his or her anger, and demonstrate how strong and controlling he or she is. Neither reaction really works if what that person seeks is a satisfying relationship. In the one case, anger is internalized and hidden beneath the surface. In the other, the controller tends to escalate the situation and make the problem worse rather than solve it, and elicit anger, concealed or not, from the partner. Finally, a partner can behave assertively when he or she is treated unfairly. In order to act assertively, however, the partner needs to manage his or her own anger first. This enables him to handle the situation calmly and effectively. Once again, it's best to start from within rather than from without. Effective anger management begins with each partner examining his or her own thinking first.

Of the three options in reacting to an unfair situation—passive acceptance, aggressive behavior and assertive behavior—assertive behavior is the one most likely to help you to correct the unfair situation. Assertive behavior optimizes the chances of finding a satisfactory solution with your partner because it helps minimize the conflict, as well as the other person's defenses. The key to acting assertively is anger management. You have to get your own hot emotions under control in order to act assertively and rationally. Once again, the first order of business is to work on your own anger prior to trying to rectify the problem with your partner.

Demanding Behavior

Another negative characteristic many angry people in relationships share is that of *demandingness*. Demandingness means that one or both people need to have things their own way. Her significant other must, has to, ought to or should do what she wants. The world must give to him and conduct itself in a way that best meets his own concept of the universe.

A good example of an individual expressing demanding behavior is Ann, who joined one of our anger groups. Ann was constantly angry with her husband, Carl. Although she rationalized about Carl's stubbornness and intractable behavior, the real reason she was angry was because Carl had the audacity to disagree with her on important matters: he had different ideas about rearing their children, managing the family finances and how often they should have sex. No matter how much Ann argued, yelled at or berated her husband, he stuck to his guns. She ended up being incredibly angry with him most of the time because he refused to see things the way she demanded that he should.

When they joined our group, Ann was on the verge of divorcing Carl. She had never encountered a person who so resolutely disagreed with her on nearly every subject. In talking with her, it became apparent that Ann always had her way growing up as an only child and had always been the decision-maker in her previous intimate relationships with men. She really had no experience with people who significantly disagreed with her. Much of the focus in Ann's therapy revolved around the idea that other people are entitled to their thoughts and opinions too and that if she was going to make this marriage work, she needed to work on accepting and respecting others' perspectives. This was a novel concept to her, but she quickly caught on and worked on it tirelessly. She came to realize that Carl wasn't intentionally disagreeing with her for argument's sake, but genuinely had different opinions, opinions that she respected. As a result, her anger diminished greatly and her relationship with Carl improved drastically.

Although some of us develop a set of distorted truths or philosophies about the world, probably a lot of our demandingness stems from childhood. Being demanding as a child gets us what we want, generally. When we're hungry, we cry and get fed. If we don't get fed right away, we just cry louder. When our diapers are dirty, we cry again. Why not, it worked when we were hungry? When we're tired or just unhappy with the world in general, we cry again and get comforted and held. The typical family with an infant child is demand-driven: the child demands incessantly by crying, and the parents respond by tending to the child's needs. It works. It also tends to foster a behavioral pattern that lasts well beyond infancy.

Since crying, complaining, and whining worked so well for us as babies in our first personal relationships, we may consciously, or most likely subconsciously, use it later on to get what we want in our adult personal relationships. After all, if we just scream loud enough and make enough of a fuss, we'll probably get our way once again. In some relationships, this fussmaking is refined further to include other things in life, such as our demands about what is fair and just.

When a freeway driver cut Bill off one day a short time ago, he screamed invectives out the window and turned to his wife and began to scream about her inadequacies. To himself and later to our group he said, "People shouldn't treat me this way." In other words, he was using the "kick the dog" rationale.

Often, the anger that we direct towards a significant other, in reality arises from anger at ourselves. We can get enormously mad at ourselves about things we did or didn't do that turned out badly and, in turn, take our discontent with ourselves out on our partners. A client of ours, Pete, was playing a very competitive doubles tennis game several summers ago when an overhead smash was hit in his direction. His first impulse was to duck, but instead he went for the ball, thinking he could return it. The ball hit him in the left eye, causing a lot of pain and some residual damage. On many occasions since then he has said, "I shouldn't have gone for the ball. I should have ducked!" Well, obviously, if he had known then what he knows now, he would have ducked. So when he tells himself that he should have ducked, he's basically telling himself that he should have known how the event was going to turn out, that he should have been able to foretell the future. How can that be? The answer is, it can't. He did the best he could at the time with the information that he had and it turned out less than desirably. About the best he can do is remember it and learn from it. Like the overhead shot which Pete should have ducked rather than gone after aggressively, there are thrusts and parries by one partner to another in a relationship. Some are innocent and may be lobbed back safely. Others, however, are dangerous shots. The trick is to quickly discern the difference and if you can't, know how to deal with the consequences. One way to do so is to change demands into preferences. In Pete's case, "I wish I had ducked" leads him to feel disappointed or perhaps irritated or annoyed, but not clinically depressed or furious with himself. In a like manner, changing demands into preferences in terms of how we view other people's conduct leads us to behaviors which focus on compromise, negotiation, and requests. We can then decrease the chances of other people getting angry and digging their heels in against our demands, while at the same time increasing our chances of persuading people to our way of thinking.

Perfectionism

Another trait we have taken notice of in the many couples we have counseled, one which plays a large role in the personality characteristics of angry people involved in unsatisfactory personal relationships is *perfectionism*. There are many reasons why this is so, but in our experienced opinion, the main reason is that perfectionism is tied in with the angry partner's self-esteem. We may rationalize, *if I can just do things perfectly, the important person in my life will love and respect me* or, *If he truly cares about me, he will behave perfectly towards me and never do anything unfair or thoughtless to me.* This perfectionist outlook usually involves trying to live up to a goal that someone else has set for a person, rather than one he has set for himself. The goal then becomes one of trying to avoid criticism from others by living up to their goals or perceived goals. Angry people also tend to expect perfection from themselves and their partners, thus their self-esteem, like perfectionists, is largely based on what other people think of them. Living up to the expectations of others is an elusive phantom that is by all accounts not worth chasing. Angry people must resolve their need for other people's approval to feel good about themselves.

If there is a conflict, the other partner must see things their way: angry people are very threatened by differences of opinion. They are threatened because their self-esteem depends on agreement with them on things that they consider important. If the other person disagrees, the angry person concludes that the other partner thinks poorly of them and doesn't value them. Conclusions like these produce further angry and upset feelings.

Basically the attitude of *I'm completely right and you're completely wrong* indicates feelings of self-righteousness and justifiableness in the perfectionist's position and intolerance towards the other partner's viewpoint. This perfectionistic attitude doesn't leave much room for compromise or negotiation, as the other person is going to feel defensive and trapped.

Possessiveness

Another typical characteristic of close relationships, we've found, is that as two people become closer emotionally, they tend to also become more possessive of each other and demand better and better behavior from each other, with each person having the ideal of perfection in his or her mind. There is an old saying that when a man and woman get married, the man thinks the wife will never change from the way she was when they were dating, while the woman thinks that after they're married, she'll be able to change the man. They both end up being wrong. Here, it's sort of a new twist on the old idea that familiarity breeds contempt. When a partner inevitably makes a mistake, as we all do, the angry person demands corrective measures. She then tries to control her significant other any way she can. If her control efforts fail, anger is the typical result. Our culture promotes the idea that for a man to be strong and masculine, he must be in control. Men who subscribe to this philosophy often find that they feel weak if they allow their partners to do things their own way or request certain behaviors of their significant others in non-demanding ways. Although we do not deal with such relationships in this book, in some instances, a sense of control, combined with certain egotistical attitudes and unresolved anger, can potentially lead to violence. In such cases, the ultimate control in the angry partner's mind is the other's submission and, failing that, in the most extreme cases, his or her death. Their logic becomes so twisted and their self-esteem so fragile that the angry partner actually would rather have his partner dead than out of his control and acting in a way that is contrary to his singular view of the universe. We've all seen such situations highlighted in the media. We hear about estranged spouses killing their partners because they couldn't make the spouses stay with them. It is important to note that anger and violence are related, but not causal. Even when angry to the point of rage, we always have choices about how to act.

The four main kinds of thoughts people tend to get when they're angry involve low frustration tolerance (e.g. *I can't stand it when she does that*), judging and damning (e.g. *He's a terrible person because he did that and deserves to roast in hell for eternity*), catastrophizing (e.g *It's awful when she does that*), and demanding (e.g *I forbade her to do that*). Each partner should examine each situation for its own consequences and specific ethics, while being as flexible as possible in incorporating all of the facts of the case.

A Sense of Humor

We've been talking of negative qualities angry people and couples have in common. Another quality we've found that angry people often have is a sense of humor. We don't know why exactly this is true, but we've found it to usually be the case. Perhaps the reason is that angry people tend to be very responsive or reactive to situations around them, both good and bad. Their readiness to laugh, as well as to fight, might be partly explained by this physical state. In any event, the fact that angry people often tend to laugh readily is a good thing. Humor is a major ally in the ability to modulate anger and other dysfunctional emotional states. It's a powerful anti-anger tool for couples to use as they seek to defuse a potentially "hot" situation.

Humor helps us to put things in perspective when we're thinking in grandiose, absolute, non-scientific and intolerant ways. Thinking in such ways tends to promote anger and a sense of specialness, whereby we see ourselves as the center of the moral universe. Using humor helps couples to not take things and life too seriously. When we're treated unfairly in a relationship, humor helps us to avoid acting passively, which promotes anxious, inhibited, and indirect behaviors or aggressively, which fosters hostile, rigid and punitive behaviors towards others. Humor can help restore equilibrium to a relationship which is off balance.

Chapter 2

The Many Faces of Anger in Relationships: How Anger Affects Your Behavior and Sabotages Your Relationships

Anger is an emotion that most people would rather not experience. The word itself comes from the Latin root *angere*, which means to strangle. In modern terms, it is defined as a strong feeling of displeasure and usually of antagonism. Fury, rage and wrath are included as synonyms. Webster's dictionary defines anger as "an intense emotional state induced by displeasure...at what one considers unfair, mean or shameful...[and] a desire or intent to revenge or punish the source of that anger."

Yet, even though anger is an undesirable emotion, it carries an important message, a message that is sometimes indecipherable to both sender and receiver. Through hostility and rage it conveys untold hurts, unmet needs and desires and violated rights.

In some couples, anger results in rage acted out, in others, the anger submerged under the surface results in a cold, distant relationship. This is often the case when one partner is unable to express anger.

In other cases, however, the inability to express anger is not the problem; rather it is the red-hot way anger is vented. Either way, suggesting a quick fix, as many self-help books on the market do, does not work in the long run. The underlying and real reasons for simmering hostility and not only the immediate trigger for a particular argument must be uprooted and dealt with by both partners. Only in this way can a relationship be healed. Anger often leaves the person experiencing it in an intellectually and behaviorally vulnerable state that tends to overpower and hinder him from coping well with his environment. When a person is angry, he's operating from a limited set of data. This tends to produce distortions and often results in flawed thinking. An angry person has difficulty thinking of other things, feeling other emotions and behaving in rational, non-angry ways.

The angry person in a relationship often feels overwhelmed, overpowered, helpless and out of control. She is upset with herself and her partner. Is anger contagious? In some ways it is, because it tends to elicit angry, defensive reactions from the other person, who automatically gears up to protect himself. Soon, both parties involved get a little "crazy," and the fires of anger are stoked to red-hot levels. Passion takes over, reason goes out the window and all real communication stops, thus preventing any real attempt at problem resolution.

Terms many people use to describe anger are often inadequate and imprecise. For instance, *annoyance* implies a condition where the person is bothered or concerned by "persistent petty unpleasantness" (Webster 1986) and, by the same token, *irritation* (as defined in Webster) implies a state of unpleasantness or excitation that is similar to annoyance in nature. It's important to note that in everyday language, when we use the terms *annoyance* and *irritation*, we mean something considerably different than anger.

These lesser emotions, in terms of the strength of feelings, suggest an emotional frame of mind that puts us more in control and causes us to be less upset than does anger. Secondly, they imply a set of attitudes and behaviors that are less cognitively and behaviorally "hot" than those that occur when anger is experienced. When we're angry, we feel physiologically "hot," both in our heads and in our bodies. When we're annoyed, we feel concerned, perhaps "warm," but we don't feel overtly hostile, overwhelmed, helpless, or frustrated. We still feel in control, can think pretty clearly and interact with others appropriately.

You might think that the only traits the angry couples we see have in common are pent-up feelings of hostility toward each other. However, in our work with hundreds of angry couples, we've found that this isn't true. Angry people share not only common characteristics such as those noted in the previous chapter, but also certain behavior patterns. More importantly, we've found that most of the time these very same characteristics have a big impact on both the arousal and intensity of their anger. As we will also show, thinking in faulty ways increases the likelihood of anger. The term *irrational anger* is used in this book to reflect the type of anger that faulty thinking produces. It stems from our failed attempts to control people and things that we cannot control. We will also demonstrate that, in the majority of situations when partners get angry with each other, it is the result of faulty thinking. The characteristics of angry people—low frustration tolerance, judgmental attitude, demanding behavior and perfectionism—make them more likely to think in faulty ways, which can lead to harmful behavior patterns.

Signs of Angry Relationships

Rage

Anger is a common emotion. We may raise our voices, maybe even yell, curse, point fingers or slam a door or two—certainly not mature behavior. None of the above behaviors promote constructive dialogues about a problem or encourage possible solutions. Still, most relationships can tolerate an occasional outburst of frustration. Multiply these behaviors times ten and you have rage: screaming, invading personal space, pounding fists, throwing objects, name-calling. When your lover is in a rage, she looks like she's out of control. Her behavior looks like more than frustration—it looks like a threat.

It took Stacey two hours and fifteen minutes to get home. There was an accident on the freeway and she is certain that the ice cream she picked up at the store after work has melted. She walks into the apartment, groceries in hand, kicking the door shut behind her.

"What took you so long?" Daryl asks, his annoyed voice has an edge.

"Don't start with me. I've been working since eight o'clock this morning. Here's your damned ice cream," she retorts, slamming the grocery bag down on the counter top. "If I hadn't stopped for it, I probably would've missed rush hour."

Daryl softens, "Hey, I'm sorry you had such a lousy day."

"Oh, well, thanks. That makes everything okay," she says in a sarcastic tone. "Why is this place such a mess? You could have helped me out a little by straightening up. You know I've been working a lot lately."

"I've only been home for an hour myself. Besides, the place doesn't look that bad."

"That bad? That bad?" Stacey's voice becomes shrill. "How bad does it have to look before you get up off your lazy butt and do something? You were waiting for me to come home and clean! Does it look bad enough now? No? How about now?" She empties the grocery bag on the kitchen floor. "Is it messy enough for you to do something *now*?"

"Go to hell you bitch," Daryl shouts as he storms out of the apartment.

Fortunately, this episode did not have a chance to escalate into physical violence. The neighbors, hearing the yelling and thumping, called the police.

Both partners, had they been able to cool down, might have asked *What is really going on here?* In this scenario, Stacey's rage masks the real issue—her frustration over Daryl's limited contribution to running their household and inconsideration for her. Instead of Stacey coming up with some division of chores or Daryl thanking her for picking up his favorite ice cream, Stacey rages and Daryl misses the point, chalking up her anger first to commuter traffic, then to her being a bitch, before losing his own temper.

Jealous Behavior

We all know what jealousy is: it's when we feel suspicious of another's loyalty or faithfulness to us. Jealous feelings come up in the best of relationships since it is human nature to worry about losing people and things that are important to us. A little bit of jealousy can be flattering because it is like our partners saying, "I love you enough to be afraid of losing you to someone else," or "You're so wonderful, I'll bet that every other man/woman on earth would be with you if they got half a chance!" Some people find their partner's jealousy charming, since part of the message of jealousy is, *I love you and I value you.*

But what about Carrie who secretly searches Sam's wallet at the end of each day looking for unfamiliar phone numbers or Chip who constantly accuses his fiancée of eyeing other men when they're out together? This is where jealousy stops being flattering and endearing and starts being unhealthy and even harmful. This is when the message starts to shift from *I love you and value you* to *I don't trust you.*

What is really underneath these extreme forms of jealousy is insecurity and dependence, that is, fear of not being good enough for our partners to stay with us and fear that we would not be able to live a satisfying life without them. So what do many of us do when we're feeling intensely jealous? We try to control the circumstances to remove the threat of loss. For example, if you ask Carrie why she rifles through Sam's private stuff, her response goes something like this:

> Sam is really a nice guy, really sweet. Sometimes I think that I would just die without him—he makes me feel so important. But he also makes me furious. He's so naïve

and friendly. I mean, I don't think he even knows when a girl is coming on to him and if he does, it seems like he welcomes it. Hell, it took two months of chasing him before he realized that I didn't want to be just another pal. So I feel like I have to kind of watch out for him when it comes to other women. Maybe he thinks they're just being friendly, but I know what they really want…they want him. What would I do if I found something that I thought he shouldn't have, like someone else's number? I'd probably burn it. Life without Sam just wouldn't be worth living.

What we learn from talking with Carrie is that while she may or may not confront Sam if she found another woman's phone number in his wallet, she most certainly would destroy the number in hopes of eliminating at least one threat to her relationship. She all but says that if she gave Sam half a chance he just might find someone he likes more, so she had better hold on tight. Clearly Carrie feels entitled to violate his privacy as a way to deal with her own insecurities.

Possessive Behavior

Possessive behavior and jealous behavior are really quite similar, differing not so much in *how* we treat our partners since both lead to manipulative behaviors, but *why* we treat them this way. While jealousy is motivated by dependency and insecurity, possessiveness arises from a sense of entitlement and self-centeredness. Possessive people see their partners as subjects for them to rule or govern as they see fit. They act as if their lovers are on earth to serve them, not to be equal partners in a relationship. Possessive people try to control where their partners go, with whom they go, what they wear, what they say and do and many other aspects of their significant other's life. The problem is that no one can ever really control another, no matter how hard they may try. And, usually, the harder a person tries to control someone else, the more the other person will resist.

Some resist in a quiet way that seems pretty innocent on the surface—like the time your boyfriend forgot to keep plans with you after arguing with you earlier that morning. This is called *passive aggression*, that is, expressing anger by doing literally nothing. The silent treatment is another example of passive aggression where not speaking to your partner is a way of letting her know that you are angry. Others resist in very obvious ways like flat out refusing to do something or throwing a tantrum. No matter how one resists control, the result is always the same—a power struggle between the two of you with one trying to control the other and the other struggling to remain free.

Possessiveness inevitably leads to disaster. Since possessive people can never satisfy their need for control, they walk around in a constant state of frustration. Consider newlyweds Joy and Keith.

Joy and Keith had been dating a total of two years when Joy gave Keith a beautifully wrapped box. Keith was surprised to find a pager inside. He was hoping for a gold watch as a birthday present. When Joy saw Keith's confused look, she quickly explained, "With you carrying a pager, you'll never be more than a phone call away from me. . .you know, in case of an emergency or something." Keith just smiled. He thought that it was kind of cute, Joy wanting to be close to him and all.

Soon after, Keith noticed that Joy was paging him several times a day. When he called her it was never an emergency. Most of the time, Joy would just ask some silly question: "Where are you?" "Who are you with?" "What are you doing?" or "What time will you be home?" Keith became more concerned when the pages began to interfere with his productivity at work. He decided to talk to Joy that evening after they went out for dinner.

"Honey, I'm starting to have some problems at work because you're paging me too much. Remember, the pager is for emergencies only."

"Sure, Hon," Joy said, not even pausing to look up from her book.

Well, rather than backing off, Joy began to page Keith even more. Keith began to feel as though Joy was just trying to keep tabs on him. As Keith said to one co-worker, "I'm beginning to feel like a dog on an electronic leash." Out of frustration, and in hopes of teaching Joy a lesson, Keith stopped responding to her pages. At night, when Joy demanded to know why Keith didn't call, he always had an excuse handy: "I must have been out of range," or, "Oh, the batteries must have died," or, "There wasn't a phone around for miles."

Keith could see that Joy was angry. She felt that she had the right to know where he was every minute of the day but Keith prided himself on being his own man. He hardly knew what to say when Joy presented him with a cellular phone for Christmas.

In the example of Joy and Keith, it is clear that the games have begun. The power struggle is on with Joy's position being, "I'll make you accountable" and Keith's being, "You can't make me accountable." As noted earlier, the underlying issue is one of entitlement: *You're my boyfriend, and that gives me the right to know your every move!* Of course, in the worst case scenario, the need to control another leads to physical force and abuse. Such extreme forms of anger are beyond the scope of this book, though the final chapter provides some brief comments in this regard.

Communication Problems

Irrationally angry people are poor communicators. Good communication is based on a number of factors like identifying problems, talking about feelings without blaming others, listening, compromising and asking questions to make sure that you understand the other. A big part of irrational anger comes from the belief that the world and everybody in it should believe what that person believes, in effect, meeting all her needs and desires. When things don't go that person's way it feels as if something terrible has happened that must be corrected, that is, made to go the way the angry individual wants it. This person is not interested in listening to other opinions, compromising, or taking responsibility for feelings. Such a person usually has serious difficulties communicating with others, seeing everyday disappointments and frustrations as personal attacks that cannot and will not be tolerated. This is the *my way is the only way* kind of person. Their anger is extreme and takes the form of threats, demands and ultimatums that are delivered with hostility including yelling, cursing and other forms of abuse. And since anger begets anger, the situation snowballs until any remaining communication skills are lost.

Evan and Diane have been married for five years, much to their families' surprise. Everybody said it wouldn't last because of their religious differences—Evan being Jewish and Diane Baptist. But things had gone well, despite Evan's history of getting his way. Diane had learned early on that Evan was the prince of his family, the only boy. His special position earned him privileges and this showed in their marriage. When Evan didn't get his way, he became sulky and Diane had to admit that she usually gave in to his pouting. As a result, few of their disagreements had escalated...until now. They had finally reached a place where Diane didn't feel that she could just give in to Evan's demands. She was pregnant and Evan had decided on his own that their children would be reared in the Jewish faith:

"Look, you knew I was Jewish when we married," Evan rationalized.

"Yeah, and you knew that I was Baptist. What does that have to do with your decision that our children will be raised in the Jewish faith? We had agreed to discuss religion when we started a family. Now it appears that you made a decision that we should have agreed upon together without me. When did you change your mind? What happened?" Diane questioned.

"What's happened doesn't matter. All you need to know is the decision is made!" Evan's voice had a steel edge.

"Well, can't we talk about this? Let's think of some ways to blend the two or compromise," Diane replied calmly.

"Diane, there is no way to be Jewish and not Jewish at the same time. Maybe I always knew that and just didn't want to admit it. Anyway, you're pregnant, a choice had to be made and I made it. If I knew how much you disliked my religion, maybe I would have rethought this marriage."

With tears in her eyes, Diane screams, "How dare you question our marriage and accuse me of being anti-Semitic! I was open to talking about this, but with your attitude, I don't think so. This is *my* baby in *my* body and I've decided she'll be Baptist!"

This is a prime example of poor communication. Evan clearly did not enter into this dialogue with the idea of sharing opinions or feelings, but rather to make a stand. This isn't communication at all; it's a declaration. Evan clearly had some pretty strong opinions about rearing his children in the Jewish faith but kept them from Diane until the eleventh hour. His style of approach and inability or unwillingness to talk about the reasons for his decision left Diane feeling manipulated. Although she tried to stay focused on resolution, eventually Diane became frustrated and angry in response. As is so often the case with poor communication, this incident deteriorated into *personalization*, that is, an assumption that a statement made about an issue is really about us; for instance when Diane suggested a compromise on religion, Evan took that as a put down of his faith declaring, "I would have re-thought this marriage." Diane responds, "I've decided she'll be Baptist." The result: threats and rigid stances by both; Evan and Diane had both become demanding and irrational. They had reached an impasse, with no resolution in sight.

Punitive Behavior

Because irrationally angry people believe that things should go their way, they often think that they have the right to punish people who don't go along with their plans. It's not so much that they enjoy punishing their partners. They see it more as encouraging them to do the right thing—as defined by them. Punishment may take many forms ranging from passive aggression at one extreme to violent confrontation at the other.

Bill, who phones Alexis six or eight times a day, has begun an inquisition of her activities at work ever since she told him she had gone to lunch with a colleague. That's a good example of punitive behavior. When Alexis did not satisfy Bill's need for control, he shortened the leash so to speak, by quizzing her and becoming enraged when she was not at her desk.

As with possessive behavior, attempts to control a significant other through punishment usually don't work. Rather than become passive and agreeable he or she may instead become secretive or more rebellious—think about all of the systems in place to control prisoners—and less sympathetic to the underlying problem of their partner's increasing insecurity. One of two vicious cycles is likely to result when you try to control your partner through punishment. Either a cycle of alternate punishment by one partner and resistance by the other emerges or a pattern of abuse begins, since no one can remedy another's insecurity even if his or her partner does comply with his demands.

Subtle Covert Signs of Angry Relationships

Attempts to get and keep our partners under our thumbs, to make them do what we think they ought to do by forcing our will can cause hostility, resentment and sometimes rage. But anger is not always this obvious. Sometimes it enters through the back door.

Passive Aggression

To be passive-aggressive is to express anger literally by doing nothing. In extreme cases it takes the form of the silent treatment. This is the person who, when angry, has nothing to say until the anger has passed or the other person has given in. As with most forms of anger, there are also more subtle forms of passive aggression.

Marc and Delia had been married for four years and had one-year-old and three-year-old daughters. Their three-year-old, Dana, was having problems with tantrums for the past year and, after reading some books, the couple had agreed to use time-out to deal with the problem. Whenever Dana started to kick and throw things, whoever was available was to carry her to her room and place her in her time-out chair, checking on her every few minutes until she calmed down.

One night Dana had begun to throw a tantrum again and Delia put her on a time-out. Marc, however, had come home shortly after with a surprise gift for Dana and in his own excitement took his daughter off her time-out to enjoy her reaction to the gift. Delia felt that Marc had undermined her authority and, more importantly, that he had no sympathy for the fact that she had been dealing with Dana, who had been misbehaving, all day. Still, Delia didn't say anything. The next morning Delia made decaffeinated coffee for Marc's breakfast, conveniently forgetting that if he didn't have his morning caffeine he'd be groggy and tired for most of the day.

Marc never even knew that Delia was angry. It's unclear if Delia herself was even in touch with her anger. What is clear is that whether or not she really forgot to make regular coffee, Marc paid the price. Delia was able to express her anger without saying or doing anything overt. Like Delia, when a person is angry, she may find herself not talking or forgetting his or her partner's needs or preferences.

Physical Distance

Most of us like spending time with our lovers, from doing mundane things like running errands or watching television together to a night out on the town. Companionship is a very enjoyable and valuable part of relationships. Of course, it is natural that in the beginning of a relationship both people may forfeit time in the gym or with friends to spend with each other. As the relationship becomes more stable, we may settle back into our pre-relationship routines, spending somewhat less time together. Still, spending quality time together is a priority. But do you want to spend time with your lover when you're angry with her? When you're angry, do you want to hold hands while walking down the street, watch the sunset together, make love or go out to a romantic restaurant for a candlelit dinner? Probably not. Most of us want to get away from people with whom we are angry.

Karen and John have been married for thirty-three years and have three grown children who live on their own. Last year John learned that Karen was having an affair. Karen ended the affair and they decided to stay married since John had presumably forgiven her. One year later, however, Karen can't help but notice how little time they spend together. John decided to return to school, taking full-time classes in night school so that he is rarely home in the evenings and is always in bed before midnight. He has even enrolled in a tutorial on Sunday mornings so that they no longer go out to brunch together, as has been a tradition throughout their marriage.

Using all of his activity as a buffer, John is able to avoid Karen and sublimate whatever anger he may feel toward her. He is also able to punish her by withholding his company from her. Of course, such spousal neglect may come with a price of its own.

Substance Abuse

All of us have felt the discomfort of anger at one time or another. It is accompanied by the adrenaline rush and guilt for our evil thoughts. Whether anger is irrational or appropriate doesn't really matter, it is rarely an enjoyable feeling. Maybe you don't deal with your anger toward your partner very well, and don't see any reason to, since anger only makes things worse. Perhaps you would rather control the feeling or avoid it altogether. If you try to avoid anger, you may have found yourself using alcohol or drugs, even over-the-counter and prescription medications to help you calm down or forget your anger.

But in truth, alcohol and drugs only get in the way of coping with the things that make you angry because they prevent you from thinking clearly and communicating well and they disinhibit impulses. With alcohol and drugs you are more likely to do something thoughtless, that you would not normally do when clean and sober, and end up in even more trouble.

Steve was driving to work aggressively and recklessly, pounding on his horn, cursing at other drivers, rolling through stop signs and traveling one and one-half times the speed limit. Earlier that morning, Janet picked up their argument where they had left off the night before: Steve was not shouldering his share of the responsibility for their twelve-year-old son, Tommy. Just because the kid had cut school a couple of times Janet thought that some deep father-son discussion was in order. And order was the right word. She'd been on his back about this issue for weeks, but Steve didn't see what the big deal was. So the kid cut school every now and then—what red-blooded American kid didn't? Why did Janet always have to make such a big deal out of everything anyway? The woman was like a pit bull—she just wouldn't let go of anything. But worse than that, she was always finding some way to accuse him of not being good enough: he was too lazy to do his chores, spending too much money at the pub, etcetera. It was always something. It wasn't enough that he alone paid the bills.

Steve wasn't sure how much more of her nagging he could take. Sometimes when he felt this angry, he got scared that maybe one day Janet would say just the wrong thing at just the right time and he'd snap, lose control and even hurt her. He'd come close that one time a couple of months ago—actually grabbed and bruised her. Thank goodness he'd had a few drinks earlier that night. If he hadn't been relaxed who knows what might have happened! Steve thought about the scene he'd have to face at home later that day. It was clear he'd be stopping off at the pub on the way home to knock back a few. He had to take the edge off his fury. Then he could let Janet nag away without even hearing a word.

The quick fix of alcohol and drugs often feels good momentarily because it stops the hurt and causes problems to retreat from consciousness. It serves to distract people from issues they do not know how to constructively deal with. The problem is that the quick fix makes us forget that there is a problem that needs attention, patience and effort. Instead of facing the problem, we tuck it away, only to have it reemerge later in disguise. However, no matter what form it takes, if it is not dealt with, you will always have the same consequence in the end: destruction. In the above example, the chronic issue of Janet's unhappiness with Steve's irresponsibility in family matters remains the same, only the details change. That is, the specifics of Janet's complaints vary—last month it was Steve's forgetting dinner plans they had made—but the underlying issue is always Steve's lack of responsibility.

Even worse than problem avoidance, alcohol and drugs short-circuit the inhibitory center in our brains that controls impulses. You're much more likely to do all of those stupid things that you only think of doing when you're clean and sober when you're drunk or high.

Steve thinks that a few drinks will calm him down, but in fact, the only time that he had ever raised a hand to Janet was when he was drunk. Alcohol and drugs may help us feel calmer at first, but then they cloud our judgment. They actually increase irrational anger by both tricking us into thinking that a problem or feeling that is avoided is a problem or feeling that doesn't exist and by decreasing our self-control. When we use alcohol or drugs, we actually give up some of the control that we really do have over anger.

Angry people also screw up their relationships by trying to control their anger in self-defeating ways. Rather than learn effective anger management skills, they choose a coping method that can actually disinhibit angry impulses. We all wish that we had more control than we do. If you could actually control your boss, your girlfriend, any unwanted feeling, the circumstances of life in general, it would be great. You could truly have it your way.

The difference between relationships where anger is mastered and those where it is destructive is that the partners in relations with mastery recognize the limits of their control. They do not routinely act as if they have more control over people and circumstances than they do. In contrast, these partners focus, more or less, on what they can do to effectively control themselves.

Our examples of obvious and subtle ways that anger is acted out in relationships are not exhaustive. There are as many different ways to express anger in relationships as there are personalities. These, however, are some of the more common relationship problems that we see in our work. The reality is that most relationship problems involve different combinations of characteristics and behaviors.

Excessive Control

What is the one behavior that Carrie, Joy and Evan have in common? They're all determined to get their ways. What is the hallmark of angry relationships? The answer is the same—excessive control. Angry people try to control their partners through jealous behavior, possessive behavior, punitive behavior, including withholding conversation and physical affection, and abusive communication, to name just a few tactics. Angry relationships are playgrounds for power struggles where partners attempt to gain control over each other. It is impossible to truly control someone else. Beyond that, most people don't like to be controlled. So, the harder you try, the more difficult your partner becomes.

Partner Homework

1. Of all of your friends and family members, identify the one per
    son who seems most angry to you. How do you know when that
    person is angry? What does he or she do or not do? How do you
    react to that anger? How does the anger affect your relationship?

2. Now answer the questions in #1 in terms of how they relate to
    you. For example, how do you know when you're angry? What
    do you do or not do?

3. If you feel comfortable enough and in control of yourself, you
    might want to ask your partner how he or she experiences your
    anger. Use the same questions in #1.

4. What aspects of your own behavior would you like to have more
    control over? Be specific.

5. See if you can identify ways in which you'd like situations or
    people to be different according to your own ideas of how the
    world should be.

Chapter 3

It's Elementary:
The ABCs of Anger
Between Two People

Intense rage will normally make you stew *instead of* do
*when you encounter unfairness; and if you act while
enraged you will often fight foolishly and badly.*
—Albert Ellis

Connections

In our practice counseling angry couples, one of the first therapies
we suggest is that each partner get better in touch with his or her
own thoughts. In over thirty combined years of therapy sessions, virtually all the couples who come into our offices complain about
some sort of emotional disturbance or distance between them: "He
doesn't understand me." "She doesn't want to sleep with me." "We
don't even talk unless we're fighting about money, sex, everything."
Never once have we had a couple come to us complaining about how

screwed up each of their own thinking was. After all, most people view psychotherapy as a forum where only feelings are explored in depth. People generally aren't used to the idea that their thinking plays a very crucial role in how they feel about themselves and each other. Books, movies and television also tend to ignore the role that thinking plays in people's problems and relationships.

The Emotional-Intellectual Link

There are connections in the brain between our emotional selves and our intellectual or rational selves. Though there is much that we still have to learn about the brain, we do know this: our emotional responses stem primarily from the limbic system and the amygdala—a small, pea-sized organ located deep inside the brain. It is from these structures that our basic emotions including rage, anxiety and lust emerge. This system first developed in animals millions of years ago. The more advanced thinking part of our brain—the neocortex, or outer layer of brain cells—developed millions of years later. It is this outer layer which helps us to reason, calculate and think through complex problems and issues. Animals far down on the developmental scale, such as reptiles, do not have either a neocortex or much of a limbic system, therefore they are not very intellectual or emotional.

The more connections there are between the limbic system and the higher cortical centers, the more interaction, interplay and involvement each has with the other. For example, research indicates that there may be some sort of short circuit in the brain that allows emotions to drive a given action, without the intellect being given much of a chance to intervene. Let's say you're a water skier in Florida who suddenly sees a log in the river that looks like an alligator. You suddenly leap out of the way, your heart racing a mile a minute, before you have a chance to carefully look at the object and discover it was only a log and to calm down. The important point we would like you to recognize here is that you made an immediate decision which had a powerful emotional component to it, without being aware of using much of these thinking processes in the course of your actions. They are usually not thought of at a conscious level, like putting your car key into the car's ignition, but they can nevertheless be very powerful determining factors of behavior. A University of Iowa neurologist, Antonio Damasio, describes how these emotional components of action enable us to make choices that we might otherwise have trouble making. When Dr. Damasio worked with patients who had the connections severed between the emotional and intellectual parts of the brain, he found that they had trouble making choices. They were just as smart as before, but they couldn't make decisions.

Some impulses, such as anger, are much more difficult to control than others. This is probably because the brain emits a tremendous volume of chemicals, called neurotransmitters, such as adrenaline, that flood the action centers of the brain when under stress. If a person is already stressed, experiencing a physical state such as hunger, exhaustion or physical pain, the threshold for release of these neurotransmitters is even lower. In either case, if you engage in some fairly energetic form of behavior like exercise or some other diversion, such as relaxation techniques or counting to ten, you will handle the situation better when these neurotransmitters are in fact released. Other emotions, like sadness and depression, involve lower arousal states. Because the type and amount of neurotransmitters in these states may be different, they are easier to control than in states of anger or anxiety. So, when physical activity occurs, a more appropriate emotion takes hold, leading the person from a negative, destructive state to calmness; from a state of anxiety to one of relaxation.

Debunking the Myth of the Sacredness of Emotions

There is a connection between thinking, feeling and behavior. Whenever any of these three conditions occurs, although one of them may seem dominant in our level of awareness, the other two are occurring as well. We just may not be as aware of them at the time. Emotions do not exist in isolation; rarely do thoughts or behaviors either, for that matter. Furthermore, when an emotional state such as anger does develop, it is affected by our thinking processes. The more pathways that develop between the thinking centers and the emotional centers, the more likely it is a quicker, more efficient response will kick in. Emotions, then, are not magical. They don't exist in splendid isolation and are not incapable of being modified. We often hear clients say, "I can't help the way I feel," as if their feelings are somehow sacred and above reproach. In actuality, they can help the way they feel. There are both stimuli and thinking components to emotions. Even if this thinking component is below the surface of awareness and we are not conscious of it at the time, we can learn to access it and change it.

Ted, a forty-year-old journalist dating Joyce, who has three children aged seven, ten and twelve, is an introvert who has always had problems maintaining close ties. He spends a lot of time alone on his computer, writing. When he is typing a sentence on his computer, he is aware mainly of his fingers moving over the keys. He is, however, simultaneously thinking about what he is typing, and feeling a vague sense of anxiety about whether he is stating his thoughts well, whether the article will sell. Likewise, when he begins discussing plans to marry Joyce, he is moving his lips, thinking about what he is going to say and feeling apprehensive about whether she will say yes, if her children will accept him and if they will be financially secure.

Thinking, feeling and behaving are all connected, sometimes in simple ways, sometimes in complex ways. Moreover, as we change any one of these variables by consciously manipulating it, we affect the other two also. If Ted is thinking that it will be awful and terrible if Joyce turns down his proposal, he is likely to feel somewhat jittery, anxious and nervous about this possibility and his speech may reflect this feeling. He may speak faster than normal, perhaps more loudly than usual or he may retreat into silence. As he discusses his desire to spend the rest of his life with Joyce, the kinds of thoughts that he is having inside his mind are affecting his feelings about the possible outcome and his behavior. This kind of interconnection of events occurs in just about everything we do, whether we consciously realize it or not. They especially occur in relationship issues where conflict and differences of opinion color the satisfaction each partner feels with the relationship itself.

Becoming More Aware of the Role Thinking Plays in Emotions

People do hundreds and hundreds of things without consciously thinking about them at the time. In fact, most of the things in their daily lives are probably done on this automatic basis. They engage in behaviors, like getting angry or arguing, without thinking specifically about these behaviors at the time. There are even books on anger which encourage us to express our anger without trying to figure out why we are angry in the first place. The premise here is that expressing anger freely leads to honest, warm relationships. However, based on counseling hundreds of couples, we know that the idea that an uninhibited expression of anger enhances relationships is open to serious doubt. Rather, it is much more likely that when couples are *not* angry with each other they are going to be able to problem solve more effectively, think more creatively, put new behaviors into place better, resolve conflicts through enlightened negotiation and thus improve their relationships.

An illustration of the concept of acting without consciously realizing the behaviors the thought process involves might be the act of getting into your car and driving. This example illustrates another phenomenon involved in this process. When you get into the car, you are probably engaging in several different activities at once. You are probably having some thoughts about where you are going, how you are going to get there and when you have to be there. You might also be thinking about what you are going to do when you get to your destination and who you will see. While thinking these things, you may also experience some feelings depending on what you are thinking at the time.

If you are running late, you may have some feelings of agitation, anxiety or anger at your predicament. If you're thinking about the kind of company you're going to encounter at your destination and you happen to dislike these people, you may have some feelings of annoyance, frustration or distaste. Finally, while all of the above is going on, you are engaging in some behaviors. You are putting the key in the car door, opening the door, sitting down, putting the key in the ignition, closing the door, starting the engine, engaging the clutch and doing all sorts of other kinds of behaviors to get the car started and moving. The interesting thing here is that you're not thinking about any of these behaviors while performing them—at least not consciously. These behaviors are done from muscle memory or what psychologists call *automatic thoughts*. You are not thinking about how to put the key in the car door, which way to turn it, how to pull the door handle, where to move your feet and legs when getting into the car, etc. You just do it. You do it because you've done it thousands of times before and don't need to think of it consciously at this point. Yet, you could think about these behaviors if you chose to.

You could break down each of the above behaviors into the most minute detail if you had to. While you are not thinking about the behaviors necessary to start the car, you might very well be thinking about some other things. Also, if you are late to an appointment and in a hurry, you're probably feeling quite anxious. This anxiety, in turn, is probably going to cause you to be less efficient in operating your car and to be clumsier in the process of starting it. The thought of being late for your appointment is thus predominating your awareness; while the thinking involved in properly operating the car is playing a secondary role.

How "Subconscious" Thoughts Influence Our Relationships

Just as we have automatic thoughts when we engage in behaviors, such as starting a car, we also have similar automatic thoughts when we are experiencing feelings such as love, anger or depression in our close relationships. Similarly, we are not aware of these thoughts at the same time we are having the feelings. Not only are our thoughts, feelings and behaviors connected; often, the thinking behind the behaviors and feelings is automatic, and below the surface of awareness as well.

This is not to say that these thoughts are unconscious, in the Freudian sense. We can easily access them if we wish to, by focusing or intentionally thinking about them for a moment. In the example just mentioned, if we were to teach a novice driver how to operate a car, we could break down each of the behaviors described above in as much detail as necessary to get the idea across to the student. Thus, muscle memory is really brain memory and can be accessed as needed and subsequently explained, understood, analyzed and even taught to others if we so desire. What at first seems automatic and natural is really the result of learning and much practice over time. This is the way we acquire any new skill.

It's important to remember these automatic thoughts as we discuss the process of anger and how it disrupts our relationship with our partner. It is one of the reasons why couples talk the way they do. "He made me so angry when he wouldn't answer me!" "She really pissed me off when she began screaming at me while I was driving the car." "He really drives me crazy when he can't make up his mind about making plans." All these partners talk as if there's a cause-and-effect relationship between their partners' actions and what they, themselves, are feeling inside; as if another person could somehow magically make us angry. People assume an outside event produces an internal feeling of anger in us. This is not the case.

You walk out of the house one morning, leaving just enough time to get to work at the exact minute you're supposed to be there. You enter the garage, but one of the tires on the car is flat. Your fiancee was driving the car last. You're furious. According to your thinking, the flat tire made you angry at her. Is this true? How can a flat tire make you angry at someone you love? An inanimate object cannot realistically cause a person to feel a certain way about another person. It sounds difficult to believe when you think about it. So there must be something else going on here.

Different Experiences to the Same Event

Let's look at it from a different viewpoint. Suppose we were to conduct an experiment and observe one hundred different people as they emerge from their houses and approach their cars. They all encounter the same situation: a flat tire. How do you suppose each of these individuals would react toward their significant other who was driving the car last? Would they all react and feel the same, identical way? Probably not. In fact, there would probably be a variety of reactions. Some of them would be enraged at their partners—that's true enough. But not all of them would feel angry. From our past observations of seeing how different partners react to the same events, our experience would lead us to predict that some would be fairly indifferent to the flat tire, perhaps thinking to themselves, *Oh well, I really don't need this right now, but the tire was getting old anyway and I could have predicted that this was going to happen some day.* Others might be depressed, perhaps thinking, *I'm never going to have a decent car, I'll probably never afford a reliable car or get the right things—I deserve to have this happen to me.* Still others might actually be happy. They might be saying to themselves, *Good! Now I have a perfect excuse to not get to work on time and if I take my time getting this fixed, maybe I can milk half a day off from work.* Different people can and do react to the same situation in different ways. Not everyone blames his partner. Something other than the tire caused this partner to become so enraged at his spouse.

The Intimate ABCs

If some outside action by our partner (let's call it *A*), causes some inside emotion and behavior in us (let's call this *C*), then we ought to feel the same way each and every time. That is, if the way we talk about emotions and events is accurate (e.g. "When she leaves the cap off the toothpaste after I've mentioned it one hundred times, I really fume"), then we ought to react the *same way* on each and every occasion that *A* occurs. In other words, if our emotional reaction to things is strictly a cause and effect relationship, such as that water heated to 212 degrees Fahrenheit at sea level will boil every time, then we should experience the same emotion—anger—to the same stimulus each and every time. The same *C* should go with the same *A* each time. However, if you are in a good mood, you may find humor in your partner's idiosyncrasies; other times you may be distracted and not notice. At those times, *A* doesn't infuriate you. Obviously, this is *not* just a cause-and-effect relationship we're talking about. Something else is happening too.

Attitudes Are Made up of Thoughts

In our chain of reasoning, we can now state that *A* doesn't cause *C*—at most, it merely affects *C*. One way of understanding the relationship between an action and our reaction is to ask ourselves what the difference is between our own reactions to an incident and other people's reactions to this same incident.

More than likely, you came up with one or more of the following concepts, or something very similar. Usually when we ask couples to do this in our therapy sessions, they wait for several minutes, then each one comes up with something like, *Well, my attitude was just different on that occasion; I was just in a good mood that day* or, *I just perceived it differently that time than I did on the other occasions when I got angry.*

When we analyze each of the explanations as to why one partner reacted so differently on a particular day, it usually boils down to the fact that the person's thinking was different and, therefore, they felt and behaved differently. Attitudes are but a collection of a series of individual thoughts. Our attitudes are just more complete expressions and the result of a series of individual thoughts that make up each attitude. For example, how we label a situation will likely affect how we feel. If we use words like jerk or idiot to describe our partner who is the perpetrator of the event, our impression and feeling state are subsequently going to be affected a great deal. Derogatory labels are "hot" words, and tend to evoke a "hot" emotional response in return. Our thoughts and attitudes are not always definite, perfect sentences. Sometimes, they just consist of what seem to be vague beliefs, ideas or images that are only half-formed or vaguely understood. If we examine them closely enough, these different entities can be formulated into more clearly defined ideas when we desire, similar to how muscle memory can be broken down into a series of individual and distinct behaviors when it is necessary to do so.

Thinking Speed

Your thinking processes are a bit more complex than they might at first seem. There are several things going on, and it's not too difficult to understand if you step back from a situation and think about it for a minute. The human brain is an incredibly powerful and complex organ. It is capable of directing several major functions in the body simultaneously. We don't, for example, think about digesting our food after a meal. We don't consciously tell ourselves to break the food down into its chemical components and send them to the parts of the body that need them. Of course not! The brain does it for us without our thinking about it. We don't tell ourselves to breathe. Our brain does it for us without our ever thinking about it. The same thing occurs with pulse, blood pressure, sexual arousal and a host of other bodily functions of which our brain is in charge.

With the brain directing all of these different functions simultaneously, it is quite capable of entertaining a host of different, discrete, individual thoughts at any given time as well. We can have several thoughts before we even know we are having them. All of this can happen in a period of a second or two because the brain operates on the principle of biochemical electricity that is generated between neurons. This biochemical electricity is extremely fast; something on the order of more than two hundred miles per hour. Since the head is less than twelve inches wide, you can see that it doesn't take long for one thought to reach the end of its journey. In fact, we can have many thoughts in a period of a second or two. In fact these thoughts come to us so quickly that they *seem* automatic, but they're not, they're just more familiar, more conditioned. Conditioned thoughts are a little bit different than consciously constructed, deliberate self statements made to ourselves or others. Deliberate self-statements are quite a bit slower. It's sort of like the difference between a person who reads a text out loud and a speed-reader who goes maybe fifty to a hundred times faster. You can have a large number of thoughts or images or meaning fragments in a very brief period of time—enough thoughts to form any given attitude or several attitudes.

Thinking Really Does Accompany Reactions

For example: Your partner insults or critiques you in front of friends. This is the *A*, or activating or actual event out there. What's the *C*? Well, it could vary, depending on how you're doing that day. It could also vary among different people. But, for the sake of argument, let's say you react with anger and tell her off, then that is the *C*, or emotional and behavioral consequence. Having found that people don't always react the same way to the same thing or that even you don't necessarily react the same way each time, we observed that this difference could be analyzed in its most basic terms as thoughts. As we've said before, our thoughts can vary and when they do, the result each time is going to be a little different, depending upon their nature.

We know you're thinking, *Usually, I'm not thinking when I get angry, I just feel angry.* Just as we can have muscle memory, we can have thoughts of which we are only vaguely aware. These thoughts can happen spontaneously—faster than the blink of an eye. Although these thoughts can be just below the level of awareness in our subconscious, sometimes they definitely are not. This is not the Freudian idea of subconscious, but the muscle memory kind of subconscious. It's the kind of memory or thought that you can access, identify, and state to others if you have to do so. These thoughts, in other words, are quickly accessible if we choose to identify them and usually we get better and better at identifying our thoughts and verbalizing them as we get more and more practice.

The thoughts of which we speak are really a part of the various belief systems we carry around in our heads. These belief systems are sometimes elevated to the status of truths that we hold immutably and rigidly without even knowing it. We are convinced, according to these beliefs, that the world operates, or should operate in a particular way and we seldom, if ever, question these convictions. Not all of our thoughts are part of these rigid belief systems, of course, but a number of them are. The kinds of thoughts that lead to anger, for instance, are generally a part of these inflexible belief systems.

We find that when couples come to us for therapy and we ask them what they were thinking when they were so angry or disturbed with each other, they often have trouble coming up with the thoughts at first. Later on, often in the same session, locating, identifying and stating the thoughts that each of them had at the time becomes easier. Both partners begin to look at their problems in a different way. They begin to understand that they both have these thoughts and that they both can choose to have different thoughts if they want to change the reaction or *C* in their equation

Some examples of this *A-B-C* connection, will illustrate in more detail how this process works. First, we'll start with some common situations (*As*), then give a typical Irrational Belief (*IB*), followed by the usual Emotional and Behavioral Consequence (*C*). Beneath it, using the same (*A*) we will point out a typical Rational Belief (*RB*), and its Consequence (*C*). Hopefully, you'll then start to have a clearer idea of how important your beliefs are and how they affect how you're going to feel in response to any given situation.

A	IB	C
1. You're telling a story to a group of friends and your wife interrupts you, finishing the story.	She shouldn't interrupt me like that! Can't she see that I'm in the middle of a story here?	Angry with your wife you scream at her, embarrassing her in front of your friends.

RB

I wish that my wife didn't interrupt me when I'm telling a story, but it's not the end of the world.	Mildly irritated with your wife, you remind her quietly that she interrupted you.

2. A stranger cuts in front of you in a movie line.	I hate it when people are so rude! Why can't they just stand in line like everyone else?	You feel hatred toward the person who cut in front of you. You feel like punching him.

RB

It would really be nice if every-one was as considerate as I am, but clearly they're not. Oh well, it's an interesting world.	Feeling disappointed at the person's behavior, you decide to ask him politely not to cut in front of you.

3. You're walking down the street and slip on a spot of ice, almost falling down.	Damn it! That was stupid of me! I should have seen that spot. I could have hurt myself.	You become filled with self-loathing, cursing at yourself loudly.

RB

Whoa! Good thing I didn't slip and fall. I'm going to to have to watch where I walk a little more closely in the future.	Maintaining a relatively calm attitude, you develop concern about looking where you walk.

4. In the restaurant where you're eating, the waiter brings you a steak that's overcooked.	Well, that's it! My meal's totally ruined. Why can't people ever do things right?	Depressed, you lose your appetite, and sulk the rest of the meal.

RB

I sure wish that they had prepared my steak the way I want it. I'm going to ask them to fix another one for me.	You feel disappointed that you are going to have to wait a little longer to eat, but you enjoy talking with your dinner companions.

Taking Responsibility for Your Feelings

In all our years of therapy, we have yet to have a couple come to our offices that, when asked what's wrong, say, "There's something wrong with our thinking." That just never happens. Almost invariably, they start talking about what they're feeling emotionally—anger, depression, anxiety—or how one or both has done something which has gotten the other upset. They never talk about their thinking. Oftentimes each partner blames the other. Sometimes to defuse the charged atmosphere we say, "If the way you're both feeling is only the result of one person's behavior, you're wasting your time by coming to the office together, since presumably neither of you has anything to do with the way the two of you feel. But, because you're here together, that sort of implies that both of you had something to do with the problem. It also means that there is something each of you personally can do to stop being upset."

You can't keep giving the other person the complete blame for how you feel. The responsibility is each of yours. Every individual's feeling is produced by that person alone. The other person may have had an effect here, but he or she didn't cause you to feel angry. There is only one person in the world who can make you angry or feel any other emotion either for that matter and that person is you. If you choose not to laugh at a comedian's jokes when you're in a nightclub, nobody else, including the comedian, can make you do so. This holds true for other emotions as well, including anger. Okay, that's the bad news. The good news is that since both of you are the ones that are largely making yourselves miserable, then each of you is precisely the one who is in the best position to fix it and if each of you does that, you're both on the way to fixing the relationship. Using the A-B-C method to identify the irrational beliefs that fuel both partners' anger plus changing those beliefs is the key to your own self-help couple therapy.

If either of you still doubt that you are thinking whenever you experience anger or any other emotion, try this exercise. Each of you take a moment right now to sit back and concentrate on getting yourself really, really angry. Give yourself about thirty seconds to do this. While you're doing this exercise, we don't want you to think about anything either of you has done to the other. Nothing at all. Not a single thought is to go through your mind. Okay now, close your eyes. Really concentrate and get yourself really angry but don't think anything. All right: go.

Okay. You should have had enough time by now to try this exercise. How did it go? Were you able to get yourself angry? We doubt it. Of all the couples whom we've asked to do this little exercise, no one has ever been able to do it. If the only thing both of you are telling yourselves is "get angry," you're both still having a thought, aren't you? Your irrational thinking and your anger are inextricably tied together. We have yet to have one single person get angry in our therapy groups without having any thoughts. In fact, a lot of people quickly see that they won't be able to do it and they don't even try. A similar phenomenon occurs when couples come to a therapy session. At first they are composed, self-assured and calm. Then they start thinking and talking about their relationship and the events that originally made them angry and they immediately get very agitated again. They quickly evoke the same, or very nearly the same, emotional response—anger. The original event hasn't recurred, but their thinking about it still generates anger. Thus, the event, or the memory of the event, may be a necessary cause for anger, but it is not sufficient cause for it. Making a judgment about that event must be added to the equation.

As therapists, we are familiar with three extreme measures to combat anger. We could give you potent psychotropic drugs, which alter the biochemistry of the brain. There are some antidepressant medications on the market right now that show promise for the control of anger symptoms and behavior, especially when the person has problems with rage. One problem, though, is that these medications seem to be effective with only about one-third of the people treated. Another problem with drugs is that they have undesirable side effects. The person taking them is relying on an external agent which he must continuously put into his or her body.

The second extreme way to alter anger which, fortunately, is not used very much these days, is psychosurgery— specifically, frontal lobotomy. This procedure cuts the connections in the brain between the emotional centers and the rest of the brain. There are several important problems with this approach. First, the solution is permanent and invariable. Second and most importantly, the procedure turns the subject into a human vegetable. Not only does the anger go away, but all the other emotions go away as well. This leaves an emotionally deadened, inert personality. The procedure was fairly widespread in this country in the early part of the twentieth century, with literally hundreds of young men and some women who acted out violently being subjected to the procedure. The result was a waste of human lives. Fortunately, it is rarely performed now.

The third, much more moderate way to control anger is through your thinking. There is no tool more powerful than the human brain to help us when we are in distress. Using your mind to control anger means that there are no undesirable side effects as there are when using drugs. When we use thinking to modify our sense of distress, there is no unchangeable, permanent damage done, as there is in psychosurgery. It is a flexible, powerful and readily available tool. One of the goals of this book is to help you individually and as a couple to become your own therapists, managing your anger through the way you think about yourself, your mate and the world in which you live.

Chapter 4

"Why Do I Get So Mad at _____?"
How Intimate Relationships Trigger
Irrational Thoughts and Anger

Because we are so needy at birth, we are born with a sort of predis-position or strong tendency to form relationships. As children, we need relationships for survival. Later in life, relationships become a key source of pleasure. We all come into this world completely help-less. Babies depend upon their mothers or some caregiver for all physical needs including food and shelter. But we also have social and emotional needs that are just as important.

We look to our mothers to provide for our attachment needs like cuddling, soothing, attention, playing and other sensory stimulation. Without this connection, infants will not thrive and may even die, even when physical needs are met. When we look at orphanages we find that many more infants die in the busiest institutions. The reason for this is that while there may be enough staff to meet the babies' physical needs, there is not enough to meet their emotional needs for one-on-one con-tact. When staff is increased and more time is spent with the babies, the survival rate increases dramatically. We are born not only with physical needs, but also emotional needs and we only do well when both are met.

Though we grow older and more able to meet our physical needs, we still need others in order to meet our emotional needs. Relationships therefore remain essential to us even as adults. We want them and we seek them out. Life without relationships would be empty—there would be no one to connect to and discuss problems with, tell secrets to, or find sexual intimacy with. Life, for most, would be pretty empty without connections to others.

Clearly, there are a lot of different types of relationships that serve different functions. Because of the differences in the nature of relationships and in what it takes to keep them going, certain types of relationships tend to be more problematic than others. The most complained about types of relationships are the ones from which we ask the most, relationships with significant others like boyfriends, girlfriends, spouses and lovers. We have found that perfectly rational, intelligent adults can become irrational and begin acting like children—with behaviors ranging from not talking for weeks at a time to acting out destructively—when there are conflicts with their partners. We have also found that after exploring the problems, no matter how they label them, the real issue is almost always underlying anger.

Irrational behaviors can be acted out in different ways. Jennifer punished her husband, Zack, with the silent treatment because he didn't phone home to tell her that he would be late. Zack, in turn, stayed out all hours of the night to teach Jennifer who's boss. When Jennifer and Zack finally came in for couple therapy, Jennifer said the problem was Zack's inconsideration; Zack identified the problem as Jennifer's poor communication. The fact is that these faulty behaviors are just symptoms of the real underlying problem, which is their anger toward each other that was being expressed as poor communication and inconsideration.

Because anger can take on so many different forms (depression, passive aggression, rage) and be acted out in a lot of different ways (inconsiderate behavior, substance abuse, abuse of self or others) it is easy to confuse the symptoms for the problem. This is one reason why it is hard for couples to confront their anger toward each other (it often looks like something else—the symptom). We have learned it is important to deal with the symptoms of anger and help couples learn how to control their behavior. However, as with anything, the most effective way to deal with the symptoms of a problem is to go to the source. With anger, this means helping each person to recognize and change the irrational thoughts that lead to anger.

While reading this chapter, look for characteristics that fit you and your primary relationship. This will help you to recognize what you need to change and how and what you can do more of to make your relationship better. Although we focus here on your love relationship, at times we also explore other types of relationships which impact on the primary one with your partner.

Relationships with Significant Others

Functions

Relationships with significant others usually serve a lot of different kinds of interpersonal needs such as like companionship, a steady, safe sexual partner, financial, physical and emotional security, a sense of being important or valued, greater acceptance from the community because our culture is geared more toward couples than singles and safety in case of a catastrophe, such as chronic illness or unemployment.

Problems

While we're familiar with the types of relationship problems that our couple clients have, we were also interested in hearing from the general population, including couples who were not in therapy. We decided to talk with some friends and colleagues to get their opinions about relationship problems and qualities that strengthen or improve relationships. We posed the following questions:

1. Name three characteristics that you think are most damaging to
    your relationship with your significant other.

2. Identify three to five characteristics that are most important for
    maintaining a good relationship with lovers.

Interestingly enough, though we chose a variety of couples
varying in terms of age, religion, ethnic background, gender and
marital status, their responses exposed many similar problems. Let's
look at one of our participants.

Marcus, thirty-nine, is an African-American attorney.
Handsome and Yale educated, although Marcus never married, he
has had a number of long-term relationships, including live-ins.
Marriage is now a priority, though he is still trying to figure out how
to let go of his unreasonable demands of a partner.

It took him thirty-eight years to realize that his standards
were impossible for any mere mortal woman to meet. He feels his
biggest problem in relationships is having too many options.

When asked what three characteristics are most likely to
cause serious problems with lovers, Marcus responded, "probably
the biggest problem is that most people can't set aside their feelings
long enough to solve the problem, whatever that may be. I come
from a family that expects a lot. A lot was expected of me in college,
and a lot is expected of me now in the workplace. So I think I expect
a lot from other people and I have been known to get pretty angry
in the past when they haven't delivered. I don't mean screaming and
cursing. I just become less communicative. I feel if that's the way
someone is going to be, then I don't have time to deal with that person."

Within Marcus' statement, a variety of problems were mentioned. He cited anger and unrealistic expectations, so we questioned why he thought they were a problem.

Marcus explained that he never realized the negative effect
his behavior had on his relationships, because in the short run, his
behavior usually got him what he wanted.

When asked what he meant by that, Marcus said, "Well, usually the women I date will give in to my demands."

Lately, however, Marcus noticed that the women he dates eventually start acting differently. They start doing little things that they knew he didn't like or stop doing things that they had agreed to do. Marcus realized that these women felt manipulated and that this response was their way of getting back at him for his attitude.

We asked him to name a third characteristic that typically causes problems.

He replied that he already did—poor communication. He explained, "Most people don't know how to sit down and talk a problem out to resolution. I've lost some pretty good relationships by skipping the talking and just getting angry or copping some sort of attitude. I think I'm getting better, though."

Aside from the three characteristics he discussed, his explanations revealed that in his relationships, he exhibited impatience with his partners as well and these women responded passive aggressively.

The next question, what do you think the most important qualities are in good relationships, was posed.

Marcus responded, "This I really have thought about a lot—sort of like a wish list: commitment, good communication, and a partner who makes you feel good about being in the relationship. If you don't have fun with your lover, what's the point? I think the woman in my life should build me up, support my accomplishments, say things and do things that help me feel good about myself and vice versa—I should do the same for her."

Since commitment was one of the words he used to define a good relationship, we asked what the word "commitment" meant to him.

He explained that he and their relationship should be the number one priority in his lover's life. He continued, "It's hard enough to have a good relationship when both people are trying; you can forget it if it takes a back seat to your job or friends or some other distraction. I know me, I need to be a priority."

We next asked about the second quality on Marcus's wish list, good communication.

"To me, good communication means being able to set aside your feelings long enough to talk about a problem and try to fix it. I'm used to having my way. I know this. So, for me, I have to really work at not forcing a situation and at least giving in a little bit once in a while. I guess it's about being more reasonable or flexible."

When asked if there is anything else that Marcus looks for in a relationship, he added, "a sense of humor always helps in tight situations."

Anger—The Real Underlying Problem in Relationships

Though we spoke with a number of people, we decided to print Marcus's interview because it differed from the others' in one important way. Unlike most others, Marcus saw the connection between his real problem (anger about not getting his own way) and how he acted that problem out (not communicating). While the absence of communication skills can cause trouble in relationships, in Marcus's case the communication problem was just a symptom of the underlying issue, anger. But in general, the public, like our clients, tended to confuse the symptom of the problem, some bad behavior, with the true problem—anger. The responses we received to the first question—name three characteristics most damaging to relationships with lovers—fell into three broad categories: inappropriate expectations, poor communication or problem solving skills, and excessive control. These are not only common characteristics of angry people as were described in earlier chapters, but also the most frequently identified problems in love relationships.

Inappropriate Expectations

Inappropriate expectations are often the source of irrational thoughts that feed irrational anger in relationships. Most people expect their relationships with lovers to meet the vast majority of their emotional and social needs. Why shouldn't we expect this when we grow up in a society where boy meets girl and they live happily ever after? When we see people in therapy we ask them what they hope for from such relationships. We often hear a laundry list that goes something like this: *I expect my lover to be my best friend, to make me a number one priority, to be loyal and committed even when I'm not, to be my primary supporter, to be my lover, to be my primary source of security, to be a good mother or father to our children, to be honest at all times, to know what I want and need without my having to ask for it.* To complicate things further, most of us have the greatest expectations of the one relationship that most times, by definition, demands exclusivity. In friendship, there are a number of people you can go to in times of need. And if one friend isn't around, it's perfectly okay to go to another. You're expected to have a lot of friends, not just one. The same holds true at work. If one co-worker can't meet your needs, you're perfectly free to find one who can. But with significant others, you want or expect the majority of your most intimate emotional and social needs to be met by that one person. If that sounds like a set-up to you, you're right. This is an enormous job for one person and a virtually impossible one. The expectations you have in love relationships are likely to lead to disappointment for you, not to mention the tremendous pressure your partner feels under the weight of such expectations. Even children, who are completely dependent upon their parents at birth, become independent with time, holding fewer and fewer expectations of their parents' responsibility to meet their needs.

It is, nevertheless, typical for people to go into relationships with a truckload of unrealistic expectations about what their partners or relationships will do for them and how their significant others will soothe old wounds and make their dreams come true. When you look at it that way, it's pretty easy to see not only why everybody wants a relationship, but also how easily it can go wrong. When our lovers or relationships don't line up with our fantasies, and few do, we naturally feel disappointed. This is the point in all relationships where the honeymoon phase ends and the commitment to the relationship is put to the test.

When we first meet up with disappointment in our relationships, we may stumble a bit. But most of us soon right ourselves and develop some skills to deal with our disappointment and unmet needs; we talk it over and negotiate some livable, less idealistic compromise. We find some other way to meet that need; we learn to live without whatever it is because enough of our more important needs are being addressed. In other words, we change or let go of some of the inappropriate expectations that fuel our anger. Because of low frustration tolerance, some people may not have developed the skills to live with disappointment. Though you may know in your head that life is not fair and people are not perfect, you still set impossible standards for your significant other. When faced with disappointment, which is inevitable in even the best of relationships, you feel wronged, slighted, downright ripped off—you feel angry. Such anger is acted out with your partner in some pretty typical ways: trying to control the situation or person, with a resultant breakdown in communication.

Excessive Control

Anytime we don't get what we want or think that things aren't the way they should be, we, as human beings, want to step in and make it right—control the situation. Our relationships are no exception. *If he really loved me he would not do X. She is deliberately doing Y to bug me. If I can just figure out the best strategy, I can make him do Z.* How many times have you had these types of thoughts? What makes these thoughts irrational is the fact that they are based on the belief or expectation that things should go your way and that if they don't, something's wrong and you're in a position to right those wrongs. Suddenly, you are the judge, jury and executioner for others; you have the right not only to feel angry when disappointed, after all, things are supposed to be a certain way, but also to act on those feelings. This is the working definition of control.

Partners sometimes use control as a way of trying to deal with anger about disappointment with each other as well as with the outside world. The fewer skills you have for dealing with life's disappointments, the angrier and more controlling you're likely to be. Your anger can take a variety of forms, from the very obvious screaming and yelling, to the subtle, like conveniently forgetting to pick up your partner's dry cleaning on the way home.

There are also many different ways that angry people try to control things. But whether you express your anger openly or subtly, the motivation is the same—control: *If you don't do what I want, I'll make you uncomfortable and if you want to avoid this in the future, you'd better do it my way.* Clearly, this type of angry controlling behavior is a problem all by itself, but it also tends to snowball in two ways. First, when our attempts to control others fail and they will because the reality is that we can't control others, we become more frustrated and angry. Second, anger begets anger. When someone does something hostile to you, your first reaction, if you're like most, is to get hostile back. Your lover is probably no different. One bad deed calls for another, starting a nasty cycle beginning with your anger and followed by your partner's retaliation. You're angry because he didn't support your decision to change your hair color so you conveniently forget to pick up his dry cleaning on the way home so he calls you a dizzy blond (it's actually a tawny auburn and your friends think it's a great color for you) so you cook liver for dinner, knowing he hates liver. He then stays out all night with the boys. It's not the unrealistic expectations that cause the problem, nor is it the anger and desire to control. After all, disappointment and frustration are part of being human. The problem is that the irrational thoughts drive you to destructive behavior with your partner. Shifting to more reasonable thoughts and expectations is the key to short-circuit this process.

Poor Communication

Anger and communication problems go hand-in-hand for most people. That's because we don't think as clearly as we normally do when we're angry. Anger is likely to lead to one of two types of communication problems: abusive communication or no communication at all.

Abusive communication is easy to spot. It's characterized by screaming, yelling, cursing, name-calling, blaming, digging up old arguments
and any other tactic that you think will result in victory. You are determined to get your way, not solve the problem. For you, getting your
way is the only solution to the problem. You don't see that getting your
way just means that you were either hurtful or manipulative enough
to force your will upon your partner this time. In which case you can
look forward to some form of retaliation in the future, leading to the
same nasty cycle described in the previous section.

Avoiding communication in relationships is another way
that excessive anger can lead to distance problems. Rather than
become verbally abusive, maybe you try to hide your anger. Storing
up anger is called *gunny-sacking*. You act as though you're not angry
but you are. Rather than confront the problem, you store your anger
away. Then, one day, your partner says or does something you don't
like and you fly off the handle with rage, bringing up every little
thing she has done wrong in the past year that you've been unhappy
about. Your partner may ignore your rage because she realizes that
you're overreacting and just chalks it up to your having a bad day. So,
feeling relieved because you've gotten most of those repressed angry
feelings off your chest, you bury the real problem again. In the
process, any motivation to actually solve the problem disappears and
the cycle begins again.

Perhaps you're not as extreme as the gunny-sacker. Perhaps
rather than pretending that you're not angry, you let your partner
know in some subtle way, like making a snide remark every now and
then, but never really making an attempt at resolution.

Joe, Jean's boyfriend, recently bought a motorcycle. Jean
didn't want Joe to buy the bike because she thinks they're dangerous,
but in the end she gave in. Now she's sorry she did. Since Joe bought
the bike, he spends all of his free time either riding or hanging out
with his new biker buddies. Jean has started to feel like an after-
thought. Rather than saying she's angry and asking Joe to spend

more time with her, Jean becomes sarcastic, referring to Joe's motor-cycle as his new little girlfriend. Joe, realizing that Jean feels replaced, decides to plan a vacation with her and says, "Honey, I've been thinking, it's been a while since we've gone away together. What do you think about us taking a weekend trip sometime soon?" Jean responds with a question of her own, "A real trip or a road trip with your girlfriend?"

Jean's anger gets in the way of what she says she wants—time with Joe. Rather than addressing Joe's lack of effort or respond-ing positively to his attempt to make amends, Jean offers a sarcastic remark. Joe in turn becomes angry as well. Resolution or reconcilia-tion will have to wait for another day—if they're lucky.

Some people, when angry with those closest to them, don't say anything at all. They punish their partners with the silent treat-ment, which could last hours, days, weeks or months depending upon how angry they are. Whether you become verbally abusive or avoidant when angered by people failing to meet your expectations doesn't really matter. The process is the same—poor communica-tion—and the end is the same—no satisfying resolution.

Relationships, by definition, involve two or more people. No matter how great your expectations or how forceful your will, there is no way that two people will see eye to eye on everything. There are simply too many ways for people to differ: values, beliefs, culture, personalities and experiences, to name a few. Of course you want your way. Who doesn't? But this is real life and despite all of your irrational demands, you probably already know that you won't always get your way. You and your relationship will be better off if you acknowledge that there will be conflict and you learn the skills you need to negotiate the next best thing.

Clients complain a lot about relationship problems with lovers. We believe that this is the case for all of the reasons just stated: inappropriate expectations, the tendency toward excessive control, and breakdowns in communication when expectations are not met.

Partner Homework

1. Don't change anything about the way you both are handling situations with each other too abruptly.

2. Concentrate on focusing inward on the thoughts each of you is having, rather than on the outward situation.

3. The next time either of you feels angry at the other person, you both should take a few minutes to write down your feelings. Answer the following: What happened just now? What am I telling myself about it? What is going through my mind? Is it accurate?

4. Remember this formula: Action—Belief—Consequence.

Chapter 5

The Origins of Anger: Where It Comes From, How It's Shaped

What we expect or demand in our primary relationships is greatly influenced by how our parents or caregivers responded to our needs when we were young. That is, whether our essential needs were more or less fulfilled, neglected or over-indulged. Problems with inappropriate expectations are usually related to a history of neglect or over-indulgence. Children who are over-indulged or spoiled have a hard time developing a healthy sense of independence. They often grow up to be very demanding and dependent adults. Children of neglect and abuse, however, tend to have difficulty forming attachments and the trust necessary to develop the most basic expectations of others. So, our earlier experiences tend to impact what we later expect from others, whether those expectations are excessive or minimal. But even adults whose needs were reasonably fulfilled are likely to have inappropriate expectations because, as humans, we struggle with the conflict between wanting freedom and independence, versus attachment and contact. As such, our expectations flip-flop and we give inconsistent or conflicting messages: *I expect you to be there for me; I expect you to give me space.* Maybe the biggest problem with expectations is that all of us just assume that our significant others can read our minds and know our expectations. Expectations are hardly ever discussed in relationships until problems arise. Then we usually find that our partners have very different expectations of us and the relationship than we do.

Kat still laughs about her early relationship with Karl:

> I'd always been focused on my career, you know, raised to be independent. Sure, I watched all of my college friends marry in their twenties, divorce five years later and then struggle through their thirties, raising their kids by themselves. By the time I finished graduate school and began to think about marriage, all of my friends' relationships were falling apart around me, and that just turned me off. Then I hit my forties and my divorced friends were starting to date and remarry, and suddenly I felt lonely (chuckles). I began to worry about my future. What if I lost my job? Who would take care of me if I got sick? Who would I grow old with? I got tired of talking about "me" when everyone else was talking about "we." But still, I'd been on my own so long, grown to value my freedom so much, that I wasn't sure if I could do the relationship thing, you know, meet at home every night at 6:00 P.M., hash out the details of our days over dinner and a martini and get up and do it all again the next day. I don't know, it just sounded so boring, so routine, so well, typical.
>
> Then I met Karl. Well, he was perfect, or so I thought. He traveled two weeks out of each month. I think that knowing that he would be gone half the time is what made it possible for me to get involved with him in the first place. I knew that I wouldn't have to give up my independence or free time completely. And just when I started to

worry that I might start to depend on Karl too much, well, he'd take off on another trip and I would prove to myself again that I still had "it"—still had what it took to make it on my own. Still, I started to depend on Karl. An example of what I mean came a few months after we started dating. Karl had developed this habit of always telling me his schedule, you know, when he was leaving town, how long he'd be gone, how to reach him and so on. I thought it was all pretty unnecessary, after all, it's not like I was his wife or something. Anyway, one day he left town for New York and didn't call me that night. I found myself waiting for his call. I guess I had come to expect it. It was a pattern. Anyway, I fell asleep waiting for his call, and woke up the next morning without any message from him on my machine, so I decided to call him at his hotel. He wasn't in, so I left a message for him to call me at work. I swear, I must have checked my voice mail at work every fifteen minutes and nothing. At first I felt disappointed. Then I tried to figure out what I might have done wrong to make him ignore me. Then as more time passed without hearing from him, I started to feel angry. I asked myself, "What is this guy, some kind of jerk? What gives him the right to treat me this way?" Well, as it turned out, the poor man's plane had been re-routed because of mechanical problems. It actually took him two days to get to New York, with a lot of hassle in between (lost luggage, multiple plane changes, stand-by, overnight in a flea-bag airport hotel, etc., etc., etc.). Like any smart business person, when he realized that he would be delayed, he called his hotel and checked in by phone so that he'd still have a room when he finally got in. When I called his hotel, the computer showed that he had checked in and the front desk transferred me to his voice mail. Of course I didn't know any of this then, so when Karl finally did call, boy, did I give it to him! "Why the hell didn't you call? If you could call the hotel, you could've called me!" Fortunately, we managed to talk things out. Karl was patient with my bad attitude and boy, was it bad. He understood that I had felt, well, I guess rejected and definitely angry. He explained that in the past he had called when he was away because he missed me, not because he felt that he owed it to me. We both came to understand that I now expected that call from him when he was out of town. It was no longer just a courtesy call. I guess that's the point when things started to get more serious between us. It's funny, despite my need for space, I still started to depend on Karl for some things, to expect certain things from him. We've been together now for six years. He wants to marry, live in one house together. I'm comfortable with things the way they are. Hell, as just boyfriend and girlfriend my expectations of him have already changed so much. The thought of how much more dependent I'd become if we actually married is too scary!

Kat has a pretty clear understanding of her struggle between wanting space and wanting attachment. For her, the struggle is to connect but not become so attached that she ends up depending on Karl for basic things, like her identity or peace of mind. She doesn't want to start to expect her partner to help her feel good about herself.

This issue of attachment versus separation actually shapes our expectations of partners. Think of it as a spectrum with independence at one end and attachment at the other. In general, Kat falls on the independence side, so she expects a healthy amount of time away from her partner, little accountability, and respect for their lives separate from each other. In contrast, expectations associated with attachment include a high degree of accountability, minimization of differences in views and beliefs, like the man who converts to his wife's religion, or the woman who switches to her boyfriend's political party and emphasis on identity as a unit, instead of separate identities. Regardless of where we fall on the spectrum, the other side is still represented. So, while Kat values her independence, she still wants some degree of attachment. We see that her expectations of Karl change, sometimes reflecting attachment by expecting that phone call and at other times reflecting independence by still rejecting the idea of marriage. This flip-flopping or change in expectations, depending on where we might fall on the spectrum at any given moment, is also part of what makes many expectations inappropriate. This problem is compounded by having expectations that are too high, too numerous, too rigid, or simply impossible, like mind-reading.

You may be saying to yourself, *Inappropriate expectations are common in relationships so what's the big deal?* Again, in and of themselves, inappropriate thoughts and expectations are not big deals but, as noted earlier, how we respond to not having our expectations or demands met is. Depending upon the level of expectation, and the need to have expectations met by our partners, we may feel hurt, abandoned or rejected, or angry. We're more likely to have strong reactions to disappointment when we take the other person's failures to live up to our expectations personally. For example, even with Kat's fierce independence, her unmet expectations that Karl should phone her when he's on the road led to negative thoughts about herself (she blamed herself for doing something wrong) and about Karl (he must be a jerk). These irrational thoughts sparked feelings of anger and acting out and were complicated by another inappropriate expectation, that Karl could read her mind. Kat expected him to know that what was once a courtesy call was now an expectation of accountability without her ever saying so.

Although Kat's irrational anger got in the way of her expressing her true concerns about Karl's safety, her possible rejection, and their relationship in general, Karl was able to stay focused, and clear up the misunderstanding. Kat's anger could have resulted in the ending of the relationship had Karl also become defensive and distracted from the real issue. Herein lies the problem with irrational thoughts or expectations. They lead to irrational anger that gets in the way of communication and, therefore, problem solving, and fuel the impulse to act out. As you begin to recognize the chain of events in your patterns of reacting to your partner, you will also learn how to interrupt that process in your relationships.

By practicing the skills presented, and following through with partner exercises, you can learn to be your own therapists, salvaging a
relationship that would have otherwise been damaged or lost.

When you're angry with each other you feel badly—tense,
shaky, flushed, tearful and you may hear your heart pounding in
your ears. When you're angry, it's easy to do stupid things like threat-
en each other, walk off, become more controlling, break things, get
drunk or binge on other things like food and drugs, to name a few.
Once the anger has passed, if you're like most couples, you spend a
lot of time and energy on what we call damage control. This can take
many different forms like apologizing, offering a gift, being repen-
tant, drinking lots of black coffee to recover from a hangover and, in
general, gluing your relationship back together. At best, this process
is painful and sometimes corrosive. At worst, it's tragic, since a broken object glued back together is rarely as strong as the one that was
never broken in the first place. This is not to suggest that anger itself
is bad or destructive, but that the ways that most of us deal with it
are. You may ask yourself, *If anger is so difficult to handle, why do we
have to feel it at all?*

The Psychological Origin of Anger

As human beings, we have a whole range of emotions that include
feeling happy, surprised, frustrated, bored, disgusted, angry and
enraged. Anger is one of the most basic emotions. We probably first
feel it as babies long before we can recognize the feeling or call it by
name. This anger is related to the first loss.

What we mean by the "first loss" is this. We all start out in
the womb where we are physically connected to our mothers—like
being one person instead of two. There, the temperature is always
perfect, we're fed before we even feel hungry, and we never have to
wait to have our diapers changed. All our needs are anticipated and
taken care of. After we're born, however, things change. Suddenly
we're physically separated from our mothers, who are not as quick
at figuring out what we need as nature was. But still, it's not bad. The

flood of attention from her sort of smoothes the way so that we can still feel like we're connected to her even though we're not. But as time passes, mom becomes a little more relaxed. She starts to expect us to be able to wait a minute or two before she responds to our cries with a bottle or some cuddling. In waiting for our needs to be met we feel frustrated. We also start to recognize that the world does not revolve around us, that we have to share our mother's love and attention with others, and that she is not just an extension of us to meet our needs but, in fact, a separate person. This realization is the "first loss."

As we grow older, our physical needs and need for attention are less likely to be met immediately. This delay of gratification causes further discomfort, frustration and eventually anger, especially if we're used to a quick response to our demands. All of this is normal. But some kids are over-indulged; their parents give them exactly what they want, when they want it. These kids are most likely to become angry when frustrated because they have been given the message that they have the right to immediate satisfaction. More than any other child, this one is likely to experience separation as a blatant disregard of his needs that must be protested, usually in the form of a tantrum.

Anger, however, is not the only reaction children have to the first loss. As we've said, our range of emotions is much more complicated than that. Some children react to the recognition of separateness with a feeling of helplessness. This is especially true for children with unreliable parents, parents whom they really can't depend on for basic things like food, shelter or comfort. As a result, the bond between such a parent and child is weak. These children tend to feel insecure about their worth and have difficulty trusting others, so that any form of separation is likely to feel like rejection and abandonment. It is not surprising that clinical studies find that these children often grow up to be clingy, depressed adults.

In cases of traumatic separation, a common response to the first loss and later losses is detachment. Children who are torn apart from parents learn early on that they are on their own. For them the first loss is so painful that many have to protect themselves from future loss by avoiding relationships with others. A good example of this is *hospitalism*. This is when young children with medical problems are forced to separate from their parents to enter an institution. These children first grieve the sudden loss of their parents, rejecting comfort from others. Later, they may protest the loss with tantrums which are followed by depression. Finally, they may detach from everyone. The pain of the first loss is so great that re-attachment is not worth the risk, even if it would be comforting.

Another common response to the realization of separation is anxiety. The truth is that although we may have a significant other, friends and family to support us, each of us is in some way alone in life. No one really knows what it's like to be in your skin, to live your experiences. This idea of being separate and alone naturally causes anxiety, especially about our safety and our ability to take care of ourselves. It's not surprising then that when people suffer a loss, even in adulthood, they often have symptoms of anxiety, and even panic disorders.

There are other possible reactions to separation, but these are the most common. Many people have two or more different reactions to separation that are affected by the type of separation and how old they were when it occurred. For example, research shows that children who were separated from their mothers after six months of age grew up to have more relationship problems than those who were separated before six months of age. It seems as though human bonds are not firmly set until six months of age or so, and, after that time, disruption of the parent-child bond can have a major impact on later intimate relationships and overall psychological functioning.

Biological Origins of Anger

Having discussed the psychological bases of anger, let's take a look at some other factors, for example, biological factors. As living beings, we need certain things like food, shelter and stimulation just to survive.

To do better than survive, to thrive, we need all of that and more: emotional support and nurturing and opportunities for growth, intellectual, psychological and otherwise.

For most animals, including human beings, survival has always been dependent upon both group and individual skills. Even cavemen realized that there is strength in numbers. By running in packs like other wild animals, they had a better chance of fighting off the wild beasts and of getting food and shelter. Living separate from the pack was simply too dangerous. Of course, life is different now: there aren't a lot of wild animals running around, you can stroll into any corner store for food, and you no longer have to arm wrestle for space in the cave. If you choose to live alone as an adult these days you can. However, this is not an option for our young because they are born so dependent. We are actually born programmed to attach and be social as a way to increase our chances of survival. So when we are faced with our first separation, and with most separations from significant others for that matter, we are likely to feel anger, anxiety, and a lot of other things. The reason for this is simple. Anger is energizing; it gets our blood pumping, our heart racing and gives us an adrenaline rush. It triggers the fight-or-flight response, the very same response that saved the caveman we spoke of earlier. The adrenaline rush from anger actually prepares us to either stand our ground and fight off threats, like screaming and crying to protest separation, or tuck our tails between our legs and run away, like withdrawing and feeling helpless in response to separation. For example, say you're strolling down a busy street in broad daylight and a twelve-year-old unarmed boy runs up to you and grabs your grocery bag. Your instinct might be to fight off your assailant to keep what's yours. However, if you were held up at knife-point in a dark, deserted alley, rather than stand and fight you might decide to flee, giving up not only your groceries, but your wallet, too. In both cases the fight-or-flight response is set into motion. The degree of threat helps you to decide what to do: fight or run away. Fortunately, you can also learn to deal with some threatening situations in more moderate ways such as problem solving, negotiation and changing your own expectations.

Sociological Influences on Anger Expression

Because feeling angry is an unavoidable part of being human beings, we all grow up seeing people express anger in very different ways. Still, we learn the most about anger expression in our first families. In a perfect world, we would have grown up in a family where anger was recognized as a normal feeling and where it was okay to be angry sometimes, just like it was okay to be happy or sad at other times. In this perfect world we'd have seen our parents dealing with their anger in rational ways: talking it over instead of acting it out; listening to others even when they were upset; setting aside their anger to solve the problem at hand. Of course, we're still human, so even rational people, in anger, raise their voices and say some hurtful things sometimes. "Rational" does not mean robotic. It does mean having the ability to recognize that the function of anger is to cue us in to the fact that something is wrong and to help get to some sort of resolution.

In the following example constructive anger communication is compared with destructive anger communication.

Tom and Suzie meet at home after work to set out on a dinner date. Tom has made the reservations weeks in advance because the restaurant is so popular. Suzie arrives home late. Notice how Tom and Suzie's conversation in the first example leaves room for discussion, while still staying focused on the problem at hand. In contrast, the "destructive anger communication" leads to blaming, defensive posturing and straying away from the topic.

Constructive Anger

Tom: I'm really pissed off that you're not ready to go. [*Takes responsibility for his feelings*] You know how long we had to wait for these reservations. [*Includes Suzie in the problem by using "we"*] I was really looking forward to a special evening with you. [*Talks about his disappointment and alludes to her significance in his life*]

Suzie: I'm sorry, Tom. [*Acknowledges Tom's feelings*] When you made reservations for mid-week I had a feeling that it would be hard for me to be on time, but I didn't want to say anything because I knew how hard it was for you to get them. [*Acknowledges Tom's efforts*]

Tom: Well, I suppose I should have checked with you first to find out what would have been a good time for you, too. [*Acknowledges his contribution to the problem, and suggests a possible solution*]

Suzie: Yeah, that would have been helpful. Look, I'll try to speak up more, even if I think you don't want to hear it. [*Acknowledges her contribution to the problem, and possible solution*] Well, we do have the rest of the evening. Maybe we can still find something worthwhile to do. (Sly smile.) [*Adds some humor to the situation after appropriately addressing the problem; communicates that time together is also important to her*]

Tom: Well, what do you have in mind? [*Argument moves away from escalation towards resolution*]

Destructive Anger

Tom: You really make me mad when you're late. (Pointing at Suzie.) [*Blames Suzie for his anger; uses physically threatening posture*] You're always late! Why can't you just be on time for once? [*Generalizes from one instance of tardiness to the accusation of always being late*] Sometimes I wonder why I even bother trying to do something nice for you. [*Attributes the problem solely to Suzie; avoids discussing feelings other than anger*]

Suzie: I'm sick of you always getting on me for the things that I do wrong! [*Like Tom, Suzie generalizes from one situation of Tom expressing anger about her tardiness, to Tom "always" being angry*] What about things you do wrong? Like last weekend you said that you would mow the lawn, but you didn't. Did I hassle you about that? [*Defensive blaming style; drifts away from the issue at hand*]

Tom: Well, it's not like you did anything last weekend but lay around and watch videos all day. [*Style is defensive; he drifts ever farther from the topic*]

Suzie: What's wrong with that? I deserve some R and R, too. [*Argument continues to escalate with blaming and subsequent attempts to defend themselves by calling up past transgressions*]

Few of us were lucky enough to have completely positive examples of constructive anger communication in our first families. Instead, most of us saw some multiple variations, variations like rage, passive aggression or self-sacrifice. As an exercise, spend some time thinking about and trying to understand your first family's style of anger expression. If you can share your recollection with each other, this will lead to a better understanding between the two of you.

Chapter 6

Leftover Anger

Why do we get *so* angry at our lovers? Why do we feel such hostility in our intimate relationships? After all, we *chose* to be with these people. They're not like family members, where we're born into a certain system and we have to play the hand dealt. When it comes to our lovers, we *picked* the hand. So, why the constant struggle?

Intimate relationships differ from other types of relationships in some very significant ways: we have greater expectations of our partners than of others; we often choose partners based on characteristics they possess that allow us to work through past conflicts and these relationships tend to be exclusive so that there aren't other outlets available to meet our needs. These are just some of the ways that intimate relationships differ from other relationships. Because of the nature of intimate relationships, whatever is left over from childhood—the good, the bad, and the ugly—our lovers are likely to get the lion's share of it... our anger is no exception.

What is Leftover Anger?

Leftover anger is anger that started in childhood and is carried over to our present relationships, especially relationships with lovers.

How To Identify Leftover Anger

If you find that:

- in your most private moments even you have to admit that your anger toward your partner is excessive

- no one else you know gets as angry as you routinely do about certain things regarding your lover (e.g., when Mitch's wife is late with dinner, he goes into a rage; when Joe's wife, Jennifer, is late with dinner, he eats dinner without her)

- your need for control over your lover is never completely satisfied

- you get equally or more angry about the same things now as when you were a kid

- you recognize a lot of similar annoying flaws between your parents and your lover

you are probably serving your partner leftovers. And we all know how bad a steady diet of leftovers can be.

The Origin of Leftover Anger

The true source of all anger is in our heads. That's right, anger comes from our thoughts, expectations, judgments—in short—our cognitive patterns. Of course, we all have certain experiences that shape our cognitive patterns and, therefore, influence the path our anger later takes, but we are indeed the source of our own anger. Although others may do things that we don't like or feel is right, only we can make ourselves feel angry. In fact, how we feel is directly related to what we think. The more irrational our thoughts, such as rigid beliefs, judgmental attitudes and unobtainable expectations, the more likely we are to struggle with anger in our relationships. This may sound strange now, but by the end of this book you will not only understand this concept, but also feel relieved by it because if you, not your parents nor your lover, are the source of your anger, then it is truly within your power to master it.

For now, however, let's explore the types of early experiences that prime us to carry anger over from childhood into our relationships with lovers. The role that these experiences play in leftover anger is that they significantly influence the development of irrational cognitive patterns at a time in our lives when we are most susceptible to being shaped. Such experiences include: maltreatment, especially by parents, such as abuse and neglect; overindulgence; and poor parental models for coping with anger. Remember, these experiences are not the cause of our anger, merely the sculptors.

Maltreatment

Children who have been grossly mistreated may think, at a young age, that it's just normal to be hit, abused or left alone for days without food and neglected. But as they get older, they realize that this is not the norm and that, while many individuals struggle with some sort of family dysfunction, this degree of mistreatment is extreme. Such maltreated children grow into adults who feel cheated for not being treated decently. Maltreated children have learned that their needs do not matter to others and that those needs will not be met by their significant others without manipulation on their part, whether obvious or subtle. They are, therefore, prone to anger. Because high expectations are also common in intimate relationships in particular, as indicated in thoughts like *She'll be my everything* or *He's my whole world*, their partners are the most likely recipients of the manipulation.

Abuse

Abused children are taught by their parents that control over others is all-important. Through abuse, parents communicate to their children that one's own needs come before others'. Many of these children learn to do to others that which has been done to them; they learn to disregard others' feelings and to expect, even demand, that others meet their needs. Although abuse is about power, the ultimate lesson is one of dis-empowerment. Being abused emphasizes one's own lack of control. Abuse results in a cycle that is self-perpetuating. Without developing a sense of empowerment, we cannot see our own contributions to our problems. We believe someone other than ourselves must, therefore, be to blame. Finally, we must find a way to make these others do the right thing.

Children of abuse often grow into adults who seek control over others, demand that others meet their needs, and blame others when they are unhappy. While these attitudes are likely to leak out in a lot of different directions—throwing a tantrum in the grocery store when the clerk ignores you; sabotaging a coworker's project because he was chosen for promotion over you—no one provides a better lightening rod for leftover anger than our lovers. If you couple the fact that most of us enter into relationships with excessive expectations of significant others, early abuse often causes later feelings of entitlement. In this way, adult children of abuse are set up for disappointment in intimate relationships.

Leila was sexually abused by her step-father, Mack, in early adolescence. One of Leila's clearest memories is of Mack telling her how beautiful she was, how sexy he found her and the fact that looking at her gave him his greatest pleasure. Mack used to give Leila presents, money and special privileges if she dressed up for him or, as he would say, got dolled up. In a strange way Leila felt as though she controlled Mack with her looks although, in the end, he always got his way.

Leila is now thirty-nine and married. She was still attractive on her wedding day ten years ago, says husband, Skip. But neither marriage nor Skip have lived up to Leila's hopes. When she realized that she was not going to be a doctor's wife as planned because Skip dropped out of medical school, but rather one half of a working class couple, Leila began to gain weight. Early on, she thought that she could entice Skip to return to school by promising sexual favors. Skip happily accepted the favors but never went back to school. After a couple of years of that game, Leila could see that it was useless, he was not going to be a doctor. Now, no matter how much her husband complains about her appearance Leila still doesn't do anything. She neglects her appearance and hygiene, something she knows bothers her husband, because he won't do what she wants (go back to school and become a doctor).

Leila was raised in a world of control or be controlled. She was taught that her only value was her physical appearance and that with that commodity, she could control others, make demands of them. True to form, Leila managed to marry a man who, like her stepfather, valued her beauty more than any other aspect of her being. Like Mack, Skip was gratified by her beauty and potential sexuality. But when Leila was unable to control Mack with her body she became angry, blaming him for their dismal existence. What better way then to express her anger toward Skip than to deprive him of what she, too, believed to be the only quality of value that she possessed?

Neglect

Unlike abuse where parents *do* something that is harmful to children, neglect occurs when parents hurt children by *not* doing something, like failing to provide food, shelter or emotional support. These children live in constant fear of abandonment, developing little sense of security about their own self-worth and even less ability to trust others. It is exactly this inability to trust, this fear of rejection that creates the need to control others, and the anger at failing to do so. This control can manifest itself in many forms, from brute force to passive aggression.

Adults who were neglected as children tend to express anger by becoming depressed and clinging closely to their partners. Because of their fear of abandonment and their belief that they are not worthy of love—they believe that if their parents couldn't love them, how could they expect someone else to—expressing anger openly is just too risky. Neglected or abandoned children may, after all, be abandoned again because of their bad behavior. Often, as adults, formerly neglected children hang on to their anger, never letting it be known. Instead of turning their anger toward their lovers, they focus it inward on themselves. The result of these pent-up negative thoughts and feelings is depression. Perhaps the most important point here is that depression can also be a form of anger and control since being around depressed people is often painful for loved ones.

Overindulgence

Children who are overindulged are often set up to have excessively high expectations of what others ought to do for them. By the same token, they are set up to be angry since they are often frustrated by others' inability to meet their excessive demands. More often than not, their expectations remain exorbitant and are carried over into adult relationships, particularly their relationships with lovers. This is, in part, due to the fact that few others would tolerate such behavior. For the overindulged, other people, especially significant others, come to be symbols of their disappointment and anger.

Do you remember that classmate growing up who always got whatever he wanted…the new bike, the newest toys, a later curfew than everybody else, dessert instead of dinner, a whopping allowance even though he wasn't responsible for any chores? Often, this was the same kid who left you cringing in the corner as he took on his parents in verbal sparring matches *and won*. He was amazing. Half the size of his mom and dad but, with twice the power, he was the envy of every kid on the block. He was also spoiled rotten because his parents gave him everything he wanted, when he wanted it.

Parents who seriously overindulge their children likely don't know the importance of setting limits, saying *no* and establishing rules. They often don't understand that, while setting limits may be unpleasant for both them and their children, doing so is as much a parent's responsibility as providing food and shelter.

Setting limits sets the stage for many essential experiences. For one, limits actually help children feel secure, even when they get an answer they don't like. After all, it's pretty hard to feel secure when, at the age of eight years old you're in charge and making all your own decisions. Second, limits help children to learn that they may not get everything they want in life. Finally, limits provide children with the opportunity to learn to cope with the frustration of not having their every need met by someone else.

While that kid may have seemed cool then, today he is pushing his wife farther and farther away with his sense of entitlement and inability to manage frustration. You see, one big difference between the overindulged person and another person is that the other person, having dealt with minor disappointment as a child, has developed skills for coping with differences of opinion and related frustration.

Parental Models and Family Styles

Experiences of maltreatment and overindulgence actually shape children's thoughts and leave them vulnerable to irrational thoughts that fuel anger. Our cognitive patterns are shaped not only by such experiences, but also by how our parents manage their own anger. Though less extreme than overt behaviors like abuse, neglect and overindulgence, parental models of anger also teach irrational beliefs about the world—unreasonable expectations, judgmental attitudes, cognitive rigidity—and how we ought to treat loved ones when angry. These models are powerful. After all, our parents are our first teachers and the people on whom we depend for our survival as youngsters.

Parental Rage: The Terrorizer

Some of you may have grown up with a terrorizer for a parent. This is the mother or father whose normal, everyday anger and frustration turned into rage. They weren't exactly abusers in the physical or sexual sense. Rather, they destroyed things with their angry words and tempers; they left behind smashed objects and bruised egos. Others of you may have had to deal with the irrational anger of an alcoholic or drug-addicted parent. They were fine as long as they weren't using, but have a drink or two or use a substance and suddenly they'd lose it. Growing up with this kind of parent makes it difficult to learn how to deal with your own anger reasonably, after all, the raging parent's message is the same as the abusive parent's: *Only my feelings matter; I'm always right, you're to blame; You must meet my needs.*

Maybe one parent raged while the other tried to passively keep the peace; perhaps both raged. Either way, it wasn't good, because all you saw were the extremes; what you learned were hurtful cognitive patterns and extreme behavior—raging or gunny-sacking.

Dave's father was a terrorizer. Dave and his wife, Mary, came to the clinic for marital therapy. It was Mary's idea because she was sick of Dave's anger and controlling behavior. Dave was never physically abusive, but he was threatening. He'd scream and yell and pound the table when Mary or the kids did not live up to his high standards. Dave had standards about how they should dress, whom they should hang out with and how they should run their lives. Most of the time, Mary just went along with Dave, even though she disagreed with his ways and felt manipulated a lot of the time.

What finally got her attention were the changes that she started to see in the children. Their teenaged son began getting into trouble at school for bullying other kids and their daughter began losing her temper with her brother, her parents and even her friends. Dave's disappointment in the kids just fueled more rages. Though the rages were nothing new and something that Mary had decided to put up with, she had begun to change her mind now that the children were being affected—Mary was talking divorce.

Looking at Dave and Mary's families, it was pretty easy to see why they had the problems they did. Dave had come to emulate the terrorizing behavior his father showed him. Like his father, Dave was controlling and rigid; he was furious when disobeyed or disappointed. Dave set impossible standards for others, then verbally abused them when they could not meet them. He manipulated circumstances to increase his control, like never letting Mary know what was going on with their finances so that she would be dependent upon him. Mary's father, who was also controlling, made all of her decisions for her, including her marriage to Dave. Thus, in some ways, her relationship with Dave had been comfortable. Though Dave hated his father's terrorism, he also believed that the only other choice for dealing with his anger was passivity. Being a terrorizer at home didn't win him any popularity contests, but at least this way he had some control in his life. As for Mary, she felt that being passive was an easy way to live; this way she didn't have to take responsibility for anything. She just did what others told her to do. Dave and Mary had finally realized that their ways of dealing with anger were hurting their children. In effect, they were grooming their kids to be third generation terrorizers. Dave and Mary decided to continue therapy in hopes of breaking the cycle.

Rage and avoidance are two extremes of coping with anger. Both are destructive, though in different ways. Rage is directed outside of yourself and usually ends up damaging things or people. Avoidance usually ends up being hurtful to you. Anger can be damaging to you and others when mishandled, and that includes when not handled at all.

Avoidance: The Ostrich

Another style for dealing with anger is avoidance. Mary is a good example of this. Instead of dealing with the reality of her anger, for much of her relationship with Dave, she buried her head in the sand, hence "the ostrich," and acted as though nothing was wrong. In this way, she tried to keep the peace on at least a superficial level. But one of the values of anger is that it is a cue that something is wrong. By ignoring such cues, problems such as Dave's overt anger towards

Mary and control issues are likely to careen out of control rather than be addressed and resolved.

As it turned out, Mary was not the only one unhappy in the relationship. Dave was too. He was frustrated because he felt that he had to do everything: make all the decisions, earn all the income, discipline the children, run the household. Sometimes he wondered if Mary was just along for the ride. But Mary believed that the best way to avoid making Dave angry was to stay out of his way and let him run the show. That's how her mother dealt with Mary's father's hostility. "Just turn the other cheek," her mother used to say to her, "You're better than that." Mary's translation: *Anger is evil and can serve no good purpose; If I feel angry something is wrong with me. I must be perfect.* As a result of these irrational thoughts, Mary avoided her own anger and the cues that there was a problem. In doing so, she further compromised her and Dave's happiness.

Passive-Aggression: In Through the Back Door

Maybe your family's style for dealing with anger was not as extreme as rage or total avoidance. Maybe you saw something more along the order of passive-aggression. These people get angry, but unlike the terrorizing parent who does extreme things when angry, this parent goes to the extreme of doing nothing. So, instead of saying he's angry and getting to the core of it, your father may have let you know by "forgetting" to go to your baseball game or giving you the silent treatment or putting off fixing the flat tire on your bike. Eventually you probably figured out that this was his way of getting back at you and others. His doing nothing was your punishment. Like anything else, if you grew up with it, it is likely to be a part of your baggage today. You may believe that if things don't go your way, you have a *right* to get angry, people *should* do what you want or it is your place to teach them a lesson.

Consider Laurie and Steve, another couple we've seen for marital therapy. Laurie complained that Steve never did anything around the house without her nagging him into it and Steve complained that Laurie was always nagging him and wished that she would get off his back. However, both were committed to the relationship and hoped to resolve this problem.

After several sessions, it became clear that Steve was not helping out around the house. He believed that running the home was women's work since he had grown up in a pretty traditional home where his father worked out of the home and his mother was a housewife. The problem was that in the past year, since putting their youngest child in daycare, Laurie had returned to work full-time and could no longer keep up with the chores on her own. Steve acknowledged the new time constraints and agreed that he too would have to chip in. So, Laurie and Steve wrote up a chore list and divided it in a way that seemed fair to both—a good example of negotiation. Additionally, Laurie agreed to scale down her expectations for a clean house to better fit the reality of their present situation. It seemed as though the couple was back on track until their fourth session.

Although their plan worked for about a month, after that, something changed. During their session, Laurie explained that for the past few days it felt like Steve hadn't been holding up his end of the bargain because he hadn't been doing anything around the house. Laurie stated that she worries that if she doesn't push him, he'll never do anything.

Steve responded to Laurie's accusations by explaining that he had just been tired lately. "I don't see what the big deal is anyway. I mean, so what if the toilet goes a few extra days before it's cleaned."

"You know how important a clean house is to me," Laurie responded. "We've covered all of this before. I've been trying to hold up my end of the bargain and not demand perfection."

Stepping in, we asked Steve why he seemed so calm and almost indifferent to Laurie's feelings. He remarked that he wasn't going to get upset just because Laurie was upset. He explained that if he did, he would be mad all the time.

This was somewhat of a turn around for Steve. We told him he seemed different than the last time we met. We asked him if something had happened in the last few days to upset him. He responded, "No, not really."

When asked what "not really" means, Steve didn't have an answer. He simply shrugged his shoulders.

Looking for an answer, we turned to Laurie for help. We asked her if she could think of anything that had happened in the last few days that might have upset Steve.

"Well, nothing, really...except I did make a few extra charges on one of our credit cards this month without telling Steve," she recalled. "We got the bill about three days ago. He might have been mad about that, but he didn't say anything."

Suddenly, Steve exploded. "Well, of course I'm pissed! I'm tired of trying to pay these damn cards off. But you know, there's just no point in saying anything to Laurie because, look, she does it anyway."

It was obvious that their finances and Laurie's shopping habits were very frustrating for Steve. We suggested to Steve that he may have been expressing his anger at Laurie by doing something to upset her, like failing to do the chores that he agreed to do.

Calm now, Steve actually laughed a little, responding, "You may have a point there. I know my not doing anything around the house irritates her more than anything I could ever say to her."

In this scenario, Steve, angry at Laurie for using the credit card, expressed his anger by failing to do something that was important to Laurie. There are many reasons why you might choose to cope with anger in this way. Maybe you learned to do it in order to avoid retaliation from the terrorizers in your life, or maybe you use passive-aggression because you believe that you will be abandoned if you are openly angry. Maybe you learned it from a parent, like Steve did. Steve grew up with a passive-aggressive mother. He told of a time when she let almost two months pass before speaking to his father after he had bought a car without her approval. The family was so upset by her silent treatment that Steve's father finally returned the car. Soon after, life was back to normal, so to speak. Steve grew up seeing that if you withhold things long enough, you can control others.

Self-sacrifice: The Victim

In looking at family styles of expressing anger, let's not forget the victim. It has long been known that if you feel angry toward someone and you don't do anything to deal with that feeling on some level, even if its just exercising to relieve some of the energy, you can end up turning that anger against yourself. The energy of anger doesn't just go away. If it's not dealt with in some way, like changing the thoughts that make you angry, confronting the problem to find a solution or channeling the energy into something else, the negative energy stays with you. When this happens people hurt themselves: deprive themselves of fun and pleasure, sacrifice themselves like some sort of martyr, neglect or abuse themselves by abusing drugs or doing dangerous things.

People who deal with their anger at others by taking it out on themselves usually do so because they think that anger destroys relationships. Their fear of abandonment is so great that they would rather hold on to their anger than risk dealing with it. Usually the victim has grown up being victimized by abusive or neglectful parents. Because they continue to victimize themselves, they usually suffer from depression and their loved ones suffer from being with a depressed partner. A former client, who was verbally abused by her father as a child, fits this profile. Kim was angry with her father well into adulthood, but never owned up to her anger because she was afraid of retaliation by her father, who was actually a very sick old man at that point, as well as rejection by other family members.

Kim hung on to her anger and complained that she wasn't able to laugh or enjoy herself, depriving herself of fun. She also had a history of hurting herself by ignoring doctors' orders to take medication she needed to control her epilepsy. Kim's boyfriend, Roy, suffered too. He lived with the pain of loving someone who refused to care for herself. Although not angry with Roy, she continued to take out her anger toward her father on herself, thereby pushing Roy away and forcing their relationship into her cycle of anger. People who cope with anger by turning it inward do not know, or fail to recognize that by victimizing themselves, they also victimize those who love them.

All In The Family

If any of the family and relationship patterns we've discussed apply to your family of origin, you may find that, in addition to that awful wedding gift they gave to you, they also gave you something else... a legacy of anger to act out in your own relationship. Luckily, just as you were able to exchange the gift for something you really could use, you can also trade in your destructive anger for skills of rational thinking, problem solving, and good communication.

Taming The Childhood Anger that Now Threatens Your Relationships

Not everyone who has problems with anger in intimate relationships does so because they have learned such behavior in childhood from family members. Some of us are simply born with more difficult, hard to please temperaments than others. Others of us develop anger problems later in life having made some erroneous association between anger and control in other relationships. But, for those of us who did learn about irrational, destructive anger in our families of origin, there are certain steps that are helpful to master anger with roots in childhood.

Understand the Displacement Factor

Displacement is taking a feeling we have toward one and acting it out with another. We displace anger when the person we're *really* angry at is no longer around, either dead or somehow unavailable or simply too high risk to deal with directly because that person may retaliate with physical or emotional threats or sever the relationship. In the case of Dave and Mary, Dave is a good example of someone who displaced his anger. Though Dave expressed anger toward Mary, the person with whom he was truly angry was his father. The more insight that Dave develops into the true source of his anger, the less likely he will be to take it out on others. To do so would be irrational.

Identify Triggers

Simply speaking, a *trigger* is any sort of stimuli that, through association, stimulates memories. It can be an object, a song, anything. For instance, the smell of popcorn may remind you of the matinee movies you attended as a child. Just as sights, sounds and smells can take us back in time so can our lovers' behavior. Returning to the example of Steve and Laurie, we find that Steve's father had a history of financial irresponsibility. Not only did he buy cars without any previous discussion with his wife, but he often blew an entire month's wages at the track, leaving Steve and his family to financially fend for themselves. Laurie's occasional over-spending was a trigger for Steve's unconscious anger toward his father.

Recognizing the triggers that transport us back to childhood anger empowers us to cope more effectively with our anger. We can: educate partners about triggers to reduce the frequency of occurrence by letting them know why a particular habit or behavior of theirs triggers an angry response; problem solve to further reduce our exposure to triggers by figuring out together ways to avoid the activities or behaviors that act as triggers; learn specific anger mastery skills.

Recognize that Your Choice of Partner is not Random

It is widely agreed upon in the field of psychology that we all choose our lovers based, in part, on the fantasy that with our partners, we will be able to work through our unresolved conflicts with parents. Acting out this fantasy has many implications, one of which is the likelihood of choosing a partner who has the same flaws as our parents, especially the parent with whom we had the most difficulty. In the case of Dave and Mary, Mary began a relationship with a man quite similar to her father; Dave was bossy, controlling and overbearing. Mary's unconscious hope in marrying Dave was to develop her own sense of empowerment in the presence of a controlling man, something that she was not able to do with her father. Instead, Mary found herself in her old childhood pattern of passive aggression. She was not able to move toward empowerment until she saw that not only were they both miserable in the roles that she and Dave had assumed, but their behavior was having a serious impact on the children.

While we are all likely to be attracted to our partners for obvious reasons, like good listening skills, physical attraction or being good providers, we are also likely to be drawn in by their flaws which provide fertile ground for us to continue our battles with age-old conflicts. This is true for most people, not just those of us who struggle with destructive anger. Consider your relationships with your parents. Identify possible conflicts you carry with you and ways you may be reenacting them with your lover. Remember that recognition is the first step necessary for change.

Clarify the Origin of Your Anger

It's hard enough to deal with our genuine anger and frustration toward lovers; throwing leftover anger in the mix is more than most relationships can bear. It is, therefore, important to be clear on whom you are *really* angry with—are you really that furious with your partner for not being attentive to your needs or are you really angry with your father who selfishly put his own needs before yours? Though we are the source of our anger because of our irrational thoughts, confronting the origin of those thoughts and beliefs can be the first step in letting our lovers off the hook of our leftover anger, where *origin* refers to the people and experiences that shaped our cognitive patterns. Confronting the origin of our irrational thoughts does not necessarily mean confronting the person who taught us such thoughts, such as an abusive father. It does mean getting clear on who taught us about anger, whether it was abusive parents who taught us that we have to manipulate to get love or overindulgent parents who taught us that our way is the right way. We must also realize how we act out our anger, and the ways in which we perpetuate our anger. Clarity can come in a number of different ways.

Direct Confrontation

Many adult children choose to confront the parents with whom they are angry. This can be a positive step in dealing with childhood anger that affects intimate relationships *if*:

- in adulthood you have developed a good relationship with that parent
- you have reason to believe your parent can now cope with conflict more effectively because you have witnessed your parent deal with conflict since then
- the mere act of confronting the parent has value for you regardless of the response because confrontation validates your feelings or confronting the truth empowers you

  Confrontation is usually not helpful if:

- the value of the confrontation is based on the quality of the other's response
- your parent must either acknowledge your point or apologize for past transgressions
- you have fantasies that the very act of confrontation will immediately resolve your anger
- confrontation will endanger you physically or emotionally

Indirect Confrontation

If direct confrontation is not beneficial because of circumstances, consider some indirect means. Letter writing is one such technique. Here, you write a letter to the person with whom you are angry without any intention to mail it. Since this letter is for your eyes only, you can be honest about your feelings. Sometimes people burn the letter, symbolizing closure of feelings, memories or incidents. Sometimes people decide to send the letter after all. Regardless of what you do with the letter, the main value of this exercise is in your confronting the reality of your anger by analyzing it and putting it into words.

Another technique of indirect confrontation is called the empty chair technique. This is when you sit across from an empty chair and imagine the person with whom you are angry sitting there. Then, you talk to the chair as if the person were there. You talk about your anger then and about how your anger hurts you today. This technique can be used replacing the chair with a photograph of the parent.

Examine Your Expectations: Are They Appropriate?

Unmet expectations are a major source of anger, and the primary vehicle for perpetuating our anger. Those of us who carry childhood anger into our intimate relationships expect a different outcome with our lovers than that with our parents, even though we often choose partners who are similar to our parents *and* react the same way to our partners as we did with our parents. This doesn't leave much opportunity for a different outcome. Even if we do manage to choose a partner who does not exhibit our parents' flaws, they exhibit other flaws.

In a society that emphasizes happily ever after, that just isn't supposed to happen. Our partners are supposed to be perfect, even if we're not. When most of us examine our expectations of ourselves and our partners, we find that the hurdles are impossible to clear. This frustration alone is enough to cause problems with anger in intimate relationships. As discussed in later chapters, it is important to examine which of the expectations we hold are realistic and which are merely set-ups for failure and subsequent anger.

Develop Other Outlets for Anger

Like it or not, our partners are convenient outlets for our anger: they're always around; since nobody's perfect, sooner or later they make a wrong move which allows us to justify and blame them for our anger; they're usually safe targets since, despite our anger, they often have our best interest at heart. However, we are likely to pay dearly for making our partners such targets, losing trust, respect and eventually love. Rather, we can find more appropriate outlets for our anger, such as exercise or meditation. Better still, we can learn to recognize the true source of our anger—irrational thoughts—and develop skills to combat the true culprit.

Partner Homework

1. How did your family members behave when they were angry? Did expectations differ according to gender or age?

2. What is the most uncomfortable aspect of anger for you (the physical response, the negative thoughts, feeling guilty because you feel angry, the rage, or something else)?

3. What irrational beliefs do you have about anger (for example, only bad people feel angry, no one will like you if you get angry, if you get angry you will lose control)?

4. Keep a journal for at least two weeks. Note feelings of anger, why you were angry and how you expressed your anger. After two weeks, look for patterns in your behavior and in what you did with your anger.

Chapter 7

Cherished Truths:
Our Cognitive Maps of the World

We see the world through a filter composed of a basic set of truths that we believe to exist about the universe. Our reality is really a *cognitive map* of the world. We don't actually know the real world, but only what our senses reveal to us. And then, it isn't just what our sensory organs perceive about the world, it is how we organize and interpret this sensory data that forms the basis of our knowledge of the factual world. In other words, we may look at something, hear something, smell something or touch something and form some idea about what it is we saw, heard or touched based upon our interpretation of this information or our perception.

Perception is, in turn, influenced by past experience and learning. Sometimes our perceptual awareness of the world is treated by us as if it were actually the world itself. For example, if a child looks at a straw in a glass of water, the child might believe that the straw became bent at the point where it entered the water. Repeated experience, however, would convince the child that the straw remains straight both in and out of the water, no matter how it appears. However, if the child had relied only upon his *visual* perception, with no other sensory input, he might have wrongly continued to conclude that straws bend under water.

Reality and Subjective Experience

In addition to the external, factual world, or reality, there is also an internal, subjective experience, or private reality, that we experience as a representation of this external world. There are several steps, or degrees of separation, between this external reality and our internal reality. First of all, the external, objective, factual world exists, regardless of whether we as human beings like it or even know about it. It is just there. Even if there were no human beings around, it would still be there. Second, in order for us to know this world, we must first detect it through our senses—seeing, hearing, smelling, tasting and touching. Third, we must then organize this raw sensory data into some sort of meaningful pattern that makes sense to our brains—perception. If we were to see a series of dots in close proximity to each other in a circular pattern, we would likely perceive it to be a circle. Fourth, we then make some kind of judgment about the perception. In the case of a circle, we might judge it to be a good circle, a dim circle or an irregular circle. Finally, we arrive at some sort of conclusion based on this judgment. If we, for example, judge that the circle is too dim, we might conclude that it needs to be brighter and take steps to enhance its color or shading characteristics.

Our Conclusions About Reality May or May Not Be Accurate

There are many steps, then, between the initial, raw external stimulus and the final conclusion arrived at by us. By the same token, there are as many opportunities for error in analyzing, organizing and concluding from this original data as there are steps in the process. There are many examples of how we mess up and make erroneous decisions based on faulty interpretation of the data. For instance, if we are going down a set of stairs in the dark and think that there is one more step at the bottom of the stairs than there really is, we may take a step downward and are brought up short with a jolt in the legs and hips when we find out that there is no last step, just level ground.

We make similar mistakes and arrive at erroneous conclusions and actions in the psychological and emotional arena just as we do in the physical world. For instance, let's say you are standing in the hallway at a party and observe your boyfriend and another friend talking to one another. Suddenly, one of them looks in your direction, points at you and then they both laugh. How do you feel? Well, it all depends on the kind of data you observe, how you judge it and what you conclude. You don't arrive at this scene as a blank slate. You bring with you all kinds of learning experiences, expectations and truths about the world. You may say to yourself, *Josh is pointing at me and laughing. They must think I'm a fool or something about me makes them think I'm a fool and therefore they don't have any respect for me.* If one of the truths that you brought to this situation was that all people that you value should think highly of you and respect you, then you will probably experience a fairly intense emotional reaction to the scenario we described. Your specific reaction will probably revolve around the specific things you are telling yourself and how strongly you believe them.

If you think, *My boyfriend should never laugh at me—how dare he treat me so disrespectfully. He doesn't care about me at all,* you're probably going to get angry. If you instead think, *Who knows what they're laughing about? Whatever it is, it must be very funny. I'll have to remember to ask him about it later,* then you are more likely to not be angry with him. Different emotions can be generated by different words and thoughts that you have in your belief system, especially when they occur in relation to the person who is closest to you.

Quickly and subconsciously, you arrive at a series of multiple conclusions depending upon the type of thinking you are engaging in and the particular truths that you use to filter sensory and intellectual data. The objective reality, on the other hand, were we to overhear what Josh and your other friend were discussing, might reveal that he was actually pointing to a poster on the wall directly behind you that pictured a silly character from his favorite comedy. You then have become very upset at a situation which, in reality, didn't even involve you. You needlessly upset yourself over misapplied and misinterpreted information that you erroneously concluded related to you. Your as-if reality gets confused with the actual reality out there in the world. Had you had accurate information about what was really happening between the two, you would have thought and felt a great deal differently. Similarly, lacking this information, if you had just treated your thoughts as theories or hypotheses instead of facts, you would have felt differently about the way your significant other was reacting to you, as well.

Our Interpretations Are Not Necessarily Reality Itself

The same thing that happens when we interpret events in the physical world can and does happen when we attempt to interpret events in the human behavioral and psychological world. We are prone to misinterpretation here too. There are a lot of ways that we misinterpret others' behaviors.

One of the most common ways people mistake their understanding of an event for reality is mind-reading. This occurs when a person, especially when he or she has come to know another person fairly well, thinks he knows why the other person behaves in a particular way. For instance, Jill doesn't respond to her boyfriend's overtures to make love. Jill's boyfriend may say to himself, *Jill ignored me because she isn't attracted to me. She must be mad at me or she just doesn't care about me.* He is taking a simple action, the failure to respond and drawing his own conclusions about it. He is also making the assumption that she understood his intentions, that his partner intentionally ignored him and that she intentionally ignored him for the specific reason that she doesn't care about him.

Often people jump to these multi-layered conclusions quickly, subconsciously and intensely, especially when the other person is someone with whom they have a close relationship. They treat their perceptions, interpretations and conclusions as if they were reality or the way the other person actually thinks. They are instead making a series of assumptions and decisions. As if this wasn't bad enough, their view of the other person's thought processes is sometimes quite distorted. Nevertheless, the accompanying emotions are often very upsetting to them. If you tell yourself that your mate didn't make love to you because he no longer cares about you, you are going to probably feel despondent, depressed or upset, at the least. You are treating your theories about what occurred and why it occurred as if they were reality. You can convince yourself and feel very strongly that you know what happened and why it happened and be mistaken. What you feel and think may or may not be the way your mate really is. Your cognitive map of reality may be accurate, or it may be distorted and unrealistic.

Even if your thinking is inaccurate, if you at least *view* your interpretations or beliefs as theories about your significant other and not as the actual facts themselves, you are quite likely to avoid serious emotional distress. In other words, if you tell yourself, *Maybe Jill didn't want me because she was tired or because she had something on her mind. She was not necessarily intentionally rejecting me.* Now you are thinking more scientifically, accurately and flexibly. You aren't jumping to rigid conclusions that you hold as truth and you are willing to accept evidence to contradict what you believe you *know* to be the case.

Other ways that we misinterpret events are by labeling them and by taking events out of context. For example, you might have labeled Jill a bitch for not returning your desires. Or you might have looked at the incident as if it occurred in a vacuum, disregarding the fact that you and Jill have been lovers for years, without her rejecting you. Whether you mind-read, label or view events out of context, you're likely to end up with the same problem: misinterpreting others' behaviors, drawing conclusions based on those misinterpretations and damaging your relationships.

Seeing your assessment of your relationship as theoretical and not forming assumptions about the other person instead of treating your thoughts as if they were unerring reflections of reality itself, the more likely your thoughts are capable of being modified by correct input. You and your partner will end up being more flexible and objective and thus able to avoid relationship crises more easily. You both will be calmer because you will not be setting yourselves up as all-knowing gods who possess the only true insight into each other and the world around you, as well as the ulterior motives of the other partner. Interpreting another's behavior is a very dangerous and potentially disturbing game. If you believe that your thinking accurately reflects what's really happening in your partner's mind, you will find it difficult to cope with the reality of your partner's thoughts, and ultimately, with each other and your relationship.

This concept is simple but not necessarily easy to apply. It takes a lot of work and practice on both your parts to stop jumping to conclusions, mind-reading and labeling but it can be done. If you practice in warm, rather than white hot situations of anger, you will both become better at refraining from rigid interpretations of each other and the world. Start today by recognizing your hypotheses for what they are—hypotheses, not facts.

The Origin of Cognitive Maps

We obtain our thoughts, truths and ideas about the world from a variety of sources. First of all, we are biologically scripted to be irrational. Emotions are given to us because they have survival value. They prepare us for the *fight-or-flight* response in reaction to possibly life-threatening situations. Imagine an early caveman coming out of his cave and spotting a snake. The rational caveman might think, *Hey, I wonder if this snake is poisonous. I think I'll go up and try to get a closer look.* Suddenly the snake strikes out and bites him—turns out it was poisonous and the rational caveman dies. The irrational caveman, however, goes out, sees the snake, gets scared and runs far and fast. It doesn't matter if the snake was poisonous or not. The question is academic, because either way, the irrational caveman isn't around to get hurt. His irrational running response has spared him from contact with the snake. The snake may well have been harmless so both the rational and irrational caveman would have been safe anyway.

Although the irrational caveman may look and act strangely, he gets himself out of dangerous or potentially dangerous situations due to his overreactive emotions and thus stays out of harm's way. In the era of the caveman, he probably lived a little longer than his inquisitive, rational cave mate. The emotional center lies in the older, core part of the brain. The outer, newer structure of the brain—the neocortex—came later in the evolutionary development of the brain. Perhaps this is why it seems we often tend to react emotionally to an event or each other before we're aware of our thinking or analysis of that event.

The Social Influences on Our Cognitive Maps

We also get our ways of viewing the world, or truths, from a variety of other sources. In addition to the genetic makeup in our brain's structure that we inherited from primitive man, we also develop our cognitive maps by learning from others. We pick up ideas, concepts and beliefs about the world in our childhood from important people in our early lives: parents or other family members, as well as other significant individuals like teachers, priests, rabbis and coaches.

There is a critical learning period in our young lives when it is very easy for us to pick up and learn information and ways of looking at things, a period in which we are particularly vulnerable to acquiring new data uncritically and non-analytically. During that period, we literally soak up hundreds of bits and pieces of information without examining them closely for correctness or holding them up to critical scrutiny as we might when adults. Our brains are like sponges when we're young and this is one reason why it's so easy to learn a foreign language at an early age and relatively more difficult to do so once we're more mature.

When you're young, people tell you things like, "Be fair to others and they will be fair to you in return," "Good hard work will always be rewarded" and "If you do well, others will respect you and you will do well in the world." When people tell you these things, they mean well and oftentimes they don't expect you to necessarily take their words literally, but young people do, all the same. As youngsters, most of us believe inherently what we are told.

We thus acquire a tremendous amount of knowledge uncritically when we're young and impressionable and a lot of this knowledge is either incorrect, when looked at carefully or distorted by us after we hear it. Some of our adult views of reality come from our own inherent genetic makeup as well as from other people. We also tend to create and form ideas and impressions about the world by interpreting, categorizing and concluding ideas from the information we get externally. We do this because it's natural to try to understand, predict and to some extent control what happens to us and the things around us. We try to figure out why things happen so that we can cope better with the world, achieve our goals and survive. It makes us uncomfortable when we don't know why things happen or why people do the things they do. We want things to be simple and orderly and to conform to certain rules or truths, because somehow things just seem safe or right when they do.

Emotional Happiness As a Couple
Depends on Accurate Thinking

One other thing should be remembered about all of this. All the truths about the world you carry around inside your head may either be accurate reflections of the way your lover and the world really is (*There is gravity and things will fall to the earth if dropped.*) or inaccurate and irrational (*There really is no such thing as gravity and if I jump out of this second story window, I will simply float gently to the ground.*). The more accurate your thinking, the better you both will be able to cope with each other, the world and the other people in it. Another spin-off from this accurate thinking involves the emotional state of your relationship. The more accurate your thinking, the less likely you are to be upset with each other.

By the way, thinking inaccurately or irrationally does not necessarily mean that you won't cope well or that you will be upset but it certainly sets the stage for it. Inaccurate thinking makes you more vulnerable and fragile and more at risk when dealing with the world and your significant other. If you think you can fly, you probably won't be in any trouble until you go to a high place and test out that notion. If you think that other people and especially your partner should always treat you fairly, respect you and you either never leave your room or you only happen to run into people who in fact do treat you well, you probably won't be upset. However, that isn't the restricted world in which most of us dwell. In the real world, you will probably run into the exception to your truth or belief about how the world and the people in it are supposed to be. If the exception is the person you love, all the worse.

Thus, you are primed to be upset by events concerning that person before you even encounter them. The particular event itself just happens to be the thing that sets it off, but that is really not the major factor that causes your distress. What's much more significant is the ongoing processes in your head. Your thinking is the real cause of your distress—the actual event itself merely sets it off or affects it. It doesn't cause it as so many people think. The event affects you, but doesn't make you angry. Only you can control that. In a similar vein, we can tell you a joke, but only you can choose to find it funny or not.

Chapter 8

Disputing Demands:
A Major Cause of Partnership Anger

How you react to your environment depends on your beliefs and perceptions. Suppose you approach the cash register in a clothing store to pay for your purchases and you pleasantly greet the salesgirl with, "Hello. How are you today?" Without responding, the salesgirl goes about her job, ringing up the items. You suddenly feel very indignant, telling yourself, *What's her problem? I was being very polite even though I didn't have to. How dare she ignore me! I at least deserve a response. After all, I am the customer. She is obviously a rude person.* Despite the intensity or longevity of your feelings of what *should* be, we predict that you will not be able to prove that this salesgirl *should* have greeted you in return. It is not written anywhere except in your mind that she must respond to you just because you spoke to her first. It is not a physical law of the universe that she must, ought to or has to respond. In fact, you can probably come up with lots of evidence quite contrary to this assertion. Her mind could have been preoccupied. Or she could have been upset because of a previous customer and, therefore, not up to her usual level of politeness.

You—and this is a very important point to remember—could also come up with a lot of reasons why it would have been *better* if she had greeted you in return or why it would have been nicer or more pleasant. After all, things would have gone more smoothly had she been polite in return; you would probably have been a satisfied customer and referred friends to the store. These things are all factual and realistic because you can prove them. What is *not* factual and realistic is that just because all of these things would have worked out better if she had greeted you, that therefore she *must* have greeted you back.

Noted author, Stephen Covey, tells the true story of a man who stepped aboard a train with his seven unruly children. The children were being loud and making lots of noise while running about in seven different directions. The nearby passengers were almost unanimous in their irritation and annoyance at both the man and his children and some were sharply critical of their behavior. At this point, the man stated that he was very sorry about all the noise, but that they had all just returned from the hospital where his wife, their mother, had died that day. Almost at once, the mood of the passengers changed from irritation to empathy and concern. Several offered to help in any way that they could. The point here, once again, is that behavior by itself is not the critical determinant of emotions. Perceptions are. When the passengers' perceptions of the situation changed, their emotional reactions changed as well. Perceptions can make all the difference in our reactions to our environment.

The Consequences of Relationship Demands and Expectations

The previous examples illustrate the ways in which our perceptions of the way that the world should be affect how we feel. We present the world with many demands. We have demands about the way that people should act and react, what they should say to us and do for us. We have demands about what we deserve and what we think others owe us. It should not be surprising then, that demands often lead to anger. But anger isn't the only effect that demands produce.

Demands also tend to create a sense of resistance, alienation and stubbornness. Think about how you react to demands. How do you feel when someone demands something of you? Chances are, you don't feel like doing whatever it is that the other person is demanding. In fact, you probably want to do just the opposite even if you originally agreed with his idea. You may resist doing it or do it grudgingly. You are likely to feel less emotionally close to that person because of the way he treated you. And we'd be willing to bet that you feel angry.

Paradoxical Effects of Demands

Demands can also have a paradoxical effect on us internally. For example, if you're a man and you begin to experience difficulty obtaining an erection and tell yourself, *I have to get an erection. If I don't get hard, it will be terrible,* chances are obtaining an erection will be that much more difficult. Unfortunately, the demand for an erection does not always produce results because the tremendous anxiety the situation creates physiologically is antagonistic to sexual arousal. Moreover, if a man feels he has his entire manhood, and thus his self-esteem, riding on his sexual performance, it is hardly a condition likely to produce optimal results.

The same thing happens when you're lying in bed at night, knowing you've got to get up early the next morning and telling yourself you have to get to sleep. The pressure usually produces restlessness, tossing, turning and emotional arousal, once again because of the demand you're placing on yourself. The same happens when you expect too much from yourself when playing sports. You can't demand that you do well, win the game or be "in the zone." Demands tend to produce tightness, tension, poor timing and coordination. What's the answer then? Once again, you had better stop making the demands, whether to win the game, have an erection or relax and sleep, because it just doesn't work. Most often it produces the opposite result of what you want. The best way to achieve these states is to relax, allow them to happen and enjoy them; don't focus on the results and take your ego out of it. Using the erection example, bridge that gap between lack of fulfillment and joy between you and your mate by telling yourself something like:

> I'm going to enjoy myself and try to ensure that my partner feels the same. Hopefully, if things go well, I'll be able to perform. If not, it's not the end of the world. There will be other occasions to have fun trying. It hardly defines our entire relationship if I fail tonight. Mostly, it just makes it a disappointing experience at this point in time. She probably won't think poorly of me, although I'm sure she'd like it better if we did have intercourse. If we can't, I'll try to please her sexually some other way.

You must strongly, forcefully and vigorously challenge your irrational thoughts when they occur in situations like this. The idea is to talk reasonably and realistically to yourself, take the pressure off and stop making excessive demands on yourself.

God or Human?: The Rigid Nature of Demands

In forming demands and expectations, we are faced with choice. An angry partner can either find out how things in the universe really function and adjust his thinking to this reality or he or she can rigidly, stubbornly and self-righteously demand that things in the universe must behave according to his or her own laws and directions.

Some partners spend a great deal of time going around trying to make their mates do exactly as they tell them. Often, angry partners spend enormous energy trying to correct the other person's flaws and mistakes, trying to ensure they'll do things the "right" way. A lifetime could be spent in this futile pursuit and there would be rather limited results.

Since one person can't control another person's thinking, he will similarly have limited success in trying to control her behavior or attitudes. He can plead with her, beg her, cajole her, set in motion various consequences for her behavior if she messes up, but he cannot make her think the way he thinks or behave the way he feels she should. One has about as much control over their spouse's or lover's mind and thinking as we do the weather.

I love him and want to spend the rest of my life with him, so he should want to spend all his free time with me. This is a demand, whether said out loud or to oneself. It is truly irrational and unrealistic because it's not factual. What he has done, and what most of us do in emotionally upsetting situations, is take a perfectly good, rational idea and push it over the top. She changed it into something mystical, illusory and dangerous. *Because I want to be with him all the time, he should ignore the other aspects of his life and spend time with me today.* When someone takes a reasonable idea to the kind of extreme where it no longer makes any sense because it simply isn't true, there is usually an irrational ending. Other ideas like this are: *Because I am very hungry and my wife usually has dinner waiting for me on the table when I get home, she* must *have it ready for me this evening* or, *Because I'm a courteous driver, other drivers must treat me courteously too.* As soon as a person starts to put himself in the assumed position of center of the universe by demanding that things and people *have* to behave a certain way—fair or unfair—he is not thinking realistically and will surely be disappointed when things don't go his way.

Different Uses of the Word "Should"

Of course, no one makes these demands all the time. But, the times when people set themselves up as the sole true masters of the universe and make these demands on their partners, it is almost guaranteed to ignite the coals of anger. There is nothing wrong, by the way, with the words should, must, have to or ought to, in and of themselves. We can use such ideas and think them all of the time and not get ourselves in trouble. And how do we do that? The fact of the matter is, we use *should* in a lot of different and appropriate ways.

The Moral Use of Shoulds

Should can be used in a moral sense, for example, you should treat other people nicely. Ethics evolved to help people get along better with each other but they were written precisely out of the knowledge that people can and do make mistakes, for example, by not treating each other kindly. Through time, wise people have figured out that things go better and more smoothly if we treat each other kindly.

Legal Uses of Shoulds

Should can also be used in a legal sense. A thirty-five miles per hour speed limit sign implies that you should not exceed this limit, because if you do it's against the law and you may get ticketed for it. You *should* obey laws. Once again, laws were made to presumably enhance our ability to get along together in a more efficient, safe and orderly manner. Do laws allow for violations? Of course they do. There are consequences for breaking the law, but people break laws all the time. Laws were created to make society work more smoothly, while at the same time punishments for infractions were created and are administered because there will always be those who break the law.

Spiritual Uses of Shoulds

Shoulds, or commands, are also used in a spiritual sense. The Ten Commandments are good examples of this. Moses, so we are told, gave God's commandments to us to help regulate people's behavior in a way that would enhance them spiritually and help achieve entrance to heaven. However, once again we see that even these commandments were "created" because people were fallible. They were doing things that their God forbade. Did people then strictly adhere to all of the commandments? Once again, the answer is no. The Bible is full of such violations. In these three examples, should, or a form of should, is a type of rule, whether ethical, legal or spiritual, that is often broken.

Contingent Use of Shoulds

The word should can also be used contingently. For example, if I want some ice cream tonight, I should stop by the grocery store and purchase some. This is still a rational use of the word, since I am not making a demand on myself to get the ice cream; only surmising that if I am going to be able to eat some ice cream at home, I had better plan ahead and get some beforehand. I am not telling myself that I *have* to get the ice cream or that I have to have it or have to eat it, either, for that matter.

Our uses of *should* ought to make sense in their own context and achieve realistic purposes. We only get ourselves in trouble when we transpose meanings for the *should idea* into one that in our own minds now means that the concept is a physical law of the universe which must be rigidly obeyed under all conditions, at any given time, forever. Confusing the above meanings of the words *should, ought, must* and *have to* gets us into serious trouble when we think of them as physical laws that are immutable. The best test is to ask ourselves if indeed they are physical laws, because if they are, we'll be able to come up with some proof for them. If we can generate some evidence for them, then our thinking is accurate. If we can't, then no matter how strongly we may believe something to be true, our thinking is probably inaccurate and we had better change it.

Chapter 9

War, Terrorism
and Anger Between Couples

On 9/11 America experienced a foreign terrorist attack. Thousands died, along with a national sense of invulnerability as the nation grieved. Many felt violated and angry. For some the anger intensified. This anger was not only expressed by individual, but in many instances resulted in couples turning their feelings of rage, frustration and victimization on one another.

Lindsay, twenty-eight, and Sabastian, thirty-one, have been married for three years. Their history together is a good one. They met in college and it was love at first sight. They dated throughout college until they married, without the typical problems of break-ups over miscommunication, jealousies or even momentary indiscretions that can plague relationships of the very young. They always knew what they wanted as a couple (e.g., to love, support and enjoy each other, to marry, buy a home, have a family and continue to grow together). Further, their individual goals fit in perfectly (e.g., graduate, establish a career and pay off student loans). They shared the values of family and quality time over professional accomplishments and money.

Three years into the marriage, they were right on track with their master plan: they graduated, married, purchased a home and secured careers, all while maintaining their values and commitment to each other. Given all of this, Sabastian was confused when Lindsay was reluctant to discuss starting a family. Hadn't they agreed that if their lives together went according to plan, they would try to get pregnant this year? After Sabastian talked with Lindsay, she had agreed to go off of the pill, albeit reluctantly. But just the next week, Sabastian had found Lindsay's pills and noticed that she hadn't stopped taking them after all. Sabastian found himself feeling frustrated, even angry about Lindsay's deception. He began to wonder, *Should I hide her pills, flush them, make her answer my questions?*

Sabastian's feelings are understandable. What he didn't know was that Lindsay's reluctance to get pregnant had nothing to do with their relationship, but rather her fear of bringing children into the world who might have to fight in a war or be killed in a terrorist attack or victimized by some other act of violence. But Lindsay didn't tell Sabastian about her fears and frustration. She was afraid to challenge their master plan, afraid of disappointing Sabastian, afraid that he might not understand. So Lindsay stayed silent and Sabastian continued to stew.

Intimate Anger as a Reaction to Terrorism

- *Terrorism:* By definition, terrorism implies a relative reduction in power, victimization and loss of control for individuals. These factors are the cornerstones of anger.
- *Victimization:* Victimization is the epitome of loss of control in which we are at another's whim, where unwanted things are being imposed upon us and we are powerless to stop them, where there is no one to look to for the protection that we are unable to provide for ourselves. There are stages that victims tend to go through including:

     Shock - This usually immediately follows the event, when the victim is not at all sure what happened, whether it was real or a nightmare. Feelings may be quite numb in this stage and victims are often withdrawn.

Denial - Victims are aware of what happened but struggle with disbelief: *This can't have happened!* Fear, anxiety and depression are often associated with this stage and victims are often hyper-vigilant.

Anger - The enormity of the incident sinks in, along with a sense of powerlessness and vulnerability, ushering in anger. The energy of anger is often used for retaliation in this phase. *Why me? This isn't fair! I'll fix them!*

Acceptance - The final stage of the victim process where the healing begins. We seize the control we do have, using it to better our lives, recognize and let go of fantasies of control over others.

In typical crime victimization cases, these phases are clearly delineated. Have you heard a story about a couple coming home to find their home burglarized? Or perhaps you yourself have had this experience. One day or evening, you come home from work and something doesn't seem quite right: perhaps the door is unlocked when you're certain that you had locked it that morning; a vase or some other object or appliance is slightly out of place. However, you tell yourself it's just your imagination. Perhaps you hear a noise from the back of your home, where your bedroom is, but still you dismiss it. Finally, you make your way back to your bedroom and see that your dresser drawers have been dumped out onto the floor, your closets have been rummaged through and your portable CD player is missing. You stand there dumbfounded, jaw hanging open and are oblivious that the perpetrator could still be in the house, endangering your safety [shock]. You recognize that you've been burglarized, but you tell yourself, "This can't be happening!" [denial]. Finally, you call the police, who come to take report. They tell you that the chances of recovery of the items are slim. Your blood starts to boil as you assess your losses and take in your sense of violation. Some slimy stranger had his/her paws on your personal belongings. Perhaps you or your partner blame each other and you fight about this [anger]. You and your partner spend the evening cleaning up the mess, talk to friends who have had similar experiences and get references for home security systems. When your new security system is in place, you feel a bit safer; then your insurance claim is processed and you chalk the experience up to life in the city [acceptance].

When we are victimized, we are likely to respond in one of a number of ways:

1. Attempt to Make Sense of the Incident – Sometimes this takes the form of self blame. We look to things that we or our partners could have done differently to have at least minimized, if not prevented, the tragedy. An example of this was the intense scrutiny that our law enforcement agencies came under after the terrorist attacks, trying to understand: INS lapses in immigration practices; failed communication between the FBI and local law enforcement agencies; intelligence breakdowns at the federal level including the FAA.

    The practical value of such self blame is clear—to problem solve glitches and develop a more effective system. More often though, the driving force behind self blame is the fantasy of control. That is, if we begin to feel guilt about the ways we could have prevented the event, we feel that we somehow participated in the tragedy. We fantasize that changing our partners' or our own behavior would enable us to prevent future victimization.

    This rationale is problematic in at least two ways. First, blaming ourselves suggests that we ought to be perfect, to know the future and act accordingly, which is a surefire road to depression. Self blame is a form of judging, a hot thought that will most likely lead to anger either toward ourselves (depression) or our partners. After all, few of us can know the future and expecting that we can only leads to frustration. Also, the practice of blaming ourselves suggests that we have control over external events, which is not true. Reinforcing such unrealistic expectations further maintains our sense of powerlessness.

2. Strengthen In-Group Ties – Cultural anthropologist Gordon Allport coined the term "in-group" to describe a subset of people

who claim membership in a group based on sharing a particular attribute with other group members. Examples of such attributes include sharing the same parents, being members of the same sorority, citizens of the same country and/or members of the same race. In-group members use the term *we* to describe themselves and everyone who shares that particular trait. Those who do not share that trait belong to the "out-group" (Allport, 1954) and are referred to as *them*. Strengthening in-group ties is the first step in delineating "us versus them," in setting up judgment of one group being better than the other (hot thought). The act of strengthening in-group ties is akin to the old west practice of circling the wagons. When we feel vulnerable, we band together with others "like us." More constructive segments of our society encouraged Americans to pull together across ethnic and racial lines in response to the 9/11 terrorist acts.

As we discussed earlier, victimization often leads to a sense of undeniable powerlessness, which is a major cause of anger. In response to anger, we struggle to get back on top of our game. From the powerlessness of victimization comes the thirst for control. It is natural to try to regain one's sense of control after a perceived loss of control. Examples of this occurred after the terrorist attacks: the development of the Homeland Security Office, heightened security at our borders, airports and federal buildings and the creation of a stock pile of small pox vaccinations, to name a few. While it is prudent to take precautions, we must remember that no amount of precaution enables us to control others or all circumstances [hot thought]. Here are some ways in which victims attempt to regain control:

1. Prejudice Against Out-Group Members: Prejudice is the act of *pre*-judging someone, of ascribing perceived attributes of the entire group, often stereotypes, to the individual without benefit of knowing the person. We all prejudge people to some extent. It's a short-cut to understanding our environment, since

we can't know everyone. Still, prejudging raises many problems, one being that stereotypes are often negative, so out-group members are seen in the worst light, enabling us to heap all the blame for our misfortunes upon them. In doing so, we reinforce the judgment that we're perfect, our judgment infallible. Another problem is that, by definition, prejudging generalizes from the group to the individual, reducing the likelihood of us taking the time to know the individual and realizing the mistake in our judgment. We see them as other than us, because they look different and/or have different beliefs and, therefore, they cannot be trusted. We determine this based on the behavior of others who we have judged to be like them, since we cannot possibly know all out-group members personally (e.g. Japanese-Americans during WWII, Middle-Eastern Americans in present day). When we fortify the boundaries between ourselves and out-group members, we reinforce the us-versus-them position, setting up competition and ill will.

2. Fight Back: Fighting back is a form of protest, a judgment that *I'm right and you're wrong*. Aggression is often used to try to (re)establish control, as evidenced by the rise in hate crimes against Middle-Eastern Americans since the terrorist attacks. Fighting, however, does not have to take aggressive forms. We can fight back with peaceful protests, as Martin Luther King did, or with union strikes and by legislating change. Remember, anger is a very human emotion; what we choose to do with it may or may not be humane.

If you or your partner have reacted to the threat of terrorism by becoming nervous, defensive or fearful, your feelings may have caused increased tension or anger towards your mate. Here are some cool-down tips: refrain from judging your own reactions or those of your partner too harshly. Be more aware of the kinds of thoughts that automatically come to mind when we feel threatened. On some levels these reactions can be quite constructive: to be able to assess our own behavior and make positive changes, to be able to seek and receive support within our own community or family, to take measures to influence what we can, to pre-judge aspects of our world so that we can organize and predict even within its complexity, to be able to stand up for ourselves in the face of adversity. All of these behaviors are necessary to survive and thrive. However, problems arise when we take them to the extreme, when we become rigid—*My way or no way; Agree with me or get out*—and the world must bend to our whims. It is angry people who take these normal responses to threat to such extremes. And it is this anger that can damage relationships.

We witnessed such extremes in a one-time Critical Incidents Debriefing (CID) Group that we ran just days after the 9/11 terrorist attacks. This was a free half-day group that we offered in our community. CID groups are a part of crisis services that are frequently offered after major disasters by community health organizations to help people deal with feelings such as anger, denial, fear, helplessness, loss of direction and shifts in values, all of which are generally associated with trauma and loss. The groups focus on support and validation, grief processing, empowerment, development of necessary coping skills, education regarding the healing phases and the universality of reactions. The purpose of such groups is to offer rapid intervention in the case of trauma to prevent more long-term, ingrained dysfunctional responses, such as depression, anxiety, withdrawal and avoidance.

Our group that day had twenty-five participants, though in the following brief description of several participants and their remarks, we will focus on eight participants who most represented the views of the other seventeen members.

Micheline is a forty-six-year-old, divorced, Protestant, African-American woman who works as a licensed vocational nurse. She has two adult children.

Shala is a twenty-three-year-old, single, Muslim, Pakistani-American woman who works full time as an office manager and is a part time student at a local junior college. She has no children.

Rob is a fifty-seven-year-old, divorced, agnostic, European-American man who works as a dentist. He has three adult children.

Allen is a thirty-two-year-old, single, Protestant, Japanese-American man who is a software architect. He has no children.

Laura is a thirty-eight-year-old married, Catholic, European-American woman who works as a bank manager. She has two young children.

Rafaat is a forty-two-year-old, married, Jewish, Iranian immigrant who is a medical doctor. He has two young children.

Patrick is a fifty-six-year-old, married, Catholic, European-American man who is a construction site supervisor. He has four stepchildren.

Barry is a twenty-six-year-old, single, Jewish, European American man who is a full time law student. He has no children.

Some of their remarks show the strain most were feeling after the trauma of 9/11.

Dr. K.: Well, as you all know, this is a free-for-all. The only rule is that what's said here, stays here. We all know why we're here. Last week our country was attacked and we are all still reeling from this reality. Lorel and I are here to give you a place to talk about the attacks and your reactions to them. We'll help keep you all on track, but this is really your time.

Dr.L.: The floor's yours whenever you're ready. [silence for fifteen seconds]

Rob: Shit! Fuck! Sons of bitches! Aaahhh...

Patrick: Yea! Fuck this shit! What are we waiting for? We should be bombing the hell out of those Arabs now! Do they really think they can pull this in our backyard? That we'll just take it? They're about to find out that *that* is *not* the American way!

Micheline: No offense to you [looks at Shala and Rafaat], but when I see an Arab I feel angry! How dare they come over here and pull this shit. I don't care how bad this may sound, but it's time for Immigration to step in and start sending these folks back home where they belong because…

Allen: What do you mean "these folks"? "Back home where they belong"? Look at you; look at me! How many times do you think they would have sent us "home" if they could? My family got locked up for more than two years during World War Two just because *Japan* bombed Pearl Harbor and my grandparents were *American*— as American as anybody sitting in this room!

Barry: We're going to end up like the Israelis and Palestinians, fighting for millennia, a tit for a tat. But we can't just do nothing.

Laura: I don't think that we should just do nothing. But I don't think we should respond in kind.

Patrick: Oh, let's not even start with this "turn the other cheek" shit. You sound like my wife and all of her friends. Do you think we got to be the only superpower by turning tail and running? Hell no!

Rob: Strike back and strike back decisively!

Laura: If we do that, we're in for another terrorist attack for sure. It's like Barry said, we'll be fighting forever. I don't know how familiar you are with the history, but it's not as though America is completely innocent in all of this.

Rafaat: This is true. I love living in America and being a citizen, but I see things that you do not, like the arrogance that goes along with being a superpower, as you say. [looks at Patrick]

Laura: These bombings are a sign that there are things we need to work out with these people, and violence never solves anything.

Micheline: "By any means necessary."

Laura: We have to sit down and dialogue.

Patrick: Dialogue? Do you even know how many innocent Americans died? Do you? If it'd been your kid bombed to smithereens, I don't think you'd be talking about "dialogue".

Rafaat: It's a tragedy. But it's a tragedy for us all. Last night I left the hospital for home. Do you know that a car full of young men began to follow me? They pulled up to the curb and called me names, threatened my life. The funny thing is, I'm Iranian by birth and there's no evidence at all that Iran is involved with the attacks. Maybe even more important is that I'm not even Muslim, I'm Jewish! But in your eyes, we are all the same, like you say, [looks at Micheline] "Arabs," and must pay alike, even though I spent my evening in the ER healing other Americans.

Shala: I'm afraid to leave my house, to cover my head with my "scarves", as you call them. My coworkers look at me like I'm an assassin. I didn't even go to work today. You are very strong to be able to face work [looks at Rafaat]. I don't know when I'll have the courage to go back. I'm so sad that this thing happened. I used to really love my freedom here. Now, I'm no longer safe. Should I cut my hair, dress American, try to blend in? Then who would I be?

Exercise: Finding Emotionally Loaded Sentiments

This was a powerful exchange loaded with blame, judgment, impatience, perfectionism and in some cases, self-righteousness. See how many such statements you can find that were made by our CID group participants.

Now try to discover how many of the statements fit with the profile of our reaction to being victimized: making sense of the incident, strengthening in-group ties, attempts to regain control, prejudice against out-group members, fighting back. Can you see the overlap between angry characteristics and characteristics of those victimized, that is, those who have lost control?

What is the impact of overtly angry participants on the other participants?

In CID we see people when they are most vulnerable. As a result, there's less emphasis on political correctness and more access to what people are really thinking, for better or worse. We hear statements of overt anger, which have characteristics of both angry people and victims:

Analyzing Angry and Victim Characteristics

Statement	Angry Characteristic(s)	Victim Characteristic
We should bomb the hell out of those Arabs!	Judgment; low frustration tolerance	Fight back
Do they really think they can pull this in our backyard?	Possessiveness, perfectionism (righteousness)	Strengthening in-group ties by using "they"
How dare they come over here and pull this shit!	Judgment, possessiveness	Strengthening in-group ties by using "they"
It's time for Immigration to step in and send these folks back home where they belong.	Demanding	Increased attempts at control
You sound like my wife.	Judgment	Separate from out-group members
Strike back and strike back decisively!	Low frustration tolerance, demand	Fight back
It's not as though America is completely innocent in all of this.	Judgment	Make sense of incident
By any means necessary	Demand	Fight back

Statement	Angry Characteristic(s)	Victim Characteristic
If it had been your kid bombed to smithereens, I don't think you'd be talking about "dialogue".	Judgment	Separation of in-group members from out-group members
In your eyes, we're all the same.	Judgment	Separation of in-group members from out-group members
My coworkers look at me like I'm an assassin.	Judgment	Prejudice against out-group members

The characteristics of both angry people and victims result in overtly angry statements. Anger is directly related to our sense of control or lack thereof and our attempts to (re)gain adequate control.

Understanding this connection between anger and victimization is crucial, because, while anger is derived from a sense of victimization (being wronged, injustice, imperfection, trespass), victimization often leads to overt anger, whether directed outwardly or inwardly, causing a cycle to emerge.

As we look over the participants' statements in the CID group, we see a number of references to the victim position:

- They pulled up to the curb and called me names, threatened my life

- There's no evidence that Iran's involved with these attacks

- But in your eyes, we're all the same

- I'm so sad that this happened

- I'm no longer safe

- Should I …try to blend in?

Reviewing these statements, we can see that Shala's and Rafaat's experiences result in feelings of being prejudged by others to be a certain religion or to perpetuate certain violent acts *just because of the way they look*. We hear their sense of helplessness: *There's no evidence that Iran is involved; In your eyes we're all the same; I'm no longer safe*. And finally, we begin to see evidence of self-rejection, anger turned inward when Shala asks, "Should I… try to blend in?"

Anger as a Reaction to War

War, like terrorism, involves violence and deadly force against a group in order to meet the goal of another group. The difference is that in the case of war there is usually a formal legislative declaration of the conflict whereas, in the case of terrorism, this declaration usually not made.

Just as with terrorism, in war a struggle for power and control is implied and victimization is inescapable. War is an overt show of force to gain control through formal surrender. It is legally sanctioned, internationally recognized anger. We see our population working its way through the stages of victimization (i.e., shock, denial, anger, acceptance) and acting out these stages (i.e., trying to make sense of war, strengthening in-group ties, attempting to regain control, prejudging against out-group members and fighting back) with all of their associated classic angry characteristics.

Anger Begets Intimate Anger

Since the terrorism and trauma of 9/11, we have seen a rise in hate crimes against people of apparent Middle Eastern descent: verbal threats, vandalized property and physical assaults. These acts are perpetuated by those who are angered and feel victimized by the events of 9/11. So far, there have not been any major civil disruptions associated with these abuses, but we must remember that anger begets anger, that groups that are perpetually victimized and scapegoated eventually respond in anger. We need not look far back in our nation's history to find examples of this, including militant groups that emerged from the 1960s civil rights movement and the American Indian Movement of the 1960s, which culminated in yet another battle at Wounded Knee in 1973. It's not just on racial and ethnic grounds that we have seen such dramatic and violent responses to being the recipient of others' ongoing anger, but also between social classes, such as in the labor movement of the 1930s and on more individual and personal levels, as well. For instance, our courts are seeing more and more cases of battered women retaliating against their long abusive husbands, in some cases actually killing them after years of abuse. There are those who believe that violence must be responded to in kind, although such reactions run the risk of creating and perpetuating the above cycle. It is important to understand that our anger fuels others' anger and, in trying to increase our control by undermining others', we create situations where they feel compelled to fight back for their own control.

It is human nature to experience differences among us as threats, whether those differences are due to race, religion or sexual orientation, because these very differences imply other differences—differences in beliefs, values and lifestyles. Further, our collective gut reaction to threat, real (e.g., terrorism) or imagined (e.g., those of different cultures) is most often one of trying to regain control through dominance or destruction. This is an even stronger trend among angry people, because they feel they must be right; it's their way or the highway; they are perfect. Anyone who is different must be wrong and will not be tolerated. They must change and, if unable to change adequately, driven out. We have seen this process throughout world history (e.g. the crimes against Jewish people in Nazi Germany) and in our nation's history, starting with forcing American Indian groups onto reservations and persisting through World War II with Japanese American internment; from segregation in the 1950s and 1960s to present day hate crimes against various members of our society. While a thorough discussion of such matters is beyond the scope of this book, we would all do well to examine our irrational beliefs associated with those whom we perceive as different and recall that we, too, are fallible.

On the Home Front

After the shock wears off that terrorism and war are realities of our world, the truth is that these events have a way of permeating the walls of our homes and infiltrating our private lives in a number of ways:

1. Overexposure:

    Media—We live in an era of information overload in which we have access to multiple domestic and international sources of information, some of which are fairly immediate: The Internet, television (with cable and satellite), radio, newspapers and other periodicals. With all of these resources at our fingertips, we are able to stay abreast on all fronts, but, as so often happens, too much of a good thing can be harmful, in this case increasing our sense of being overwhelmed and causing our most intimate relationships to be more tense.

    Family/Friends/Coworkers—Even when we're not tapped into the media, we routinely hear about the state of affairs at work and sometimes go home and discuss or agonize over the situation. While information is power, overexposure can add to our sense of victimization: *I just can't seem to escape this.*

2. Increased Emotional Stress Levels: Regardless of whether the nation is at a Stage Yellow or Orange alert, the fact is that we are all more vigilant than we were before 9/11. Our sense of security and invulnerability has been violated. We no longer feel safe. We know that a new violence *can* happen at any time. Further, we are reminded of this with the increased police presence, longer security check lines at airports and recommendations from the Homeland Security Office about how to handle parcels received in the mail, among other things. Our minds do not automatically separate external

stressors (e.g., national crises) from internal stressors (e.g., marital problems). We just register *stress* and act it out in our typical fashion (e.g., demanding behavior, anger, drinking, avoiding).

3. Increased Sense of Physical Threat: Since 9/11, we have experienced two terrorist attacks, evidence of thwarted attempts (e.g., the would-be shoe bomber, Richard Reid) and continued threats of terrorist attacks to come. Thus we have a greater sense of physical danger.

4. Financial Stressors: The associated expense of two wars and beefed-up domestic security, increased unemployment, tax cuts to stimulate a weak economy and the ups and downs of the stock market have led to deep financial cuts in education and other benefits nationally. These financial burdens have been passed on to us and we *feel* it. In our individual lives we're cutting back, not taking that annual vacation, spending down our savings and questioning the feasibility of our kids' private school educations. We feel vulnerable financially as well as physically and emotionally.

5. Forced Separations: Many whose mates are in the military are experiencing loneliness, financial difficulties and problems with children enduring separation from mothers and/or fathers.

With these difficult factors seeping into our personal lives and relationships, we all feel some loss of control and may try to regain control (by demand, avoidance, manipulation, playing the martyr). If left unchecked, these behaviors may lead to serious anger problems with our loved ones.

Averting Anger on the Home Front

There are a number of things that we can do to address anger issues that emerge around or because of terrorism and war to decrease their negative impact on our intimate relationships and family.

1. Limit Exposure: Decrease the amount of time that you or your partner or children watch television news programs and listen to

talk radio. You *are* in control of the remote and dial—use them! Of course we all need to be aware of national and state news but we need not have 24/7 coverage. Watch or listen to the news at selective times. At others, change the channel to something lighter. By the same token, limit exposure to print media. Perhaps read only one section of the newspaper or limit the number of articles that are read on any given topic. Similarly, use discretion about electronic news sources.

Likewise, just because friends/family/coworkers or even your partner may wish to talk about current events ad nauseam, that doesn't mean that you too must always participate. When a subject is, in your opinion, drawn out unnecessarily , respectfully excuse yourself from the conversation, introduce a new subject or simply acknowledge that you're feeling a bit overwhelmed by that day's information overload. Instead, suggest limiting the time that you talk about the news of war, terrorism or the economy before moving on to more positive topics. You'd be surprised at how receptive most people are to these interventions, especially because they're often feeling similarly overwhelmed, but choose to avoid acknowledging their own sense of loss of control.

2. Empower Yourself Emotionally: The first step here is to acknowledge that we're feeling vulnerable. We get ourselves in trouble when we pretend to feel something other than what we really feel. When we feel vulnerable, we often take on an air of bravado that can lead to problems. An example of this is someone who is feeling anxious about possible future terrorist attacks and so goes out and defaces the local mosque to make himself feel more powerful in the face of vulnerability. It is better to admit feeling vulnerable so that we can go about doing something constructive to empower ourselves. Constructive empowerment might include:

    a. Joining a peaceful rally that represents your views
    b. Writing to your local officials/politicians about your position; spearheading a petition to further your agenda
    c. Volunteering to contribute time and/or money to your particular cause

3. Use Physical Strategies to Manage Physical Stress: Remember that threats to our well being, which is what terrorism and war are, send our bodies into the physical state of fight-or-flight. This stimulates the production of stress hormones such as corticosteroids, which add to our experience of bodily tension. Symptoms such as panic attacks, muscular tension, headaches and hypertension are often lessened by exercise and various forms of meditation. Of course, check with your physician before starting any exercise regimen.

4. Address Financial Stressors: One of the most important aspects of coping with financial stress is to avoid the temptation to ignore the problem, as this will only result in the problem mushrooming. Rather, check in with your anger management skills of identifying irrational demands and fantasies of control. Use problem solving skills to negotiate a plan of action. Apply quick fixes to keep stress reactions to a minimum in the short run. Make use of all resources, including financial advisors and consumer credit agencies. Any/all of these will help to increase your sense of empowerment.

We have addressed, in abstract, a number of ways that anger associated with terrorism and war can impact our relationships. Let's take a look at how these issues played out in one of our therapy cases:

We first saw Dotty and Mac about one year ago. They came to us complaining of marital problems. Actually, it was Dotty who wanted therapy.

"Mac's angry all the time now," Dotty lamented. "I don't know what's wrong. Maybe he's just tired of the pressures of married life. He's bossy all of a sudden, always telling me what to do. He was never like this before. We used to talk about things."

According to Dotty, this trend started about one year before they came in to see us. It started with Mac demanding that Dotty drive their thirteen- and fifteen-year-old daughters to and from school each day, rather than the girls walking the half mile, as had been the custom.

"What'd we move to this high rent area for if it wasn't to be within walking distance of good schools for the girls?"

"What's the big deal, Dot? It takes you five minutes. I don't ask you for much—just do it!"

Dotty continued, "Next Mac comes home with individual cell phones for all of us. We had a cell phone that Mac and I shared for when we were away from home. We only need one since I'm a stay-at-home mom. Now he wants us all to carry one day and night."

"It's just so I can reach you if I need to," Mac explained.

"Mac, where would we be if not at home or school? You don't trust us? Don't you trust me?"

"Why are you making such a big deal about this?" Mac asked. "Is it going to hurt you to carry a five ounce cell phone? I can't stand it when you argue with me about little shit!"

The session went on like this for some time, with Dotty pointing out all of Mac's new demands and with Mac questioning why his requests were such a problem for Dotty. We noted that the time frame of Mac's change was around the end of 2001 so, knowing how vulnerable people were feeling with respect to the terrorist attacks, we began to explore this with Mac.

"You know what it's like not to be able to protect your family?" Mac asked, looking at Lorel. "I leave home every day and I don't know if I'm going to see them again, if our home will still be standing. If Dotty's with the girls, I feel like they're more protected. If I can reach them at anytime, I can know that they're okay. A man's supposed to be able to protect his family. For the first time, I feel like I can't do enough and I swear, some days it makes me crazy."

As the session came to a close, Mac was able to talk about his anger at being targeted by terrorists, of feeling like a victim and of having an elusive perpetrator who he could not take on directly. Mac felt bad about his own limits and was doing all that he could to control a situation that was largely beyond his control. Consequently, Mac demanded, "Just do it!" and exhibited low frustration tolerance: "I can't stand it when you argue with me about little shit!" Beyond that, Mac judged himself a failure for being unable to correct his situation entirely: "A man's supposed to be able to protect his family."

As we look at the four home front stressors, we see in the first session alone that Mac is really struggling with at least two of the four: increased emotional stress and an increased sense of physical threat. Mac told us that he needed more reassurance about his family's well being when he issued cell phones to all so that he could reach them at any time and know that they were okay. Similarly, he assigned Dotty to the job of the family's own personal Homeland Security Officer when he demanded that she escort the girls to and from school. While Mac took these measures to try to insure his family's safety, they, especially Dotty, experienced his behavior not as loving, but as hostile, controlling and restrictive so Dotty resisted. The more she resisted, the more frustrated Mac became.

What's interesting is that despite the fact that it was the terrorists at whom Mac was really angry, it was his family that bore the brunt of Mac's anger and frustration. Often we can't address our anger to those with whom we're truly angry for one reason or another (e.g., they're too powerful, they may retaliate). This was true in Mac's case. He was unable to identify those with whom he was angry—terrorists. In situations like these, we often take our anger out on others, that is, "kick the dog." It's one version of the blame game, *I'm unhappy; it can't be my fault, it must be yours.* "The dog" often ends up being our partners for several reasons. One, we usually have a lot invested in our relationships with significant others and the way the equation works is the greater the investment, the stronger the emotion, even if it's triggered by outside forces. Two, our partners are *convenient.* We live with them and/or see them frequently. They're always there. Three, and most important, our partners are *safe.* They love us, are committed to us and, more to the point, they promised to stay with us *for better or worse.* For all of these reasons and more, our partners sometimes get the worst of us.

Back to Basics

We've discussed some very practical ways to cope with the impact of our anger/frustration associated with terrorism and war on our personal relationships. While specific interventions are always help-ful, the most important part of coping with anger in our relation-ships is to focus on our internal thoughts, the fears that are covered up by hot thoughts, not the external events.

Mac's Case: Hot Thoughts

Victim Thought	Hot Thought	Rational Preferences
I can't protect my family.	A man's supposed to be able to protect his family.	I wish I could guarantee my family's safety.
I'm worried that my kids might get caught in an attack.	Dotty's at home all day. She should drive the girls to and from school.	It would be nice if Dotty could guarantee the girls' safety, since I can't. But I know that she's a good mother and does all that she can.
I'm anxious about what I may or may not find when I get home each day.	I can't stand it.	The truth is that nobody can guarantee that life goes as he or she hopes. The best I can do is take reasonable precautions and let my family know that I love them.

A Final Thought

It is important for us to remember that external stressors have a way of permeating the boundaries of our personal lives. And when this happens, our significant others are most vulnerable to our anger and frustration. We often can't control *what* happens to us; where control comes in is in *what we choose to do* with the circumstances of our lives.

Chapter 10

The Sandwich Generation

We live in a stressful and complex society in which people all over the world are exposed to multiple stressors daily. The nature and quality of the stressors varies, of course, depending on the specific country and culture in which we live. One factor that appears to be widespread though is the role that family members play in producing stress.

Different countries and cultures have their own specific influences on families and family members. In the United States, we have many familial customs and traditions governing how parents, children and the various generations within families work, communicate and play with each other. A person's place in a family, whether that person is a son or daughter, parent, sibling or grandchild will determine the kind of role that person will play within that family. The kind of behavior and words you use daily will differ greatly if you are, for example, a parent, as opposed to a child.

Webster's Dictionary defines a sandwich as: "two or more slices of bread, having between them meat, cheese, etc., or any combination of alternating dissimilar things pressed together." As a transitive verb it means: "to place between other persons or things." Have you ever felt "placed between other people?" This is a common occurrence with people in middle age. The sandwich generation is a term coined a few years ago to denote people who are responsible for two sets of family members: their parents and their children.

This usually begins when a married couple is approaching middle age. As time goes on, their parents are getting older and have health problems and other issues. Meanwhile, the couple is raising their own children. A couple in their forties may conceivably have two sets of parents, both in their late sixties or older, as well as children of their own, often in their teens or late teens. Both sets of family members are approaching ages at which they respectively require huge amounts of attention for different reasons. Has this ever happened to you? Do you ever feel like you were a piece of meat between two very demanding slices of bread; sandwiched in between two equally clamoring forces, neither of which could get your full attention; finding it frustrating and draining, day in and day out, trying to meet the needs of these two very different sets of family members?

The needs of aging parents are sometimes financial in nature. Perhaps they never saved enough money to fully support themselves in their old age and need your assistance to help them out of the tight spots. Or perhaps they suffered some economic catastrophe late in life and lost most of their life savings. Serious health problems and the resultant medical bills may be a factor. Oftentimes, however, the financial situation, even if difficult, is the least of the many problems that older couples face. Also, there may be problems of loneliness, because their peers have either died or moved away. One partner may pass away, which is usually a major blow to the survivor. In such a case, older people and couples often rely on the persons they feel closest to for company—which is usually you! Sometimes the demands on your time can be exceedingly great, to the point that you feel you are spending every spare minute keeping them company. If they live some distance away, the toll is even greater on your time.

Issues other than financial ones or problems related to loneliness can be even more severe. One of the worst problems parents may face and thus you are forced to face, is that of physical illness.

The physical illness can be life-threatening or just debilitating to the point of making one or both of the grandparents immobile. Even if they are merely immobile, the chore of taking them to doctors appointments, shopping, the occasional meal out, can be very stressful for you. If they are sick enough to require constant care, but not sick enough to reside in an extended living or skilled nursing facility, then often the only option, given the sorry state of care for the elderly in this country, is for you to take them into your home to care for them. The added stress of having infirm or handicapped elderly people in the same house with two other generations can be significant.

At the same time that your parents' needs are increasingly becoming an issue, the your children are usually at the age where their needs begin to loom large. Generally speaking, children require huge amounts of attention no matter what their age. However, the nature of that attention changes as a function of how old they are. When they are infants, the care, feeding, bathing and monitoring of them is a twenty-four-hour-a-day job. When they get older, the physical needs are less, but the emotional and structural support needed becomes greater. The emotional needs of children are generally greatest during the teenage years when a variety of things can go wrong if they aren't provided the proper guidance by their parents. This often requires enormous energy and time. Thus, in the natural order of things in traditional families, the timing is often exquisitely ironic to produce the maximum amount of stress for the "sandwiched" parents: just when their children are getting into their most demanding and difficult years, their parents are approaching the age of infirmity, financial dependence or senility. Since there is little available care for the elderly in our country and little care for the fostering of needs of our teenagers, it falls to the lot of the parents to care for both groups. This is an ideal situation in comparison to children being reared in one-parent households (in California, one-half of all marriages eventually end in divorce). The amount of stress that would normally fall on two people in an intact marriage, must now be dealt with by one parent alone in a one-parent household, virtually doubling the stress level. It doesn't take a giant intellect to calculate the emotional drain, anger and desperation that this would create.

Bill and Carol are a couple facing "sandwich generation" issues. They are in their late forties, live in a small town in southern California and have three children, two girls, aged seventeen and fourteen and a boy, aged ten. Bill's father died when he was seventy, but his mother is still alive and lives in a small apartment thirty-five miles away. Prior to a few months ago, his mother, Emma, had been able to function completely independently. She clothed, fed and entertained herself nicely. She had lots of friends who played bridge with her every Wednesday night and a church group that she played bingo with every other Saturday. Until recently, she had been living a comfortable, autonomous lifestyle. Two months ago, though, she had a massive stroke, which almost completely paralyzed her right side, leaving her unable to move her right arm or leg and therefore unable to move about without assistance. Her speech was severely affected and she was obviously very depressed. She had a history of high blood pressure most of her adult life and had anti-hypertensives prescribed for her, but she refused to take them as it was "too much bother," and besides, she felt "fine."

The night of the phone call from Emma's neighbor informing them of Bill's mother's stroke almost completely overturned Bill and Carol's normal routine. Bill and Carol were agonized. After hearing a loud noise next door (the result of Emma's fall), a neighbor had rushed over to find Emma lying on her side in the bathroom, unable to speak clearly. She called 911 and Emma was taken to the hospital. The neighbor had gone to Emma's address book, found Bill's number and called him. Bill and Carol rushed over to the hospital. After hours of neurological testing, the doctors confirmed that Emma would need constant assistance for the next six months until she was physically rehabilitated and able to function without twenty-four hour assistance.

When they finally got home, Carol and Bill spent the rest of the night and most of the next day thinking through their options. They came to the conclusion that they could afford part-time nursing care, but would have to be there the rest of the time during Emma's recovery. Bill earned a good salary, but he was the only wage earner in the family, as he and Carol had long ago decided that she needed to be home to help rear the children and be there when they needed her. (They were very fortunate in this respect, as the results of inflation and job market changes in the last twenty years have largely mandated that most families become two-income families just to make ends meet.) That decision, made seventeen years earlier, turned out to be quite fortuitous now. Realizing that they could not afford twenty-four hour daily nursing care for Bill's mother, Bill and Carol had to figure out how to cover the evening and night hours. That left a period from 8:00 a.m. until 8:00 p.m. when Carol needed to be there to care for Bill's mother. They thought they could handle this division of labor for the next six months. It was going to be difficult, but they thought they could manage it.

As they talked, they turned to how they would handle this new responsibility while maintaining a focus on their children. The two older girls were both in high school. Beth was in her junior year and Ann was just starting as a freshman. Carl, the youngest, was in fourth grade. The children had always been good kids, but there were some rough spots. The older girl, Beth, was dyslexic and needed help with her reading assignments on occasion, which Carol was always happy to provide. Ann had always been an athlete and was very good at soccer in grade school, where she had been the star of the team. Now, though, she was attending a very large high school where the competition was fierce and she was in danger of not making the junior varsity soccer team. The coach was very understanding and told Bill and Carol that with a little extra coaching provided by a coach at the YWCA nearby, she had a very good chance of making the team. This would necessitate her going to the Y twice a week for probably at least two months. Finally, Carl, the youngest, had ADHD and needed to be on medication, which he was not totally reliable in taking on his own. Therefore, either Carol or Bill often needed to remind him to take his anti-hyperactive meds in the mornings and, occasionally, on some evenings. Since all of these issues were important and affected the whole family, a family meeting was called the afternoon after Bill's mother's stroke.

The children were told of the medical condition of their grandmother, how she needed constant care and supervision for at least the next six months and what their limited financial resources allowed them to afford in terms of professional nursing care. The kids seemed to understand all of this quite well, but when Carol told them she would be gone most of the day and would not get home until around 8:15 in the evenings, it gradually dawned on the girls that their needs were going to have to take a backseat, at least for the time being. Beth was going to have to find someone else to help her with her reading assignments and Ann was going to have to find another way to get to her extra soccer practices, as she was too young to drive herself. Carl, fortunately, could still be monitored on his meds, as he was still at home before Carol left to care for Bill's mother and Carol would be home before Carl went to bed, to insure that he took his evening medications.

As it turned out, Beth had a close friend she met in home-room who was sensitive to her situation and graciously offered to help her with the necessary reading assignments at school. This was mostly satisfactory, but often the homework didn't get done at school and Beth was on her own at home to finish it up on those days. Ann found a senior who lived two blocks away who swam at the Y every night and was therefore able to take her to her weekly soccer sessions. It looked as though things were going to work out okay. And they did—for the first three weeks.

However, in the middle of the fourth week, Ann's friend came down with a severe case of the flu and was bedridden for two and a half weeks. Ann was left without a ride or any other means of transportation to the Y. Playing soccer was very important to Ann and she realized that missing these important coaching sessions placed her status as a potential team member in significant jeopardy. She became sullen, moody and her grades began to drop. She wanted to talk to her mother, but, by the time Carol came home, it was Ann's bedtime and there was barely enough time to eat and say goodnight.

Beth's friend turned out not to be as patient as her mother

and it soon became apparent to her that her new "student" relationship with her friend at school was not going to work out. She terminated her study with her friend and refused to talk with her again.
She felt hurt and humiliated and began sleeping late some mornings
instead of going to school. Carol found this out after a telephone call
from Beth's school counselor on the third day that she had reported
to school late. The counselor was very concerned about Beth's academic status, as she was scheduled to take her SATs that year and they
all knew that her scores on that test would play a huge role in the
kind of college to which Beth would be accepted.

Bill was having his own worries and problems. He maintained a very successful job as the senior agent in an insurance
agency. He was well-respected in his workplace and was the top
salesman in the firm. He paid a price emotionally for this, of course.
Although affable and charming on the outside, he was a bundle of
nerves internally, often having to take medication to calm his stom-
ach. Prior to his mother's stroke, he was managing well enough, but
he always felt he didn't have much else to give to his job or any other
endeavor, for that matter. He had no hobbies and only occasionally
allowed himself the one luxury that he loved, playing a round of golf
on Saturdays. After his mother's health problems started he didn't
play golf for six weeks and was feeling deprived and frustrated. He
felt that his life consisted of all work and no play. Even when he came
home, he felt the pressure continue. Whereas before, he could come
home, slip into his shorts, read the paper and chat with the kids, now
there seemed to be constant problems. As Carol was attending to his
mother, he had to get dinner started and make sure that the kids
were all right and that Carl was taking his medicine. Bill also started
taking over some other jobs that Carol could no longer do since she
was with his mother. Bill cleaned up the kitchen, vacuumed,
straightened up the house and generally did most of the laundry. He
was beginning to feel utterly devoid of energy.

Carol was probably the one most stressed by the situation.
She and Bill's mother had never been on close terms and related to
each other with effort. After the stroke, Carol's life was turned upside

down. Now that she was spending twelve hours a day with Bill's mother, Carol felt that she had to be extra nice to her, not only because she was going to be in such close contact with her for such long periods, but also because she felt sorry for what had happened to her. The strain of caring for Bill's mother started to get to Carol over the next few weeks. Despite Carol's best efforts, Emma was often cranky and short with her, showing little patience or appreciation for all the efforts that Carol was making to help her day in and day out. By the time Carol came home in the evenings, she was frazzled.

As if that weren't enough, the scene that awaited Carol in her own home was becoming difficult to deal with. Although Bill was trying hard to be a good housekeeper, the house was not as clean or orderly as when Carol did the housework. Little things were left around the living and dining rooms and the dishes were not as clean as when she did them. She was most particular about the glasses being cleaned until they were crystal clear and Bill just wasn't doing it right. On top of this, Bill seemed to be chronically cranky and uncommunicative. He was polite enough, but she could tell that he felt "put upon" and, at times, he seemed to act like a martyr. Although she had some empathy for his emotional state, she was too wrapped up in her own emotions to give him the amount of emotional support he seemed to need.

Finally, the kids seemed to be angry and depressive because of the family stressors. The girls were screaming at each other frequently, arguing about the most inconsequential things and saying how they "hated to be living in this household, where nothing seemed to be normal anymore." Both Carol and Bill were upset with each other and started arguing over minutiae. The smallest things seemed to be blown into big deals and became the subject of heated and lengthy fights. Finally, one night Carol came home and the household seemed to be in complete disarray. Bill came home late, walked in the door half-apologizing, because he had "stopped to have a drink with the guys," and proceeded to their bedroom. The girls were in the kitchen, making peanut butter and jelly sandwiches for dinner, mumbling about how they wished they could go live elsewhere, while Carl was running around the house and throwing things, because he had not taken his evening medication. At that point, Carol went into the bathroom and sat down on the floor, sobbing hysterically.

She was so angry, frustrated and bitter at their situation that she just felt like throwing in the towel and asking for a divorce. She sat there thinking for a long time, agonizing about their family situation and her frazzled nerves. Finally, she emerged from the bathroom and went into their bedroom, telling Bill in a calm voice, "Either we're going to get some help in therapy with all this or I'm asking for a divorce—I just can't take it anymore." Bill looked at her for a long time and quietly agreed—they needed help.

The next morning, they called their HMO and made an appointment with the psychiatry department. On the day of their appointment, they sat down with us. This first session was scheduled for an hour and a half and they used all of it to itemize their list of complaints about their current situation, starting from the beginning, when Emma had her stroke, and ending with a list of all the things that had gone wrong in the family since then. They revealed how angry they were with each other, with their children and with themselves as a couple for allowing themselves to get into this mess in the first place. They were filled with a sense of guilt and self-recrimination and felt a profound sense of despair. The one bright spot was that they hadn't totally given up hope about the possibility of resolving their anger and their predicament.

We spent several weeks with Bill and Carol, meeting with them once a week to help them work out their issues. The couple had each been in therapy briefly before, when they were having a period of difficulty early in their marriage. They found that our approach was very different from what they had experienced previously. We didn't just sit there, nodding our heads and sagely agreeing with what they said. We were not passive at all, but active and involved, and explained that our job was to help them eventually become their own therapists, but first, they had to know how to do that. We told them that good therapy was like good teaching or good coaching. People went to coaches because they wanted to improve their games, but didn't know how. In this case, the "game" was learning how to deal emotionally and behaviorally with their current circumstances. We explained that people didn't handle problems well, communicate effectively or think creatively when they were upset and angry. The first order of business was to help Bill and Carol get calm and emotionally in control concerning their present plight. Until they did that, we said, they were unlikely to put into place an effective coping plan that would see them through this crisis.

We explained how their thinking was contributing to their anger and despair. We helped them become internally focused instead of externally focused, to adopt a problem-solving attitude rather than a blame-directing one. "How are we going to do THAT?" they asked. Simple, we said. By concentrating on being aware of your own thinking and then determining whether that thinking is rational and realistic or irrational and unrealistic. We pointed out to them how unrealistic thinking almost always sets people up to be disturbed by people and events. At this point, Bill asked, "What am I doing wrong? Everything I tell myself seems to make sense to me." Our response was, "Well, let's divide this up into more manageable pieces. Bill, what are you telling yourself about your mother?"

Bill looked at us for a few minutes and then, after glancing at Carol, proceeded to tell us after the initial shock of his mother's stroke had worn off, he began to get really furious at his mother. He found himself getting worked up in the therapy session just thinking about it. "If my mother had just taken her damn medication, then none of this would have happened! She should have taken it, damn it! She should have known something like this could happen if she didn't follow the doctor's orders. How could she have placed all of us in this horrible situation? It's really a terrible thing to have happened to us and I just can't stand it! I feel like shaking my mother to get her to see the light." The more he described these things to us, the more upset Bill could feel himself become. "It's funny," he reflected, "when I first came in here, I was sad but calm. Now that I'm thinking about all of this, I can feel myself getting really pissed."

"Good," we said. "You are getting the point." We proceeded to point out to Bill the connection between his present thinking and his current anger. Bill nodded in new understanding. We then began to address each statement Bill had made and go over it with him, making sure that Carol was part of the conversation. We pointed out that while they were currently dealing with Bill's issues, Carol could also learn a great deal about what causes anger and then apply those same principles to her own anger. It was important that both Bill and Carol realize that while the specifics of each person and anger episode are unique, the dynamics and principles are general and apply in most, if not all, instances of anger outbursts.

First, we addressed the issue of Bill's telling himself that his mother should have taken the medication. "Sounds like it makes sense, right? After all, you are absolutely correct. The odds are very good that if your mother had taken the medication as prescribed, she wouldn't have had the stroke. Now, does that prove that she should have?" Bill looked at us. "Of course it does," he said.

"Okay, where's the evidence that Emma SHOULD have taken the medication?" we asked. Bill repeated his argument, but we were persistent. "Just because she would have spared herself and her family all this misery if she had taken the pills, how does that PROVE that therefore she MUST take them? Where is it written in the universe that your mother HAD to take the pills just because good things would probably happen if she did? Is there some physical law that states your mother MUST do the right or prudent thing?"

Bill looked agitated and fidgety. He wanted to prove his therapists wrong, but for the life of him he couldn't come up with any evidence that things MUST go the way he demanded that they should go. Despite all his logic about how good things would have been if she had taken the pills, how much suffering she could have avoided if she had taken the pills, he couldn't make the connection, empirically or rationally, that therefore things HAD to be a certain way. He finally admitted that he couldn't PROVE that his mother had to take the pills. All he could come up with was that it would have been a really, really good idea to take the pills for all of the above reasons.

We had reached a crucial point: "Bill, how do you feel when you merely tell yourself that you WISH your mother had taken the pills, that it would have been a GREAT idea if she had, while acknowledging at the same time her fallibility and lack of foresight? In other words, recognizing that just because YOU would have taken the medication doesn't mean that other people will do likewise."

Bill was silent for a long time. Finally, he said, "I feel calm. I feel very sad and disappointed in my mother that she didn't do the best thing for her health. I feel sad, but I don't feel angry like I did five minutes ago." He went on to describe how much better he felt thinking this way. How, no matter how strongly he wanted something to happen, sometimes things just don't go the way he knew was the best way for them to go. He thought this was sad, but he felt an enormous relief fall across his tired shoulders. He felt relaxed and clear-headed. He realized that he was starting to think empirically and rationally, rather than in a self-defeating, demanding, intolerant way. He felt good about that. We led him through the rest of his thinking regarding his mother.

We addressed the issue of Bill's demanding that his mother should have known this would happen, that they were now in a "horrible" situation and that they couldn't stand it. Bill discovered the mistake in his thinking: Obviously, if his mother knew then what she knew now, she indeed would have taken her pills. Since she is an imperfect human being, who often makes mistakes and lacks the ability to accurately predict the future, she does the best she can at the time. The mistake is using a retrospective analysis to produce a prospected decision about something which has already happened. If we could foretell the future with perfect accuracy, most of our actions would probably be different.

As to the "horror" of the situation, Bill discovered that, bad as the situation was, it could be worse. His mother could be blind and speechless. He could be penniless. Carol could be a quadriplegic. And so on. The point is, when we use the word "horror" to describe something, we have nowhere else to go. Horror implies that things can't be worse, that the most terrible thing has occurred. If we use words, even loosely, like horror to describe grim events, what word do we use to describe even grimmer events? Things can always be worse and even the worst things we can think of can be worse. As to whether we can "stand" grim things, we can indeed stand them. We can stand anything that doesn't kill us. To imply otherwise unduly limits our strength and frustration tolerance. No matter how bad something is, if we're still alive at the end of it, we are indeed "standing it!"

Bill, with the help of therapy, began to see that he was further agitating himself by thinking irrationally. He began to see that when he thought he "couldn't stand" something (which he really was standing) that he made himself feel even worse. Not only that, but he was making himself feel worse by telling himself something that simply wasn't true. He was standing it!

All of these comments and perceptions were not lost on Carol. Curiously enough, just by listening to us counsel Bill, she was able to apply the same principles to her own situation and she began to figure out what her own demands were. She felt renewed strength as she realized that, in fact, this was not a "terrible" situation and that she could stand it. Just because she didn't like Emma didn't mean that she had to hate her or condemn her to severe punishment because of her poor behavior. In short, Carol, for the first time, began to feel in control of her life and her family situation.

After a few more weeks of counseling, in which the above points were consolidated and Bill and Carol discovered on their own that what we said was true, they began to have the emotional energy not only to see the present family crisis through, but also to begin to explore more creative solutions to dealing with the problems caused by Emma's illness. They began to have more patience with themselves in finding solutions that often initially eluded them. They also began to see the light at the end of the tunnel. Even though the current crisis was significant and would last for several months, eventually it would be over and life would go on. They felt better about handling stressful events with grace and deliberation and proud that their anger was largely limited to brief periods of time when they momentarily neglected the things they had learned in therapy. They realized that managing anger and life's crises was an ongoing endeavor, but not an overpowering one. Rather, it was one that was challenging and increasingly presented an adventure in developing their skills in rational thinking.

While millions of families in the world fall into the category of the sandwich generation, their situations are not hopeless. While acknowledging the increased challenges of multi-generational living situations, it is hoped that you appreciate your own powerful resources that can be utilized to cope with these pressures. Realistic thinking and rational perception are the keys to your ability to handle one of life's toughest challenges.

Chapter 11

Holiday Blues

Holidays can be difficult times for everybody regardless of which holidays you celebrate. In the United States, Christianity happens to be the most popular religion, so we see an increase in clients around the time of major Christian holidays, especially Christmas. The fact that Christmas is sandwiched in between two other major nonsecular holidays, Thanksgiving and New Years, only adds to this phenomenon of greater demand for counseling services November through January. However, there is nothing unique about Christianity in this respect. In other words, we would expect to see similar trends around major holidays of other religions if the majority of Americans celebrated them instead. If Judaism were the most popular religion in the United States, we might expect to see an increase in clients in the fall, when the High Holy Days of Rosh Hashanah and Yom Kippur occur. Or if Islam were the most prevalent religion in the United States, then we might see this trend around Eid celebrations following Ramadan and Haj. That's because inherent in holidays are certain unspoken demands and expectations that are virtually impossible to meet. This translates to *stress*.

Holidays *Should* be Fun!

Hmmmmmm…there's that word again, *should*. By now, you know
that any time you see the word *should*, trouble is not far behind.
Should is a cue for us to look for irrational expectations and there are
a truckload of them associated with any given holiday. But if we were
to sum up these expectations in one word, it would be "perfection."
Most holidays, regardless of whether they're religious or secular in
nature, include preparing one's home for a gathering of friends and
family for some form of ceremony and/or celebration. Such celebrations include the recognition of a nation's independence, the birth
or death of an historical and/or religious figure or a victorious battle, to name a few.

   Holidays often involve family dinners and sometimes gift-giving or exchange. Because we only get one chance per year to make a
holiday everything it *should* be, the pressure is on. We must cook the
perfect meal. For some this means a twelve-course feast, with each
course more impressive than the one before it and perfectly timed
(heaven forbid the candied yams grow cold while awaiting the
Thanksgiving turkey!). For others it simply means preparing a feast
that's better than last year's meal *and*, needless to say, far superior to
those of our neighbors'. Further, this perfect meal must be served in
perfect homes, cleaned from top to bottom during the days and weeks
leading up to the holiday. Lavish, though tasteful decorations adorn
our homes, with all of our holiday finest out on display. Oh, but we
mustn't forget the gifts. As we noted, some holidays involve gift-giving
and so we set out to find the perfect gifts—something our loved ones
do not have, but covet and something that's better than last year's gifts,
that others will take note of and possibly envy. These perfect gifts also
communicate just how important these people are to us, while at the
same time reflecting well on our taste and generosity. Finding such *perfect* gifts often involves exorbitant hours of shopping, while at the same
time exceeding our budgets. Finally, we strive for such perfection
because holidays are often spent with our families who, in our day-

dreams, are perfect, right? Well, let's look at this a bit more closely. There's Aunt Patti who always ends up drinking just a little too much, cousin Peter who, let's face it, only shows up to collect his gifts and Mom and Grandma, who go twelve rounds each year arguing on the surface about whether the turkey is finished cooking, but who actually have long unresolved issues. Everybody else is trying not to mention brother Stevie who has recently been incarcerated on an assault charge. We know our families, like everyone else's, have flaws. Somehow, however, we expect them to morph into the perfect Disney movie family during the holidays. They are *supposed to* somehow become loving and harmonious and the general feel in the home is *supposed to* be warm and fuzzy. When this doesn't happen, tension results, which often leads to difficulty with our significant others.

How Your Approach to the Holidays Pushes Your Own Buttons

In truth, with such impossible standards (i.e., irrational expectations) the most probable outcome is failure. After so much work and preparation, so much commitment to a single celebration, such a failure is likely to trigger anger within a love relationship. *It's not fair; I worked so hard to make this holiday a success* [demand]; *What's wrong with them? Why aren't they having a good time? They're just ingrates* [blame]. *And you're the worst of the bunch. You haven't said a word about all the things I've done to make you happy* [blame]; *There must be something wrong with me. I just can't get anything right, even our relationship* [self-blame]; *I can't stand this anymore* [low frustration tolerance].

We would be remiss if we did not take a moment to note that in most cultures, the pressure to make holidays perfect is felt more by women than men. This is by virtue of the fact that, even in the twenty-first century, women continue to have more responsibility than men do for matters on the home front. This is reinforced by gender differences in how we rear girls to nurture and take care of others, while rearing boys to protect and provide.

Managing Holiday Couple Stress

Holidays are demanding times, not only because of the extra work that is on our plates to organize celebrations, but also because of the big helping of expectations that we ourselves have and, of course, the most demanding of these expectations is what we expect from our mates. Get clear on your expectations of holidays. Are you expecting to be the perfect host/hostess, or for your family to morph into the Brady Bunch? Are you expecting your significant other to show the extent of his or her love? Watch for your demands for perfection from yourself and others. Reflecting back on previous holidays is a good way to stay grounded in reality, since the best prediction for the tone of current holidays is the tone of past holidays. Discover meaning in the holidays for *yourself*. In other words, are holidays a time for you to: reflect upon things for which you are grateful; give back to others who are less fortunate; strive to rise above petty family arguments; demonstrate by verbal means or gifts the depth of your commitment to your mate? Look for meaning that you have control over, rather than validation from others' behavior over which you have no control. Remember that at best, you can only control your own feelings, behavior and experiences—not others, not even the person you love.

Here are a few more tips for couples coping with the holidays:

Stick to Your Regular Routine: Because of the time demand associated with holidays, we often disrupt our routines and start cutting corners on self-care. We get less sleep, drop our stress-reducing exercise regimens and let our diets fall by the wayside as we increase caffeine intake to keep up the pace and sometimes use alcoholic beverages to relax and unwind from the high stress. Routines are most important when we're feeling overwhelmed, because they provide structure and a sense of familiarity, both of which are counter to stress. So, as much as possible, you and your mate should stick with your regular routine, making only those modifications necessary.

Share the Responsibility *and* Joy of Holidays: One of the most important skills any manager learns is that of delegation. For example, instead of shouldering the full responsibility for the holiday feast, share it with others and have your mate participate. Ask your guests to each bring a dish. Involve family in preparing the house for holiday guests. When you and your significant other participate in the preparation, you both have taken responsibility for the outcome and will enjoy the holiday more. This helps dissipate the friction between you that is caused by one person acting as master of ceremony and allows you both to join in the festivities. Divide the chores as much as possible.

Manage Your Time: For the most part, holidays scheduled according to the Christian/Western calendar come around the same time every year. And while holidays scheduled according to the lunar calendar (used by Muslim and Jewish people, for example) may fall on different dates from year to year, the same holidays are recognized each year. The point is, there are no surprises here, folks. And that's a good thing. What this means is that with a little planning and discipline, the two of you can start preparing for holidays early and avoid that last minute rush to cook, shop, clean, decorate, etc., etc., etc. And remember there's that little thing called the Internet, which allows us to shop online at our convenience, avoiding lines and crowds.

Manage Your Finances: With holidays that traditionally involve gift exchange, we need to be careful not to overspend and lose sight of the meaning of the holiday looking for that perfect (and expensive) gift. It's easy to become caught up in the shopping frenzy. To minimize this, try going in with others on gifts. This saves time and money. Also, set spending limits with friends and family. Most people are happy to do this, since gift-giving holidays are such a financial stress. Finally, many couples see the giving of holiday gifts as the perfect opportunity to express their love for their partner, but you needn't break the bank to show you care. You both can make gifts if you have the time. The personal touch is always appreciated.

For most, holidays are meant to be a time to gather with loved ones, share a meal and reflect on what is good. Demanding perfection from each other can only detract from the beauty of holidays. Remember that coming together for holidays year after year despite imperfections is validation enough of the significance of holidays and sharing the holiday with the one you love is the most important thing.

Bonus Section: Avoiding the New Years Trap

Most cultures celebrate the passage of time in one form or another. One common way to do this is with New Year celebrations. While many cultures maintain different calendars and so have the first day of their new year other than January first, most do recognize the end of an old year and the birth of a new one. As this happens, couples naturally assess time gone by, taking stock of where they stand in the plans for their lives. Most couples have things about themselves and their lives that they would like to be different and the coming of a new year is a traditional time to reflect on such matters.

In one word, the New Years expectation is a positive *change*. This change takes place in two forms. One form is letting go—letting go of unhealthy parts of our lives (unhealthy habits such as substance abuse, negative thinking or foul language) and letting go of past transgressions through atonement. The other form of change expected at New Years is embracing a healthier life style. This might include: (re)committing to virtuous goals of a religious or spiritual nature, starting an exercise program, adhering to better diets, working on improving your relationship and making amends, continuing education or starting therapy, for example.

Now all of this sounds pretty good. The problem is that we make these commitments to serious change in our lives and we do it not because we're ready and prepared for change, but because the year has changed. Think about it. On the first day of the new year we wake up in the same bed, with the same partner and the same relationship challenges. And in this new year, we go to the same job, pay the same bills, follow the same routine and on and on. If so much is the same, what makes us think that we can change?

Change is hard in the best of circumstances, but there are some things that we can do to make it less difficult and frustrating and more successful.

Be Specific About Desired Changes: If you and your mate want to be "healthier," define what that means to you both in terms of *behavior*. For example, a healthier life style might mean that you and your significant other exercise more, eat less chocolate and monitor your blood pressure. Then objectify the behavior, that is, describe it in terms that can be measured. *We will work out for fifteen minutes three times per week; We will eat no more than two ounces of chocolate each day; We will check our blood pressure two to three times each week.* When couples define the desired new behavior, they can monitor it and tell whether they've reached their goals.

Start with Small Steps: One of the reasons people fail at change is because they bite off more than they can chew. In other words, the expectations are too high and once people fail on one level, they are often too discouraged to continue their efforts. So if you and your partner want to make change, we recommend breaking down goals into manageable parts and not progressing to the next step until you've both mastered the current step. For instance, if being "healthier" was your goal and being healthier meant eating less chocolate, exercising more and monitoring your blood pressure, we'd ask you both to choose one of these three things to focus on before incorporating the next change. This increases your chances of success, which then increases motivation and confidence to move on to the next step.

Use Moderation: Oftentimes we get caught up in the enthusiasm of the moment and in doing so, set extreme goals which we are not likely to sustain over time. So, for example, if you both want to diet, rather than vowing never to eat chocolate again (a likely story!), start with a goal that reduces previous intake, then scale back the bad behavior over time if that's the ultimate goal. Remember that you and your partner want to break down your goal into obtainable parts which will help you both to maintain your motivation in the long run.

Evaluate Your Strategy: Most New Years resolutions are retreads, that is, you've both failed to achieve these goals in the past and now you want to improve your relationship and succeed. Assess your past strategy (what worked? what didn't?) and use your past experience to modify your current approach. If you both know something didn't work, don't set yourself up for failure again by using the same strategy. Try something new.

Elicit Support: Friends and family are there to help us with our challenges. Ask for their support. Ask them to assist you and your mate in your goals. You might be surprised at how happy people are to help.

While the desire to change our relationships by positive initiatives is healthy, setting ourselves up for failure and frustration is not. Change does not have to be overwhelming, especially when it is a choice that you both make and for which you both can plan (unlike change brought about by natural disasters, being struck by serious illness, or being a victim of a crime, for instance). Each of you can empower yourselves. Create a strategy for change and enjoy the success you achieve together.

Chapter 12

_____

Financial Problems
and Anger Management

Conflict and anger, as we've discussed, are a part of every relationship. This is especially true of those with significant others, because of the level of expectation and dependency that naturally develop in such close relationships. As we're now aware, certain situations tend to fuel anger, namely when things aren't going the way that we think that they ought to *and* when we can't effectively impose our will on outcomes.

Beyond the sense of inadequate control many of us now feel in our individual lives, circumstances of the new millennium have served to shake our sense of control as a society. Recently, America, like other nations, has suffered terrorist threats and attacks, on our own soil, which has largely in the past been an oasis of safety. The most calamitous event, of course, occurred on September 11, 2001. We have also fought two wars (Afghanistan and Iraq). In addition, in Europe, Asia and in America, there has been a significant economic downturn. The result: our collective stress is palpable and we see it manifest all too clearly in our relationships. While we may have to allow the politicians and military authorities to deal with matters of war and defense, we cannot adopt this approach when it comes to the impact of the economy on personal finances. When we don't have enough money to pay bills, when our needs outstrip our supply, anxiously we watch our families experience deprivation and feel desperate and unable to do anything. Often internal anxiety rises and this plays out in our relationships.

Looking back, the current economic downturn began to manifest itself in everyday life several years ago. The slowdown was the result of many factors converging including: the burst of the technology bubble, decreased consumer confidence in the stock market due to evidence of domestic vulnerability following terrorist attacks, exposure of corrupt conglomerates (e.g., in America, the Enron scandal of 2002), as well as other factors. The trickle down effect has been devastating for the average person: entire businesses and corporations closing, hostile takeovers and reorganizations ushering in layoffs, work furloughs and demotions leading to loss of pay. Also, there has been a loss of savings and devaluation of pension plans due to stock market losses. The result in many countries is higher than average unemployment rates and reduced consumer consumption, which further impacts the economic sluggishness.

The economic scene is reminiscent of that old song, "The neck bone's connected to the back bone, the back bone's connected to the hip bone, the hip bone's connected to the thigh bone…" and on and on. One circumstance feeds and maintains another, which in turn feeds and maintains yet another, all parts inextricably connected, harming each other and impacting lives.

Money plays a huge role in relationships. And while "money can't buy me love" (The Beatles, 1964), financial problems are one of the three most commonly cited reasons for divorce (the other two being sexual problems and conflicts about how to raise children).

The Root of All Evil

Aren't relationships supposed to be about love, communication, companionship? Well yes, *and* relationships are also about two different people coming together with different needs, values and perspectives to share one life. As a result of those differences, skills in negotiation, compromise and letting go are essential to minimize power struggles that naturally arise between two people of different backgrounds.

One aspect of relationships with significant others is that we share our money. Many times, when we live with our significant others long enough and certainly if we enter into domestic partnership or marriage, by law certain aspects of money become blended. As such, one partner loses some control over his or her own money. This is significant for two reasons. One, a reduced sense of control is often at the root of anger. Two, there is a great potential for irrational thoughts associated with money. Add to that the fact that our partners' financial decisions directly affect us, even if we've had nothing to do with their decisions and we have a potential powder keg on our hands.

One of the couples we counseled had serious anger problems stemming from difficult financial circumstances.

Harriet and Hank had been married for seventeen years when Harriet first came to see us. They had sixteen-year-old twin sons and a fifteen-year-old daughter, all of whom were already college-bound. Harriet, an office manager for a prominent law firm, was devoted to her children and concerned about their future. Hank, a civil engineer for the state in which they lived, was much more focused on his work, at times achieving national recognition for his cutting-edge bridge designs. Over the years, Harriet had learned to cope with Hank's workaholism and general neglect of the family. She accepted her role as "a married single-parent" and, in some ways, relished her unique position. On the initial visit, Harriet came to us, with Hank in tow, complaining of his irresponsible spending. Hank had always "borrowed" from household funds to further his designs, buying drafting instruments and tables, hiring contractors to convert their garage into a design studio, hosting parties for coworkers, buying materials to build models. Hank had led Harriet to believe that the state would reimburse these funds. However, Harriet started noticing an increase in credit card debt. When she confronted Hank, he confessed that the state did not reimburse employees' outlays of cash. She was further horrified to learn that while the state did not reimburse such expenses, they would have paid up-front for many of Hank's expenses had he simply submitted formal requests. Hank's defense was that the paperwork would have hindered his progress so he just used the family's money to expedite his projects. In fact, Hank had "expedited his projects" to the tune of tens of thousands of dollars worth of credit card debt.

Harriet was furious. She saw herself and her husband sinking further and further into debt that she had no ability to stop or manage. "If he loved me and his family, he wouldn't jeopardize our financial standing. He would control himself!"

When she learned the real truth, Harriet talked to Hank about her concerns and he agreed to reign himself in. However, credit card statements in the next months told a different story: Hank had continued to run up charges on their credit cards, charges for which he did not consult Harriet and for which she was equally responsible by law, despite the fact that the credit cards were in Hank's name only. And no matter how many times Harriet asked Hank to "cease and desist," and no matter how many times Hank agreed to do so, he continued to make credit card purchases. Eventually, Harriet filed for divorce citing financial problems as the primary reason: "I'm just not willing to assume any more of his debt. I think I'll have better things to do with my golden years than to work my fingers to the bone to pay off his debt!"

Besides the fertile ground for anger that is inherent in many committed relationships because of the legal blending of assets and debts, there is also the matter of the irrational beliefs that we all have about money. In modern society, money is associated with power and control:

• *Personal Freedom*
"Man, if I were rich, I'd tell my boss to shove it. I wouldn't take another minute of his crap!"

- *Power*

"Shoot, if I had that kind of money, supermodels would be tripping over me, too! Who cares whether they'd really love me. I'd have enough money so that they'd have to *act* like they did!"

- *Happiness*

"If I were independently wealthy, I'd live everyday as if I were on a Caribbean vacation without a single responsibility or a care in the world!"

- *Control*

"Everybody has a price—and with enough money I could afford to pay it!"

In short, we tend to have the belief that with enough money and control, happiness is guaranteed. Think about how many times you've wistfully thought or heard someone say, "If I could just win the lottery..." and all of the fantasies that you associated with the big bucks.

Irrational beliefs about money and unrealistic expectations about its panacea-like nature are powerful motivators, driving many individuals to seek control of what money they do have. However, as we saw in the case of Harriet and Hank, we don't have complete control over money in our relationships. Therein is the problem: our inability to control is at the root of anger, making financial conflicts a potentially volatile part of any relationship.

Up Close and Personal

Recently, in a Saturday morning focus group, several couples explored the effect of recent economic changes on relationships:

Bart, fifty-seven, and Peg, fifty-two, have been married for thirty years. They have three sons, ages twenty-nine, twenty-eight and twenty-six years old. After seventeen years on the job, Bart was laid off nine months ago from his position as president of Human Resources in a major Silicon Valley technological corporation. While he received a generous severance package—one year full salary with full benefits— he had been unable to find steady employment. Peg is a homemaker and has been awaiting Bart's retirement, with plans to travel together, both as a couple and with their grandchildren.

Joey, thirty-five, and Clarisse, thirty-three, have been married for eleven years. They have two children, a ten-year-old daughter and an eight-year-old son. Joey is an emergency room nurse and has worked at a private hospital for the past ten years. Clarisse has worked as a massage therapist at a swank spa for the past five years. In the past two years, Clarisse has been given fewer shifts due to the decreased demand for services.

Kathie, forty-three, and George, forty-nine, have been married for eight years. They have two sons, ages three and five. Kathie is an assistant professor at a local community college, where she has worked for the past seven years. George is an elementary school teacher and just received a pink slip for the fall, after ten years on the job. George's lay off was due to his state's budget problems. George likes the idea of being a househusband and looks forward to staying home with the kids. Kathie's not sold on this idea.

Mike, fifty-three, and Gary, fifty-seven, have been domestic partners for seventeen years. Gary has a twenty-three year old daughter from an earlier marriage. He took early retirement in 1999 from his position as an architect in a prestigious firm. Mike is a former antiques shop owner, turned full-time day-trader during the bull market of the late 1990s. Mike initially did well in a series of investments he made for the couple's future, enabling Gary to retire early. However, the couple lost everything in the market correction of 2000. Since then, Mike has re-entered the job market and currently manages an antique mall. Gary has come out of retirement but has only been able to land episodic contracts. "I think it's because of my age," he observed.

Sheila, twenty-three, and Carrie, thirty-five, moved in together eighteen months ago; neither have children. Sheila has worked as a pharmacy technician for the past two years, but was recently demoted to on-call status, thereby losing her benefits. Carrie is a dental hygienist and has worked at a county dental clinic for the past twelve years. Sheila wants to enter into domestic partnership with Carrie both because she loves her and because she needs medical insurance. Carrie is worried about increased financial responsibility during lean times.

David, forty-three, and Roberto, fifty-one, have been domestic partners for five years and have no children. David has worked as a high-rise window cleaner for the past twenty years. Downsizing led to mandatory over-time, which according to David led to over-work and a strained back. He's been on medical disability for the past nine months and is trying to stretch out his disability due to fears of being terminated when he returns as his company has been downsizing. Roberto has been a chef at a popular bistro for the past twelve years and believes that everybody, short of those on their deathbeds, ought to be earning a living.

McKayla, twenty-five, and Dwight, twenty-seven have been married for three years and have no children. McKayla has worked as a secretary in the corporate offices of a major grocery store chain for three years. Dwight has been a warehouse worker for the same chain for the past two years. Corporate has let it be known that the majority of warehousers will be laid off before the end of the fiscal year. McKayla wants Dwight to begin looking for a new job now. Dwight has decided if he is laid off he will collect unemployment for a few months and get a much-needed rest.

Initially, we met with the couples together, focusing on such questions as: *What is the impact of the economy and your financial changes on your relationship? What is the toughest part of your financial problems? What have you learned about yourself and your partner in all of this? How do you talk about financial problems? Where do you see control becoming a problem? How do you make sense of your recent economic struggles?*

We found, however, that we didn't get very far with this focus group when both members of the couple were present. Participants seemed reluctant to talk, other than to say that they felt scared and seemed to have less fun together. So we decided to separate our participants into two groups, putting one member of a couple in each group. Boy, did we get an ear-full!

Dr. L.: Okay guys, now that your partners are safely stowed away in another room, we're going to ask this question again…How have your recent financial changes affected your relationship with your significant other?

Bart: I think it's bullshit! I gave that company the best years of my life and they reward me by laying me off just because they hit hard times? That's just not the way it's supposed to go down. I don't care what kind of severance I got!

Dr. K.: You sound super frustrated, Bart. Tell us how all of this affects your relationship with Peg.

Bart: Well, Peg is a good woman. Hell, why wouldn't she be? She's had it pretty easy lounging at home for the past thirty years! But you know, she sees me hustling every day, trying to get work and she never once offered to look for a job so that she could chip in for a change. As always, the situation is left for me to fix. I deserve a break…hell, I *need* a break. She should be out there hustling for work after thirty years on the gravy train, not me! If you ask me, she's just plain spoiled.

George: I know what you mean, man. Kathie's constantly riding my back about getting another job. Everyday she nags me about money. She's turned into a real bitch now that she can't run to Nordstrom willy-nilly.

Dr. K.: Sounds as though things are pretty rough. Let's hear from some of the rest of you. What's the hardest part of your financial problems?

Bart: Hell, not being able to just stroll into a fine liquor store for a bottle of Chivas Regal without having to think twice about the cost! [laughs]

Dr. L.: Seriously…

Sheila: Well, I don't know about the rest of you, but all Carrie and I do anymore is talk about money. Or, I should say eat, sleep and fight about money. Sometimes it's hard to remember why we're together. If she'd just file for domestic partnership so I could get on her insurance, everything would be back to normal. Clearly she thinks I'm good enough to you-know-what, but not good enough to marry.

Dr. L.: What have you learned about yourselves and your partners in all of this?

David: That my partner's a selfish money grubber. My back really hurts sometimes, but Roberto cares more about the paycheck I bring home than me! And getting back to your point [gestures toward Sheila], is anyone still getting *any*? Do you even want it with your partner anymore? Just look at Roberto…if I ain't good enough to support, then I sure as shit ain't good enough to sleep with. If he wants to play this game, well, I'm the master at holding out!

Gary: I don't know. Sometimes I feel like a real schmuck. I mean, Mike's supporting me now and I was the one making the money. But you know, if he'd been a better investor, if he'd really known what he was doing, he would have seen signs of the bottom falling out and he would have protected our money.

McKayla: Yeah, what's with this not reading the writing on the wall? Dwight knows he's facing layoffs and he's somehow decided, all by himself, that it's okay for him to bring home some bogus unemployment check and to hang out with his buddies while I skip off to work to make the money we need to *survive*. What he needs to be doing is looking for a job *now*. I'm not about to pay his bills while he's kickin' it at home!

Clarisse: Well, I just feel like Joey's slave or something. Now that I have lost hours at work, my chores around the house have mushroomed.

Joey thinks that I should do everything because he is supporting us…cooking, cleaning, hell, he even has me keeping his calendar and making his appointments. Oh yeah, and as for sex, as far as he's concerned, I should be good to go whenever he wants it since I'm just sitting around on my ass all day. Joey has it so good he doesn't even want me to increase my hours if I could. He doesn't care about my feelings, only his own. I don't know about the rest of you who are making less money because of changes at work, but as soon as I can I'm increasing my hours and getting out from under his thumb—even if it means going to work as a clerk somewhere. I don't care what he wants. This little Miss Suzie Homemaker business is killing me! I don't really say anything to him about it—what'd be the point? He'll only try to change my mind to see things his way. I'm just going to come home with a new job and he can start chipping in around the house like before. This is no example to set for our kids!

Here's how things went on the other side. Our group included Kathie, Peg, Carrie, Mike, Roberto, Joey and Dwight.

Dr. K.: We know that sometimes it's easier to talk when our partners aren't around, so we wanted you all to have a chance to say what's really on your minds about how these financial problems are affecting your relationships.

Kathie: All I have to say is George needs to get a job like yesterday! If it weren't for his joblessness we'd have been able to keep the kids in private school. But their tuition is a killer. And I know that it sounds crazy, but sometimes I close my eyes and I swear I can just see myself pushing one of those little carts with all of our stuff piled in it. This is all really freaking me out. And the fact that George is not in any hurry whatsoever to get a job…well, he's nuts if he thinks that we can afford to live on my salary alone. Besides, as one of my old college roommates used to say, "All able bodies must work!" I am not here so that he can live the life of Riley.

Mike: Well, Gary and I have been together a long time and through a lot of stuff. You know, like we were gay before gay was cool [smiles]. But I just don't know if we can ride this one out. I know he blames me for losing our nest egg. And the way he looks at me…I just don't know. It's like he's so resentful. When I try to approach him, you know, sexually, he just pulls away.

Carrie: Well, I don't even know why you'd want any these days, Mike. Does *anybody* here feel like curling up with your partner? I know I don't. This whole experience has helped me to see what Sheila is all about. She just wants to be taken care of and she thinks that I'm the one to do it. Like the lady said, "All able bodies must work." This is *my* money she's living off of now. I finally put my foot down and put her on a budget. Honestly, I'm just looking for a way to bail out of this and find a partner who will carry her own.

Peg: My situation is a little different than all of yours. Bart and I agreed years ago that I'd take care of the home. That's what I've done and intend to keep doing. What I can relate to is having a partner who needs a job but who is taking his sweet time about it. Sure Bart got a healthy severance package, but it won't last forever. I see my main job now as encouraging him to get a new job. This is more important than anything else I do as his wife, since even he would agree that the idea of me getting my first job at the age of 52 is pretty ridiculous.

Dr. L.: Joey, Dwight, Roberto, how do you feel about all this?

Roberto: I guess I feel a bit like Carrie—really disappointed in David. He thinks just because he's bringing home a disability check that he's making some real contribution. Truth be told, that check covers less than 25 percent of our expenses. He's placed the rest squarely on my shoulders, when he could be and should be working. Instead, he's decided to milk the system for all it's worth. I wonder if he's not doing the same with me. We argue all of the time now—he says I'm insensitive, I say he's on the dole.

Joey: I'm actually okay with Clarisse being home. I like the fact that she's there taking care of me and our home. This is the way it was supposed to be. I have to pull double shifts a few times each week to keep us afloat but it's worth it. It was a little tough for her when I told her that I was cutting her allowance since I'm the only one really working, but she'll be okay. I'm sure she understands.

Dwight: Wow Joey, you sound pretty cool. I wish that Mac [McKayla] could be that understanding with me. What's the big deal if I take a break? I guess I feel as long as I'm bringing home a check, Disability, Unemployment, what not, I'm still contributing to the household. Hey, I'd support McKayla if she needed a break. Isn't that what marriage is supposed to be—supporting each other in the good and bad? She shouldn't look at me differently or love me less because I might lose my job. That's not love, that's greed.

There are many ways that these relationships are buckling under the weight of financial stress. Take a few minutes to do the following exercise and identify specific pitfalls in your relationship.

Exercise: The Economic Pitfalls of Relationships

1. Identify five to eight statements that are consistent with the characteristics of angry people: low frustration tolerance, judging, demanding behavior, perfectionism, possessiveness and humor.
2. Can you find any statements of rational preferences?
3. Reflect back on the last discussion about money that you had with your partner. Which of the six characteristics of angry people most characterized your discussion?
4. Chose any one of the statements from item #1. Rework it from an irrational statement to a rational preference.
5. Which couples have deteriorated the most from the couple unit to the me-versus-him/her position and why?

As we review the responses in the focus groups, we see that there is an abundance of fuel for anger:

- *Low Frustration Tolerance*: Clarisse, "This little Miss Suzie Homemaker business is killing me!"

- *Judging*: David, "Roberto cares more about the paycheck I bring home than me."

- *Demanding*: Kathie, "George needs to get a job like yesterday!"

- *Perfectionism*: Gary, "If he'd been a better investor, if he'd really known what he was doing, he would have seen the signs of the bottom falling out..."

- *Possessiveness*: Carrie, "This is *my* money she's living off of now."

- *Blaming*: Kathie, "If it weren't for his joblessness, we'd have been able to keep the kids in private school."

When the chips were down, our couples no longer saw themselves as couples, as "us," but rather as two separate people at odds, e.g. me-versus-you. This position ushers in competitiveness and underscores the sense that there aren't enough resources to meet demand. When resources are limited, it is human nature to be self-centered, to "get mine first." Often, the fewer crumbs there are, the harder the fight, the greater the need for control. The picture, for couples who handle anger over finances in these ways could not be any bleaker, so new ways of thinking and reacting as a unit are necessary. In the next chapter we will offer some preventative and coping strategies.

Part 2

Solutions

Chapter 13

Partnership Anger Gauges

Life, marriage and loving relationships are adventures, not tests. People we love can act their best when they feel they have the freedom to act as they wish and the independence to do so. If we want our significant other to act differently, it would be better to concentrate on ourselves first. In most caring relationships, the more one partner sees the other become less demanding, perfectionistic and rigid, the more likely he or she is to change for the better as a result of this new behavior. By the same token, increasing expressions of demanding behaviors can produce similar negative results.

The fatal error in logic made by a perfectionist partner is that his significant other will love him more the better he does. The rationale is that if he can just do things perfectly, he'll get undying devotion from his partner and in turn feel eternally good about himself. Of course, since we're human, we can never do things perfectly, because everything in the universe can be improved upon. When we don't do things perfectly and fail to live up to the impossible standards that we've set for ourselves, then we become disappointed and either angry or depressed. In between those times, we're going to be anxious about whether or not we can continue to succeed or accomplish everything we attempt. Even when we do well, the feeling of accomplishment is usually quite short lived. The perfectionist has to keep doing well in order to feel good about himself. The result is that the perfectionist tends to be chronically angry, depressed or worried, with only very brief periods of happiness in between. He can only feel good about himself if he does well. Continually grading himself and conditionally liking himself depending only on how well he does, he will always tend to feel anxious and nervous.

Once again, the way out of the trap is to stop equating your or your partner's behaviors with your value as people. In terms of our existence, our behaviors are a part of us, but not our totality. Self-acceptance, not self-rating, is the key to peace of mind. These same principles, incidentally, apply to the commonly accepted version of self-esteem of which we spoke earlier. Self-esteem is a very elusive, transitory concept that is bandied about in the popular press. It always involves a rating and judgment. Consequently, when your self-esteem is on the line in your closest relationship, instead of accepting yourself, you judge and label yourself depending on how well you do in getting your way. If your standard for good self-esteem is perfect behavior in your love affair, you are setting yourself up to be consistently angry or depressed. Oftentimes, people don't know how high they have set their internal standards and don't realize the extent to which they are setting themselves up for being emotionally upset. This is the problem that occurs when we set perfectionistic standards for ourselves and those we love.

Judgments and Labels

It's dangerous to draw quick conclusions about what the person closest to us thinks of us based on any given action on their part. If we do that, we tend to generalize that a specific action is indicative of an entire impression they have of us. We then tend to assign labels to the other person and demand that they be different. This whole process is often based on just one specific action on their part. For example, if a woman tells herself: *If he really loved me, he would know how much I want to see that show on my birthday and he will get tick-ets,* she is setting herself up for disappointment if her partner makes other plans for celebrating her birthday. Besides the arbitrariness of that definition of love, there is a more serious flaw in reasoning here. She is telling herself that he has to be the way she wants him to be. Well, how can he be? He is the way he is—the product of his own genetics, background and experience. No matter how much his girl-friend may want her partner to fit into her own model of an ideal mate, he is going to be the way he is, not the way she demands or expects that he be. We must resolve our own demands for perfection in our loved ones as soon as possible, to minimize what could be potentially serious problems. Partners occasionally mess up. So do we. One way to modify this perfectionism is to focus on thinking accurately and accepting each other, without distortion or general-ization.

When a significant other makes a mistake, it's much better to not demand perfection—which is unobtainable anyway—and take a step back from the situation itself, focusing on the whole problem instead. This problem-oriented approach helps avoid blaming and fault-finding. If preparing dinner is a problem for two people, both of whom may work, there is an underlying problem of deciding how to share responsibility. Both people should focus on that, rather than divert their energies to arguing about less produc-tive areas. In the process, each partner can have several levels of thoughts on his internal heat scales, ranging from boiling thoughts to cool thoughts. A boiling thought might go something like this: *My wife should do what I tell her and when she doesn't obey me, she's pur-posely provoking me* or *My husband treats me like I'm his servant.* This level of thinking leads to judgmental attitudes and an unwillingness to communicate needs or accept negotiated settlements.

One partner may have hot thoughts: *I really hate it when my wife goes out with her friends without leaving me something to eat for dinner; she should treat me better!* He can have tepid thoughts: *My wife should do a better job than she's doing. Why can't she get this right?* Or he can have cool thoughts: *I don't particularly like it when*

I have to make my dinner, but I know my wife loves me, and she can't do everything to please me one hundred percent of the time. The cooler his thoughts are, the more likely it is that he will be in control of himself and his angry feelings. Similarly, the more likely it is that the thoughts he is having will be accurate and not irrational ideas in which he comes up with faulty data or imprecise logic to come to a conclusion that he wants. The aim is rational thinking in which we view a situation on its own terms, with no distortion, and arrive at conclusions that are justified by the data. Here are some more examples of boiling, hot and cool thoughts:

Boiling Thoughts	Hot Thoughts	Cool Thoughts
1. I hate when he goes out with his friends. He can be such a jerk!	Why does he have to go out with his friends on my day off?	I wish he would make me as much a priority in his life as his friends.
2. When my wife takes too long getting ready, making us both late, I explode!	Why can't she be more punctual?	I would really like it if my wife would work on being on time.
3. I can't deal with her when she shouts at me!	It's really annoying when she yells during our arguments.	It would be nice if she lowered her voice in discussions like this.
4. This meal is terrible. I'd like to throw this plate at him.	This is the worst meal he's made in a long time.	I've certainly had better meals than this.

Individuals who feel intense anger at spouses for minor things need to first practice thinking accurately and taking time arriving at conclusions. Analyze the situation and pinpoint what about your partner's behavior is actually angering you. Make a point of not bringing past arguments into the present one. Check your data and conclusions with others. You will begin to see a change in how often you get angry with each other and how intensely you regard things. You will also find yourself staying angry at your partner for shorter periods of time. When you do get angry, as we all do despite our best efforts, try not to put yourself down. This produces secondary anger, which just slows down your abilities to work on the original problem. Remember, you're fallible too. If you find yourself getting angry about being angry, use self-therapy. Ask why you need to be angry at yourself or your mate for being human and making mistakes. Once you have resolved that issue, you can begin to work on the original problem between you and your partner.

If you are the angry partner, you will find that your attitude towards not only your significant other but also towards the world will change as your views start changing. You must learn to rethink your anger issues. Inside your mind, you have a cognitive map of reality, just like a driver has a road map of a new city he visits. If you have a faulty map, you will undoubtedly get lost. Having an accurate map of reality helps you to cope with the world and the people you love much better and helps your behavior to become more appropriate. You will also begin to feel better emotionally.

Important Points for You Both to Remember

One way of telling whether you and your partner have unresolved feelings of anger is for you both to ask yourselves if you have many of the qualities we just discussed.

- Individuals who feel angry usually have a sense of impatience, low frustration tolerance, a judgmental attitude, a keen sense of humor, a demanding nature and tend to be perfectionistic. When these qualities are added together they form a nucleus influencing the quality of your relationship.

- Begin today to try to learn from each situation and resolve together to problem solve much better in the future. Later we will deal more with the specifics of what causes your anger.

Partner Homework

Here are some exercises to decrease each member's anger quotient so that you and your partner can deal with qualities of perfectionism and improve self-acceptance and mutual acceptance.

1. Three maxims to repeat several times a day:
   a. Perfection does not equal happiness. I resolve to make our relationship more satisfying, not perfect.
   b. Even masterpieces have flaws. I will accept my own and my partner's.
   c. The process, not the outcome, is important. I will live more in the precise present.

2. When a partner does something obnoxious to you, rate the trait or behavior, not the person. Interact assertively to try to correct the behavior and refrain from condemning the person. Work on communicating your preferences and feelings about how the behavior contributed to your being upset.

3. When either of you catches yourself feeling anger building up, practice slowing each other down no matter what you are doing. Take a time out. Tell yourself to slow down your motion and speech rate to about one half of what it is at that moment. You will be surprised at how much more relaxed and in control you will feel. You'll feel more clear headed and more competent. In moments of anger, work on breathing deeply and slowly. This will involve a conscious effort at first, but will produce excellent results in stress relief during angry situations.

4. In other stressful moments, whether at the supermarket, bank, office, in traffic or another situation where anger seeds, stop

yourself mentally. Take a series of deep breaths. Resolve to accept that there are things you can't control and that you will not take such situations out on your partner later.

5.   The next time you leave for work, leave fifteen minutes earlier than you normally do and choose the slow traffic lane on the freeway. One member of an angry couple we were counseling used to drive himself crazy playing a game of seeing exactly how long it would take him to get to work and home on any given day and then seeing if he could beat his previous time by a minute or two. Such a tactic got him agitated quickly. Later, he and his significant other would invariably fight. Practice raising your low frustration tolerance to more competent levels and slowing down the pace of your life and sense of urgency.

6.   Agree that both partners will have the assignment of doing some things imperfectly or different than is expected—making a bed, taking the dog for a walk, preparing dinner, or shopping. Try risking by anticipating good results with your partner, rather than fearing poor results. Risk expecting the best instead of the worst. Does each of you feel any differently?

7.   Cultivate a playful attitude with each other. Do some humorous shame-attacking exercises. These exercises should help both of you to get over the idea that each of you must be perfect in order to feel valued and get approval from the other. Angry couples are composed of two people who are other directed and feel they and their partner must perform perfectly. Most people are bad predictors of how other people will react when they screw up in public and/or think it would be horrible to experience the feedback. They're just wrong the vast majority of the time. The truth is, people will hardly notice and even if they do, you'll get through it much better than you thought and learn to stop living as if you were in a tight closet in the process. Here are some shame-attacking exercises you and your partner can do. To know whether or not you're really doing a shame-attacking exercise ask yourself if you feel

some apprehension when contemplating doing it. If you don't feel
at least a mild level of anxiety, you probably aren't doing a genuine
shame-attacking exercise.

a.   Eat a meal backwards with your partner in a restaurant.
b.   Go into a large department store and yell out the time of day
     in a clear voice.
c.   Both of you ride in an elevator backwards, facing the rest of
     the people, and smile.
d.   Go into a diner, order two eggs, one fried, one scrambled.
e.   Design your own exercise with your partner.

When a perfectionist partner or couple gets over needing other
people's approval to feel good about themselves and each other,
they will be taking positive steps towards building a more satisfying life and relationship.

Self Evaluation of Anger Gauge

How Angry Are You?

First, both partners should do this exercise separately. Check any
item that either of you feels applies. This test may be shared but
should not be used by either partner as a basis for labeling the other.

1. I find it very difficult to wait for things. If I'm waiting for an ele-
    vator and someone newly arrived pushes the elevator button
    after I've already pushed it, I get very upset because I've already
    done that necessary chore (do they think I'm just standing
    around stupidly without pushing the button?).

2. If I go "Dutch treat" for lunch with a friend and I feel he doesn't
    pay his fair share of the bill, I get a knot in my stomach.

3. I hate it when people do a poor job on an item I've taken in for repair. If the mechanic spills oil on the paint job of my car, I think about suing the garage.

4. Whenever I remember an incident where someone treated me unfairly, I get angry all over again.

5. I've been so angry at my spouse or significant other that I've screamed at her on several occasions and felt badly about it later.

6. I just hate it when someone squeezes in front of me on the freeway.

7. I can't stand it when someone crowds in front of me in line and I feel like putting them in their place!

8. If my child, significant other or boss ignores me when I'm trying to talk to him I get so furious I feel like I'm going to explode!

9. When I see the owner of a new car intentionally taking up two parking spaces, I feel like "keying" the car.

10. I think my boss is a total jerk who deserves to lose his (her) job.

11. If I were a better parent I'd be able to control my kids better. I can't **stand** it when they talk back to me!

If you checked three or fewer items, your temper is probably pretty much under control. If you checked four or more, you're likely to have unresolved anger to people close to you.

Here's another quiz each partner can take to determine if he or she is likely to be chronically upset and have a temper problem. This quiz was adapted from the Institute for Advanced Study in Rational Psychotherapy (founded by Dr. Albert Ellis) in New York City.

1. I believe that it is awful to make a mistake when other people are watching.
   (Disagree - 1) (Sometimes - 2) (Strongly agree - 3)

2. I believe that it is intolerable to be disapproved of by others.
   (Disagree - 1) (Sometimes - 2) (Strongly agree - 3)

3. I believe that it is shameful to be looked down upon by people for having less than they have.
   (Disagree - 1) (Sometimes - 2) (Strongly agree - 3)

4. I believe that it is horrible if one does not have the love or approval of certain special people who are important to one.
   (Disagree - 1) (Sometimes - 2) (Strongly agree - 3)

5. I believe that it is intolerable to have things go along slowly and not be settled quickly.
   (Disagree - 1) (Sometimes - 2) (Strongly agree - 3)

6. I believe that it's too hard to get down to work at things it often would be better for one to do.
   (Disagree - 1) (Sometimes - 2) (Strongly agree - 3)

7. I believe that it is terrible that life is so full of inconveniences and frustrations.
   (Disagree - 1) (Sometimes - 2) (Strongly agree - 3)

8. I believe that people who keep one waiting frequently are worth-
   less and deserve to be boycotted.
   (Disagree - 1) (Sometimes - 2) (Strongly agree - 3)

9. I believe that it is intolerable when other people do not do one's
   bidding or give one what one wants.
   (Disagree - 1) (Sometimes - 2) (Strongly agree - 3)

10. I believe that some people are unbearably stupid or nasty and
    that one must get them to change.
    (Disagree - 1) (Sometimes - 2) (Strongly agree - 3)

11. I believe that things are too rough in this world and that there-
    fore it is legitimate for one to feel sorry for oneself.
    (Disagree - 1) (Sometimes - 2) (Strongly agree - 3)

12. I believe that it is awful for one to have to discipline oneself.
    (Disagree - 1) (Sometimes - 2) (Strongly agree - 3)

13. I believe that people who do wrong things should suffer strong
    revenge for their acts.
    (Disagree - 1) (Sometimes - 2) (Strongly agree - 3)

14. I believe that wrongdoers and immoral people should be
    severely condemned.
    (Disagree - 1) (Sometimes - 2) (Strongly agree - 3)

15. I believe that people who commit unjust acts are bastards and
    that they should be severely punished.
    (Disagree - 1) (Sometimes - 2) (Strongly agree - 3)

16. I believe that it is horrible for one to perform poorly.
    (Disagree - 1) (Sometimes - 2) (Strongly agree - 3)

17. I believe that it is awful if one fails at important things.
    (Disagree - 1) (Sometimes - 2) (Strongly agree - 3)

18. I believe that it is terrible for one to make a mistake when one has
    to make important decisions.
    (Disagree - 1) (Sometimes - 2) (Strongly agree - 3)

19. I believe that if one keeps failing at things one is a pretty worth-
    less person.
    (Disagree - 1) (Sometimes - 2) (Strongly agree - 3)

20. I believe that strong emotions like anxiety and rage are caused
    by external conditions and events and that one has little or no
    control over them.
    (Disagree - 1) (Sometimes - 2) (Strongly agree - 3)

After you and your partner take this quiz, each of you should add up all of his or her points. If one or both of you scored forty or more points, that person probably has trouble with anger. You may both be surprised to find out that anger is a "couple" trait, not an "individual" one. If so, this book will help you both as individuals and as partners in a relationship to understand your anger and work through and resolve it so that your relationship, instead of being stunted and diseased, grows strong and healthy.

Chapter 14

Addressing Financial Issues

Prevention:

Since financial problems are one of the top three culprits in divorce, couples ought to spend some time talking about money before they begin to commingle funds. This means discussing:

1. Concrete aspects of money: how much money each makes; one's current budget as a single person; debts and assets; credit card use and practices.
2. Philosophical aspects of money: values and beliefs that each holds about money (e.g., buys happiness, the root of evil); how money was managed/talked about in each person's family of origin (e.g., talked about money openly; invested, saved or spent).
3. Strategies for commingling funds: develop a budget before commingling funds; establish a concrete understanding of ownership of prior assets and debts; discuss expectations about household contributions; identify who will manage routine bills; discuss comfort level regarding savings (e.g. one month's versus six month's worth of rent/mortgage in savings); explore each person's philosophy regarding the role of insurance.

So often these matters are not discussed, because they take

us out of the bliss of the moment. Let's face it, financial discussions are not romantic and they're definitely not sexy. Further, most of us know that money is a sensitive area. How much money we have is tied to our self esteem, self image and feelings of self worth. There's almost an inherent sense of inadequacy when it comes to money, especially if there's never enough. Money is a topic that few of us bring up, especially when we're having a good time—which is exactly the right time for such discussions. Rather, we wait for a crisis and then try to resolve the problem at hand, while stressed out and most likely under time pressure.

Intervention Program:
You may not have taken financial preventative measures during good times. If either partner, or even both partners, finds themself in situations of red hot anger due to financial concerns, here are intervention measures which can cool down your and your partner's sparks.

1. Confront the problem: Because money is such a loaded topic, you may be tempted to avoid talking about the situation. But we know to be solved this problem must be addressed. Otherwise, the risk of continuing misplaced anger and/or anxiety may escalate.
2. Take a deep breath, step back and consider your own irrational demands and expectations in the situation: Look for the five problematic characteristics of angry people, e.g., Kathie, whom we met in chapter 12, said, "George needs to get a job like yesterday."
3. Change hot thoughts to rational preferences: For instance, Kathie could focus on statements of rational preference such as "I'll feel more comfortable when George has a job" in contrast to the hot demand above.
4. Take a few moments to recall what's good about your relationship: When one aspect of our relationship is going poorly, it's easy to go to the extreme and see everything as bad. The problem with this is two fold: we lose our focus and thus are less effective at problem

solving; we then feel less empowered and, therefore, primed for anger. Think of what your partner *does* contribute to the relationship, even if it's not money (e.g., rearing children, running the household, lending a sympathetic ear) and what you enjoy about your partner (e.g., sense of humor, loyalty). Resist this all-or-nothing trap.

5. Check in with yourself: Are you equating your partner's behavior with who your partner is. For example, if your partner is out of work, is she then "lazy" or a "free loader?" Remember, we judge the act not the person.

6. Negotiate a plan of action:

    a. Use a solution-oriented approach—Avoid blaming, "If you hadn't lost your job, the kids would still be in private school." Rather, focus on financial and budgetary matters.

    b. Communicate preferences, not judgments—For example, Kathie might say, "I would like to maintain our current standard of living, but we can't do that on my salary alone. You will have to work if we are to maintain the lifestyle we now enjoy."

    c. Brainstorm about solutions: they come in all shapes and sizes; some will be more attractive to you than others. This will be a joint decision. In Kathie and George's case, George may return to work or Kathie may increase her hours, they could relocate to a less expensive home, use savings to maintain their lifestyle, seek the professional help of a financial planner or consumer debt agency.

    d. Agree to check in with your partner regularly—It's human nature to avoid the unpleasant, therefore it's important to schedule check-ins with each other to assess progress with your plan of action and to modify it if necessary.

7. Use short term quick fixes: Remember, while quick fixes do not help to solve the underlying problem of anger, they can help us calm down in the moment in order to help us be more effective at dealing with the real problem. So go ahead, count to ten, take

some deep breaths or a brisk walk, distract yourself for a moment with a computer game, then gather the tools that you now have and get to solving your problem.

8. Remind yourself that you don't have to solve the problem instantly: Coming up with solutions takes compromise and negotiation, which take time. While you may not have months to solve your financial problem, you can allow yourself and your partner a short interval to regroup when necessary.

9. Be aware that you only control yourself: Anger is about our unsuccessful attempts to control that which is beyond our control. Always remember that everything outside of you falls in that category, including your partner. All that you can do is offer to be a part of the solution. If your partner refuses to participate, you need to consider your own limits and whether your partner's personality is a good match for you.

Applying Interventions:

Here are some ways to apply these interventions to one of the real-life couples whom we met in chapter 12. In the case of Bart and Peg, there is little reason to expect Bart's employment situation will change any time soon. In fact, the best predictions suggest that Silicon Valley will still be down 50,000 jobs (in comparison to 2000) a full decade from now (Econ.Com, 2003). Bart and Peg are likely to have to make some real changes to survive as a couple. Realizing this, the couple took us up on our offer of three sessions to coach them through our Intervention Program.

Day One:

Introduce the Intervention Program: We simply walked Peg and Bart through the Intervention Program outlined on previous pages, explaining each step in some detail.

Address the Problem: Our next step was to look at how well Peg and Bart had met the criteria of the Intervention Program. We assessed the extent to which they had addressed their financial problems *together* by reviewing transcripts from the focus group with them.

Initially, in the focus group, Peg and Bart, like the other couples, had little to say with each other present. Once separated, it became clear that each one had some very different ideas about how Bart's joblessness *should* be managed. This alone suggested some tendency to avoid talking about problems. The other clue that we had about their past practice of avoidance is that while Bart said that Peg should chip in and help by getting a job, it appeared that Bart had not mentioned this to Peg, as she clearly found the idea of her working as laughable, "…since even he [Bart] would agree that the idea of me getting my first job at fifty-two is pretty ridiculous!" With respect to their addressing the problem with a team approach, Peg and Bart had room for improvement.

Identify Irrational Demands and Convert to Cooler Preferences: While Peg and Bart had not addressed their financial problems directly, it is clear that they both entertained some pretty irrational ideas about Bart's return to work and their financial predicament— hot thoughts that they could shift to cooler preferences. So in the final step of coaching for Day One, we sent the couple home with an assignment: we listed the hot thoughts for each from the transcripts, as well as the angry characteristics that each thought represented. The couple was instructed to work together to generate cooler preferences for each thought.

Day Two

Identify Irrational Demands and Convert to Cooler Preferences: On Day Two we started off by reviewing the previous day's homework:

Bart's Hot Thoughts	Angry Characteristics	Rational Preferences
I think it's bullshit!	Judgment	I wish it didn't happen like this.
I gave the company the best years of my life and they reward me by laying me off just because they hit hard times?	Judgment, low frustration tolerance, expectation of fairness	In the best of both worlds, loyalty would be rewarded. But we don't live in a perfect world. At least I got a good severance package.
That's not the way it's supposed to go down.	Demanding	It would've been nice if I'd been able to stay with the company until *I* was ready to retire.
She's [Peg] had it pretty easy…in the past thirty years.	Judgment	Peg has been a great support over the years; putting up with my crazy schedule could not have been easy.

Bart's Hot Thoughts	Angry Characteristics	Rational Preferences
She never once offered to look for a job so that she could chip in.	Judgment	It would be nice if Peg offered to work, just to take some of the pressure off of me. I suppose I could ask her.
As always, the situation is left for me to fix.	Judgment-*life should be fair,* generalization	Sometimes I feel alone in solving our problems. But I can ask Peg for help.
Hell, I *need* a break.	Low frustration tolerance	I'd really like to take some time off.
She should be out there hustling for work after thirty years on the gravy train, not me!	Judgment-*should*	I'd prefer that Peg work for a while, while I take a breather.
She ought to work for a while and not be so lazy.	Judgment, confuses the action with the person	I know that Peg has worked hard in our home all of these years. I wonder if she'd be willing to trade places with me while I catch my breath.

Peg's Hot Thoughts	Angry Characteristics	Rational Preferences
It's not fair that I can't buy what I want when I want.	Low frustration tolerance- *entitlement*	I wish I had the financial security I used to, but at least we've managed to keep a roof over our heads.
Bart and I have an agreement and I refuse to change the terms.	Demanding	I prefer to keep working in the home, but I'm willing to change if necessary.
Bart's taking way too long to find a job.	Judgment, low frustration tolerance	I'm not sure Bart's working as hard as he could be to find another job.

Looking over Bart and Peg's statements during the focus groups, we see that Bart in particular is heavy on judging and demanding and, to a lesser extent, has low frustration tolerance. Later, in reviewing their rational preference statements, it is clear that both Bart and Peg are beginning to utilize this exercise and are slowly but surely working toward communicating.

Emphasize What Works: In addition to Bart's tendency toward judging and demanding, the early transcripts also revealed some true strengths that we pointed out to the couple: Bart is enthusiastic about talking (even if it's not with Peg, per the initial focus group encounter); Bart has a good sense of humor; Bart is able to recognize that Peg is a "good woman." When we coach couples, we not only look at the potential to change dysfunctional behavior, but also opportunities to capitalize on strengths. We reason that the more time you spend doing something well, the less time you have for irrational thoughts and behavior. That shift alone can improve relationships and reduce anger potential.

We encouraged Bart to talk more with Peg about his job and financial stress and to do so using his strengths of humor and validation. After all, it's hard for a couple to be defensive when laughing with one another and even harder to separate from someone when telling the person that he or she is appreciated. Rather, we feel more open and are more likely to reciprocate when validated. We developed homework exercises to illustrate the power of these two strengths in defusing anger. We developed statements emphasizing Bart's weaknesses (judging and demanding) and strengths (humor and validation). Bart's assignment was to think of Peg's likely response to each and then evaluate the impact of his statements on their relationship. Peg's exercises concentrated on developing her listening skills and expressing her views without flailing out at Bart.

Day Three

As this final day began, we reviewed Bart and Peg's homework assignments:

Bart's Strength	Peg's Likely Response	Result
Humor – I gotta tell you, I think the part that gets me most is not being able to stroll into any store and pick up that bottle of Chivas without a thought. Ha!	Yea, that and my Kenneth Cole pumps!	Returned humor, commiseration, moving closer to couple status from the me-versus-you position.

Bart's Strength	Peg's Likely Response	Result
Validation – You know, Peg, I've been hustling to get work and you've been hustling trying to run the household on a shoestring. You're a good woman. All those years you've been my companion, manned home base and in some ways raised the kids as a single parent, what with my crazy schedule.	Wow! I never knew you noticed. But you know, Bart, without you supporting us, I couldn't have done all those other things.	Movement from the me-versus-you posture back to a couple/team

Bart's Weakness	Likely Response from Peg	Result
Judging - If you ask me, she's just plain spoiled.	Spoiled? Hey, I'm here running the house and doing my job. You're the one who's not living up to your end of the bargain.	Blaming, defensiveness, separation to the me-versus-you position.
Demanding - Hell, I *need* a break. She should be out there hustling for work…	You never asked me to work! Besides, we had an agreement when we married.	Movement from the couple/team position back to their adversarial roles.

Looking at these statements side by side, one sees that cooler thoughts made with humor and validation are more easily accepted whereas hot thoughts of judging, demanding, perfectionism and low frustration tolerance can be destructive. The cooler statements are antidotes to irrational thoughts.

Check In With Yourself: Remember, self-assessment is crucial and that is the cornerstone of our coaching and homework. We can't change anything unless we 1) can see what needs to be changed and 2) have some idea of how to change. As our session continued, Bart began to recognize that his need for control was largely dictated by irrational thoughts of the judging and demanding type and that he could address these issues by using cooler preferences as well as his strengths of humor and validation. We discussed how Bart would also do well to note that he, like many others who struggle with financial stress and anger, easily confuses his evaluation of his partner's behavior with the partner. Bart felt that, because Peg hadn't offered to seek an outside job having worked in the home throughout their marriage, Peg was "spoiled." Generalizing from the way one partner sees a behavior to a concept will often lead to inaccurate conclusions. Was it being "spoiled" that got Peg up for two A.M. feedings for three babies, that enabled her to get the children off to school on time *with* lunches and still clean the house, manage the finances, prepare dinner and help with homework for more than eighteen years? Such generalizations can lead to misconceptions and red hot thoughts.

Negotiate a Plan of Action: Since Bart had now become aware of his trigger thoughts and his communication-enhancing skills, he was ready to begin work with Peg on developing a plan of action to address their financial problems. Peg was feeling more receptive after having her contribution to the family recognized and more relaxed after knowing that she and Bart could still laugh *together* (key word).

They felt like a couple again after working through the first part of the Intervention Program.

In the final phase of Day Three, Bart and Peg were instructed to develop a plan of action. At this last session, we were present only to observe:

Bart: Well Peg, I know we've both been stressed about money since I was laid off. I really want us to talk and come up with some sort of plan of attack. [Wants Peg's input, emphasizing a couple-decision, not just Bart's]

Peg: Okay, what'd you have in mind?

Bart: Well, before we get started, I just need to remind myself that our financial problems are pretty deep so coming up with a solution today might not happen.

Peg: Yeah, but it's a start.

Bart: I also need to remember that if you or I need a breather from this talk, it's okay. This whole money thing is scary and it's not like we're kids anymore. So can we agree to let each other know if we need a break, like to go scream in a pillow or have a stiff belt? [smiles, uses humor and acknowledges the role of quick fixes in immediate anger management]

Peg: Sure.

Bart: Well, I guess I might as well dive in…The way I see it is I have about three more months of severance pay. I've been looking for work in my field for about nine months without a bite. The fact is, there might not be anything out there. [getting down to the nuts and bolts of budget issues and job prospects]

Peg: Honey, you'll find something.

Bart: Well, that's just it, Peg. I might not. I've looked at our savings and we have about enough to cover six months after my severance runs out. I think it's time I start looking for work in other fields.

Peg: Well, okay…

Bart: But here's the situation, Peg. If the only positions I find are in other areas, I'll make less money and we might not be able to hang on to the house. [begins to address consequences]

Peg: Oh.

Bart: The way I see it is we have two choices if that happens. We can either sell the house and cut back to fit my lower salary, or you can get a job and maybe between the two of us we can hang on to what we have [identifies the limits; seeks feedback to maintain collaboration and couple-hood]

Peg: Wow. I never thought about work. I don't know what I could do. I have no experience.

Bart: Does that mean that you're willing to explore the possibility of work? [accepts the fact that he cannot *make* Peg do anything]

Peg: Well, I suppose.

Bart: I know things are tough. But we've always made things work before. Remember when we had two kids in diapers? We were in real trouble then. I think if we pull together in the same direction, we can get through this too. [humor, use of "we" to underscore togetherness]

Peg: You know, Bart, we really don't need that big house anymore. The kids are out on their own. I think we should take some time, look into selling the house, getting something more manageable with less upkeep. You know, see about downsizing our lifestyle so we have some idea of how much we need to live comfortably.

Bart: You'd rather do that than work?

Peg: Well, I don't know. Look, whatever job I get is probably going to be close to minimum wage, which is only going to help so much. I guess I think it's a good idea to do both—look for work *and* explore down-sizing. [starts brainstorming]

Bart: Okay. How 'bout we spend a few minutes thinking about ideas for work that we can both begin to look into.

Peg: Yeah, I think I could use some help. I'll call a realtor and start crunching some numbers and check in with Frank. [turns to us] He's our accountant.

Bart: Sounds good. [reviews cheat sheet] Let's agree to report back to each other once a week to stay on top of things? [sets up accountability]

Peg: I'll bring the Chivas!

Having arrived at this final day of intervention training, Peg and Bart did a good job using humor and "we" statements to stay connected, even while negotiating the sticky details of their financial problems. Of course, things don't always go as smoothly. Sometimes as problems persist, partners forget to use their new coping skills and instead, revert back to old bad habits (I-SLIP). This is a particular risk given the duration and intensity of the current economic downturn and the generally conservative predictions regarding how long full recovery will take. If you and your partner have fierce financial problems and can't agree on a solution, remember, none of us is perfect. We can only change our own behavior and hope that those changes have a positive influence on our partner and our relationships. When we've given our best effort and sought help and still fall short, we need to first examine whether our expectations are realistic and second, whether the current relationship is viable. The decision is truly yours!

Chapter 15

Mastering Your Anger, Mastering Your Mind: How You and Your Partner Can Combat Irrational Thoughts

Recognizing and Disputing Irrational Thoughts

Earlier, we addressed the various causes of anger and how thinking plays a crucial role in the way each partner feels. This chapter addresses a central issue in our discussions of anger in your relationship: learning how to recognize and dispute your irrational thoughts. Here you will learn how to be your own best therapist when you get into emotional trouble with your significant other or with yourself. We will show you how you both stoke the fire of anger and what each of you can do to stop igniting that fire and get yourselves back in control. Once you've managed to do that, each of you will find yourself in a much better position to handle the relationship difficulties coming your way, whether they have to do with finances, in-laws, sexual intimacy, children or other red hot subjects that previously kept you feeling unresolved anger with each other.

Most of the anger books presently on self-help bookshelves have tools that you can apply in a vague way to a variety of anger-producing situations. These tools focus on exercises like hitting a punching bag (which research shows just increases the likelihood of you becoming angry more easily in the future), counting to ten, exercising, taking a walk to cool off, imagining nice things about the person with whom you're angry, trying to minimize the importance of the event by placing it in perspective—often without showing you how to do this—and distraction techniques such as imagining the person you're angry with dressed in diapers. You end up with a multitude of methods to apply to a huge variety of situations and your job is to try to memorize which method to use in a given situation. This can be difficult.

Furthermore, even if you were able to commit these techniques to memory, they still wouldn't be enough to help you master your anger, especially when it's directed at a significant other, because they fail to get at the *core* of the problem. These temporary solutions don't deal with the person's thinking or what he is telling himself. They don't seem to recognize that people talk to themselves all the time, particularly when they're upset about something. These books deal with the present feelings at a surface level; the person may temporarily *feel* better, but that feeling usually doesn't last. The old, bad, angry feelings reappear once the person starts thinking about the episode that caused the anger in the first place. Especially when the episode is with his or her loved one, these techniques simply don't deal with the real issues, which are the person's underlying attitude, long held truths and a philosophy of life which is destroying the most important relationship in his or her life.

By developing a simple, clear and concise method of reducing irrational thoughts, partners can get their anger under control. This method will work to significantly improve your relationship with your partner; in fact, it works with anybody you're upset with, including yourself, and it does not require a lot of memorization.

Best of all, this method results in lasting improvement, not tempo-rary fixes. In fact, the more you practice these simple principles and procedures, the better you'll get at it and the quicker you and your partner will feel better anytime you get angry with each other.

Rational (Realistic) Versus Irrational (Unrealistic) Thinking

People talk to themselves all the time. We talk to ourselves on a daily basis. Sometimes we know when we're talking to ourselves and other times we just do it, sort of subconsciously. You might be worried about what your partner is doing when he or she is away from you. You might be concerned about some bill that he or she has charged or a problem at work impacting your home life. Your mind is on some important issue. Have you had to go back and reread some-thing because you weren't paying attention? As you are thinking, your thoughts are either more or less accurate.

There are a lot of steps between the external world and our internal, subjective version of it. The external world exists objectively and is detached from our perception. The first step in knowledge of this world is to notice and perceive it through our senses. This is the input and selection process. We focus on some external stimulus and then select it from competing stimuli such as other external objects, other physical sensations, and other thoughts we may be having. Once we have that selected perception, the next thing that we do is define and describe that stimulus. This is the cognitive part. Let's say there is a furry, four-legged creature out there that we perceive and select. We next define that object as a dog. Notice, it is not the dog we perceive, but the object itself, to which we ascribe a name. It could be a wolf, after all. We are now dealing with a *representation* of the environment—our object that we named the dog, not the environment or animal itself.

The next step in the process involves an *interpretation* of this representation that we call dog. This interpretation can be relatively specific—this dog is energetic—or general—all dogs are energetic. These interpretations that we make involve one of the many filters that we use to understand the external world. These interpretations can be formed very, very early in our lives and can come to achieve the status of truths we carry around with us about the nature of the world and the people in it. We use these truths to collect and analyze data about people and events. These truths can mirror the objective reality out there quite closely, but they can also be quite removed from that objective reality, depending on how accurate they are. If a person, for example, has the truth that all dogs are evil and malicious, his truth is quite removed from the way dogs really are in the external world. Notice that at each step we are further and further removed from the reality or object itself and more and more subjective in focus.

The next step after an interpretation involves an appraisal. This appraisal can be positive, negative or neutral in nature: *I hate energetic dog,* or *I love energetic dogs* or maybe *Energetic dogs are okay.* This appraisal process is a crucial step in our emotional episode. If the appraisal is neutral, the emotional consequence is likely to be quite bland, if there is one at all. If I tell myself that all dogs are energetic and that energetic dogs are okay and I can take or leave them, then I am likely to have no affective response when I see a dog. The more positive or negative a person's appraisal of an object or person, however, the greater the emotional arousal that will follow. If a person hates energetic dogs, then whenever he sees an energetic dog he is going to probably feel angry or upset. If he likes energetic dogs, he will feel warm and happy when he sees one. The greater the deviation from neutral, the greater the emotional arousal is going to be. A key step in doing your own therapy, then, is what we call disputing: engaging in an intellectually honest and earnest reappraisal of each of your interpretations of reality and your appraisals of it.

Once a more accurate interpretation and appraisal is made, a more appropriate emotional response will follow. With this new emotional response, new behaviors will also develop. These new behaviors, in turn, produce different feedback from the environment than previously experienced and, as a result, the person interacts differently with his environment. Following through with the above simple example, if we can get a person to acknowledge that some dogs are energetic and some aren't, his appraisal of dogs in general is likely to change from a single categorical response of either hating dogs or loving them to a more complex reaction. He will now feel warmly towards some, neutrally towards others and negatively toward still others. This produces a new set of behaviors toward dogs, depending on his interpretation and appraisal in any given situation, and the dogs in turn will provide him with different types of feedback, depending on how he now deals with them.

The more realistic your thoughts, the less likely you are to be disturbed emotionally with your partner. The more distorted your thoughts, the more likely you are to be upset, angry and not coping well with each other. If much of your thoughts are distorted, inaccurate and not in synch with reality, then you must seek professional therapy. This is, after all, the definition of psychosis—being out of touch with reality.

Your involvement in how you perceive, interpret and appraise people and events profoundly affects your emotional and behavioral response to them. When both partners try reappraising their thoughts, they will have gained a major key to beginning to think rationally rather than dogmatically and reflexively, feeling more appropriately and behaving in more flexible and creative ways. How rigidly you both hold onto your previously cherished truths and how willing you are to look at and integrate new data will affect how quickly both of you as a team are able to start feeling and behaving better. Once you can begin to stop stoking the fires of anger and start quenching them with the cool rationality and human understanding which you must extend to each other, you will be on the path to achieving a mutually satisfying relationship.

Anger is really the result of two factors. The first part of the puzzle is the precipitating event, the thing going on that you and your partner are upset about—your spouse cutting you down in front of others, her ignoring you when you talk of things that upset you, etc. The other piece is your subconscious reaction to the event that just happened, that is, what each of you had to say to yourself about the incident. These are the thoughts, images and half conscious ideas which started floating around inside both of your heads about the event that just occurred or the situation that you're in. When these thoughts are irrational, one or both of you is primed to become upset, *very* upset.

The question of where each partner's thoughts initiated is often one which emanates from your relationship with your first family. This complex initiation to rules and roles involved your parents and siblings setting up family scripts which governed how each member thought, felt and behaved. These buttons, developed in childhood, impact your relationships when significant others push them.

To stop being angry, both partners need to get themselves centered in reality. How do you do that? By thinking realistically and rationally. If both partners are thinking rationally, neither is going to be furious. You'll be in control and you'll handle the situation and your relationship much better. This is why we're going to spend time detailing how you both can learn techniques of rational thinking. It is a key process in helping you both to stop being angry and start being in control. But, you've got to know how to do it first. You've got to know how to determine if your thinking is straight or crooked.

Tests for Partners to Determine Whether Thinking Is Rational

1. Stop and reflect. The first step in rationally thinking through upsetting situations is for each of you to pause and reflect upon what you're thinking or telling yourself. Stop. Ask yourself: *What's going on in my head? What am I telling myself? What else is at work here?* It is rare that either you or your partner has to act or say something right away. These moments of reflection can, in themselves, be a key tool in helping you both to begin to calm down.
2. Determine logic. After each of you has figured out what you are indeed saying or thinking or feeling or at least having some mental image about something, the next step is to determine

whether or not it is realistic (or rational) or unrealistic (or irrational). There are several kinds of tests that you can apply to determine whether it's one or the other. (We'll get back to this later.)

3. Decide if the facts add up. Perhaps the best as well as probably the
    simplest way to tell whether our thoughts are rational and realistic
    is whether or not they are *factual*. What do we mean by factual?
    Well, let's say you have a core belief that any person that you are
    nice to should be polite and nice to you in return. Suppose you go
    to the bank to make a deposit. When it is your turn, you approach
    the window and graciously say hello to the teller, asking her how
    she is doing. She mumbles something that sounds like hi and,
    when finished with your transaction, curtly calls out, "Next!"
    Angry, you tell yourself, *What the hell is wrong with her?? I was
    really friendly and polite and spoke to her when I didn't even have to.
    She should have been friendlier. After all, I am the customer here.*

    Okay, then, let's apply our rule of whether or not your self-talk
    is factual. Which statements are factual? You could get feedback
    from people that you indeed did speak to her, that your voice was
    friendly and polite (etiquette books would confirm your politeness
    in greeting her first) and that you didn't *have* to speak to her (you
    could have remained mute or been physically unable to speak). The
    manager could have confirmed the fact that you were the customer.

    How did you get yourself angry here? It wasn't from any of
    those things that you were earlier telling yourself (notice that we
    are analyzing the above interaction in terms of your self-talk).
    All of those statements were factual. But wait, there is one more
    significant statement that we haven't discussed yet. You also said
    to yourself (because all of those other statements were true, and
    you did indeed initiate conversation with her) that she *should*
    have been friendlier! Is this statement also correct? If it is, you
    should be able to apply the factual test to it. You can do this eas-
    ily by asking yourself: *Where's the evidence that she should have
    been friendlier? Can I prove that she should have acted more*

friendly? Where is it written in the universe that this teller, at this point in time, in this bank must respond in a friendly manner if I politely greet her first? Where is the evidence?

You just feel she should have been friendlier. You may in fact *feel* this very strongly. You may have felt it very strongly for a very long time in your life. You might even consult a friend and ask his opinion about whether the teller should have been friendlier and he might agree with you. (However, not all people are rational or reality-based in their thinking. In fact, a majority of them are quite the opposite—they are very irrational in their thinking.)

Does 2 plus 2 equal 4 or some other number? Do you make lots of *logical errors,* that is, errors which appear to make sense on the surface but are based on some wrong essential facts. Tom, who is in one of our anger groups, came to group the other day telling us about an event that happened at home with his wife. He arrived home to find that, once again, his wife, Tracy, had not changed the oil in her new car as he had asked her to do. This was a sore spot for him since he had asked her on two previous occasions to do this and she hadn't. He was really counting on it being done this time and was incensed that it wasn't. We talked for a while about the situation as well as some of the underlying reasons for his anger, specifically, financial concerns, that they had paid more than they could afford for a nice car for his wife and that she didn't appreciate it. Then we turned back to the particular situation, and it emerged during our conversation that on this particular occasion, Tom arrived home *before* Tracy yet he was mad because he had expected the car to be in the garage with new oil in it, and it wasn't there. Tom made an error of logic in his thinking. How in the world could his wife have the car in the garage, fixed, if she wasn't even home yet! Tom innately knew this but was so caught up in feeling frustrated about finances and Tracy's lack of appreciation for the sacrifice once again that he forgot this simple fact. As a result of his irrational thinking, he immediately got angry. He could have said to himself, *Well, Tracy may have messed up, but I don't really know that. How could I?—she isn't even here yet! I can deal with that tonight.*

4. Determine if your thinking promotes your relationship or endangers it. If Jill is angry at Bob for his extramarital affairs and repeatedly attacks him physically, unable to forgive or accept his faults, this may have very disastrous consequences for her. Clearly, this sort of acting out does nothing to improve the quality of Jill's life, let alone the odds of her happiness because Bob can either leave her or stay with her, making both of them miserable. Even if she seriously hurts Bob, the possible moment's satisfaction would hardly be worth the pain, suffering and loss of freedom which would probably result.

    If you and your partner can agree that your major goal is to have a mutually satisfying relationship and that you are going to use this criterion as a categorical imperative, a measuring stick, to apply in "hot" situations, you will take an important step towards adopting a very important mutual goal.

5. Understand your emotions. A fifth gauge for you and your partner to apply as to whether your thoughts are rational or realistic is to understand the frequency and intensity of the feelings that you both experience. And this brings us back full circle to point one, for the kinds of emotions that we have are going to be generated mainly by the kinds of thoughts that we have. If we have irrational, unrealistic, rigid thoughts in relationships, we are setting ourselves up for disturbing, upsetting, and distressed emotions—the kind that we want to avoid.

    Having realistic, rational thoughts produces less distressing emotions. When we have flexible, tentative theories, we will probably feel concern rather than anxiety, irritation rather than rage and sadness rather than depression. We are in control. We have a sense of being in charge of our lives and our love relationships.

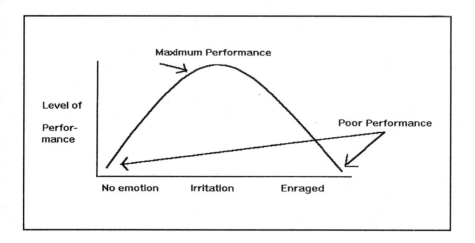

This is because we are thinking in healthy, flexible, problem solving ways. We are not blaming the universe or each other for our troubles. We are trying to deal with our life together as effectively as we can, given the cards we are dealt.

We might present the correlation between performance and problem solving ability graphically as follows. The vertical axis represents the level of performance that a person is capable of achieving within his own level of abilities. The horizontal axis represents his degree and quality of anger. You can see from the graph that when a person is presented with a problem and he has little or no emotional reaction to it, his degree of motivation to solve that problem is small, resulting in poor performance. On the other hand, when he gets himself enraged by the problem, his level of performance is also small, because he becomes so consumed by his anger that he tends to be blinded by it, and this results in confusion and ineptitude at dealing with the situation. On the other hand, when he is merely annoyed or irritated, he is both motivated and focused on the task at hand, enabling him to deal with it most effectively.

6.   There is a sixth way both partners can tell if their thinking is

on the correct track. It has to do with achieving both short and long-term goals. What if your friend Johnny came to you and said, "You know, I really enjoy smoking. It feels really good to inhale a really fine cigarette. I've been smoking two packs a day now for twenty years and I've enjoyed every minute of it. I don't believe all this propaganda about smoking and lung cancer. I think that I can continue to smoke as much as I'd like and live to a ripe old age." What is wrong with this picture? Well, Johnny's thinking is not rational, in that his belief that smoking two packs a day will not affect his longevity is just plain wrong and against the scientific evidence available to us. Smoking will definitely shorten his life span hence not leading to his long-term goal of living to "a ripe old age." Moreover, even his short-term goals are affected. While smoking may taste and smell good to the smoker, potential other goals he may have, such as saving money, being cough free, having clean fingertips or pleasing his significant other by not having smoker's breath are not being met. Johnny's thinking is not conducive to achieving either long or short-term goals. To achieve his goals, he'd better take a closer look at possibly modifying it.

Decide if your thinking interferes with or promotes a meaningful, productive relationship. If Mike thinks that he can treat his wife, Christy, any way he wants to without any consequences and his wife should cater to his every need because he's the "man of the house," it will probably have a negative impact on their relationship. He may think, *I don't feel like going home right away after work tonight so I'll just go out with the guys and have some fun. No need to call Christy. She'll be okay. I can explain it all when I get home.* This kind of thinking is faulty in that it doesn't accurately reflect the reality of the situation. Christy is more than likely going to have some strong feelings about Mike's just not showing up for several hours when she expects him home after work. If Mike makes this error in judgment enough times, the relationship is going to suffer and possibly deteriorate irreversibly.

The criteria we've discussed are useful when recognizing whether or not your partnership thinking is on track with reality. If it's not, applying the steps we've suggested will improve your and your partner's ability to deal with the real situation at hand.

Chapter 16

Changing Irrational Thoughts

Once you have learned to recognize irrational thoughts and understand the connection between thoughts and feelings, in order to master partnership anger each partner needs to go one step further: you both must start to replace those irrational thoughts with rational preferences. Each of you can do this by going back to the reality of the situation in which you and your partner had an angry response and dispute the long held irrational truths that you previously held to be immune to change. The main test of whether your thinking is realistic is whether or not it is factual. Again, each of you ask yourselves, *Where is the evidence that it must be this way?* This will help both of you to begin replacing unrealistic thoughts with realistic preferences that are reality-based and that reflect more accurately what's really happening. Simply taking a step back from your thoughts in order to gauge their basis in reality can prevent an argument. Remember, the more accurate your thinking is, the less upset you and your relationship will be!

The Rational Use of Preferences—Developing a Desiring, Rather Than a Requiring Philosophy of Life

The main component of relationship anger then is the unrealistic set of demands each partner places on himself. When you use *should* in a rigid, uncompromising way in relation to events that occur in the world or between you and your partner, you are setting yourself up to be irrationally angry, furious and even rageful. If, on the other hand, you stick to rational preferences, wishes and desires, you will minimize your upsets. In all of our years of practicing psychotherapy, we have never seen anyone who was thinking rationally and realistically about a situation be outraged by it. The person may be annoyed about it, but not angry.

If you stick to preferences, desires and wishes and resolutely refuse to allow them to revert back to unrealistic demands upon each other, you both will remain in control of your emotional lives. Preferences are rational because you can prove they exist in the outside world of reality. It is only when you take basically good, healthy ideas and, because they seem like such good ideas, change them into immutable, autocratic demands that you get yourself and your relationship in trouble cognitively and emotionally. Here is a list of "Must Statements" or demands that people often make, along with a list of rational preferences or alternative statements that lead to more productive results because of their flexible and problem solving nature.

Demands	Preferences
1. I must get this promotion.	1. It would be great if I got this promotion and the raise that goes along with it.
2. I shouldn't have to work so hard at my relationship.	2. I wish I got along better with my husband. Maybe we can sit down and discuss how I'm feeling.

3. People who treat me poorly need to be taught a lesson.

3. I wish certain people would treat me better. If they don't, it's more a reflection of their problems than mine.

4. My wife had better always love me—I couldn't bear it if she left me.

4. I certainly hope my wife continues to love me, but if she doesn't, I'll find a way to survive somehow.

5. I can't make any mistakes in this relationship.

5. I hope I can make my partner and myself happy in this relationship, but if it doesn't work out, I'll know I tried and we'll both move on.

Bill and Debbie are both busy professionals with full working schedules in the San Francisco Bay area. Since they both work, they take turns preparing dinners at home. Let's assume it's Debbie's turn and Bill tells himself, *When I get home tonight, I would really like it if dinner was ready. If it isn't, it won't be the end of the world, we'll just prepare dinner together.* If Bill arrives home and finds that, indeed, dinner is unprepared, he's going to be disappointed, maybe even irritated, but not out of control, not in a rage and not likely to escalate this minor episode into a fight.

On another day, however, Bill forgets what he has learned about self-talk and slips back into demands. He tells himself, *My wife must have dinner ready. I'll be furious if she doesn't again. I won't be able to stand it if it's not ready and next time it is my turn to cook, I'll make sure she has to wait for her dinner too.* Now when Bill gets home and finds dinner unprepared, he will likely feel very angry and will probably raise his voice or start an argument. He may even resort to violent behavior.

It is important to remember that even when you are very, very angry, you are always in control of your thoughts and actions.

If you fly into a rage or verbally/physically attack your partner, it is by your own choosing.

You are always capable of making a decision and even though it may be very hard to restrain yourself, you *are* capable of doing that as well. Preferences lead to appropriate, problem solving behavior and appropriate, moderate emotions; demands lead to rage, condemnation, blaming and escalation of poor behavior. Preferences lead to choices, flexibility, and being in control. Demands lead to forced decisions, rigidity and being stuck, along with difficulty staying in control.

The theories we've gone over in the past few pages can be applied to some typical, everyday situations. This will give each partner some practice in working on self-therapy and putting out those flames of anger. Following is a list. In the left-hand column, ten common irrational and demanding types of thinking are listed. Before you look at the second column of rational counterparts, see if you can figure out what the realistic way of looking at things would be. As you're doing the exercise, try to put yourself in each example. Imagine yourself thinking the irrational thought and then imagine yourself thinking the constructive rational counterpart. Do you feel any different emotionally when you're thinking the two kinds of thoughts?

Demands and Preferences

Irrational Demand	**Rational Preferences**
1. My wife should always keep our house neat and clean.	1. I wish my wife would keep our house cleaner; I would feel more comfortable since that is what I was used to as a kid.
[*Implication: if she does not keep a neat house, she's less than a good wife; She doesn't have much respect or love for me, so she needs to be chastised*]	[*Disputing thought: if she doesn't keep a neat house, it isn't the end of the world; it hardly means that she doesn't love me—and besides, I can pitch in to help a little too. After all, she works just like I do*]

Irrational Demand	Rational Preferences
2. My boyfriend should always keep me apprised of who he's with, where he's going and what he's doing at any given moment. [*Implication: If he doesn't tell me everything he does during the time we're apart, he's trying to keep something from me; I can't trust him when I'm not around*]	2. I like it when my boyfriend tells me about his day but I can wait until I see him to hear what he's been up to; and if he doesn't tell me everything, that's okay too. I don't necessarily tell *him* everything that I do. [*Disputing thought: we can each have some moments of privacy; it's impossible to keep each other totally informed one hundred percent of the time; if we don't tell each other everything, it doesn't mean we are hiding things from each other; we can trust each other*]
3. There are certain (gender-related) jobs around the house that the man should do and others that the woman should do. I should not have to do *his* jobs. [*Implication: there is only one right way to do things*]	3. Sure, I'd love it if my boyfriend did *all* the yard work but then I can see that that would be ridiculous given the number of hours that he works. [*Disputing thought: just because my parents did things a certain way does not mean that we have to do the exact same thing; where is it written that only men do yard work? Women mow lawns too*]

Irrational Demand

4. We've been together for a long time now. My husband should be able to tell what I'm thinking at any moment. [*Implication: by now he should know me well enough to read my mind; he's being uncaring and cold if he doesn't; he probably doesn't love me*]

Rational Preferences

4. I wish I didn't have to be so open with my thoughts to my husband. I prefer when he just knows what I'm thinking, then I don't have to risk telling him things that are hard for me to talk about. [*Disputing thoughts: my husband tries hard most of the time to work with me on things; I appreciate how hard it must be for him to communicate with me when I have trouble talking about certain things; because he makes an effort, I know he cares*]

5. My back has been hurting for two weeks now. I asked my boyfriend to wash the car last Sunday and that lazy jerk still hasn't done it! [*Implication: he should do things on my timetable; he's an irresponsible and inconsiderate lover because of his indifference*]

5. I wish that the car would have been cleaned by now, but it's not the end of the world. I'll talk to him and find out why he hasn't done it yet. After all, I sometimes procrastinate doing things myself. [*Disputing thoughts: it doesn't follow that he doesn't love me or doesn't care about tasks that need to be done just because he hasn't washed the car; he may not have had time; he's not perfect—nobody is—and I can't expect him to be.*]

Irrational Demand

6. I'm always the one to call Sharon; she never calls me! [*Implications: I like Sharon more than she likes me; I exert more effort in our relationship; she really places no value on our relationship; she is inconsiderate*]

Rational Preferences

6. I would prefer it if Sharon would call me more often, but it hardly means she isn't a good girlfriend. Even though we spend weekends together, I will tell her that I would like to hear from her during the week. [*Disputing thoughts: It's okay that I usually have to call her, after all keeping up with people is one of my strong points; Sharon does other things for our relationship; I can't expect her to know how I feel when I haven't told her*]

Partner Self-therapy—The Easy Way

The major steps to take in order for each of you to master your anger are really quite simple to understand and hopefully you will start applying them right away. They involve a few key things:

1. Each partner should start by focusing on his or her internal thoughts, rather than the external situation that got you both angered in the first place.

2. Look for the *should!* Look for the demands you are placing on the other person, yourself or the situation; these are usually in the form of some *should, ought to* or *must* statement. This is the most common form that an irrational thought that is producing your anger takes.

3. Start doing your active therapy now: uproot and extract that demand from your mind by disputing it, arguing with it forcefully and getting rid of it after a hardheaded discussion with

yourself about why it simply doesn't make sense to hang on to it. No matter how intensely you may feel something has to be a certain way, if you can't prove it, then you'd better get rid of that silly notion.

4. Replace whatever illogical demand you had with rational, realistic preferences, wishes or desires. These preferences are your guide to recognizing that you indeed have wants and wishes about how things will go and how people will act, but at the same time you acknowledge the fact that people and events will act in accordance with forces outside of your control. You have a right to your rational preferences, but realize that your partner may not always agree with them or act in compliance with your view of things.

After you have done these steps, you will notice an immediate change in your emotional state. The anger will have changed into an emotion much more adaptive to the situation and one which leaves each of you considerably calmer and more in control. The emotion will probably be something like disappointment, sadness, irritation or annoyance, depending on the precise nature of the realistic preferences you have replaced your irrational thoughts with. Once you have done your own self-therapy, you have developed a skill that you can use over and over again whenever you choose. As both partners practice this, you will find that it becomes easier and easier to do over time and that, moreover, as a couple your general philosophical approach to life shifts to a more flexible and reasonable process.

Other Irrational Thoughts
Leading to Partner Anger

If demands are the main component of anger, this does not mean that they are the only causes of anger. There are many other types of irrational, unrealistic ideas that we tell ourselves that get us into relationship trouble too. Demands, however, are the easiest type of irrational thoughts to identify. Once you dispute them, uproot them and replace them with healthy, rational thoughts, you are going to be largely out of trouble emotionally and your relationships will be unlikely to suffer any great damage from anger. However, because the human brain can process a huge number of thoughts in an incredibly short period of time, it is important to discuss these other irrational thoughts since they can get you into trouble easily.

Catastrophizing and Low Frustration Tolerance

People are capable of many, many upsetting, unrealistic thoughts, the nature of which often directs the emotional response related to it. If, for example, I emphasize the fact that it is *horrible* if my girl-friend or boyfriend isn't home when I call and doesn't return my phone call immediately when they do get home, I'm more likely to be depressed and downcast in the event that this happens.

A low frustration tolerance emphasizes the *I-can't-stand-it* attitude leading to anxiety and irritation. Telling myself that some-thing is horrible or terrible gets me into a depressed state very quickly. Albert Ellis calls this type of thinking catastrophizing or awfulizing. The cure, once again, is realistic thinking, thinking that will put the occasion into its true perspective. How awful and horri-ble is it, really? Is it life shattering? By calling to mind worse situa-tions, you quickly defuse the present one to its true place in the scheme of things. One can do this quickly, easily and efficiently, even with a small amount of practice, just as one can quickly and vigor-ously dispute and argue oneself out of crazy, demanding thinking. After all, if not being called back is awful, then what do we call a really difficult situation? If by saying something is awful we imply that it can't be any worse, that it shouldn't exist and that we can't stand it when it does exist, then we are clearly in an unrealistic realm of thinking, because bad things can and do exist. They can always get worse—you may not get a call back tomorrow either. But you can tolerate that, too.

On a superficial level, if I say I can't stand my girlfriend not being home when I call, I may mean one of two things. I may mean that I really, really don't like it when my girlfriend isn't home and doesn't immediately return my call. We do, in fact, often talk to each other in this rather inaccurate but seemingly harmless way. Or I may mean that I really can't stand it and it's horrible, but this quickly gets us into trouble. We strongly urge you to be very careful whenever you tell yourself that you can't stand something. It is a bad habit to get into and it can quickly get you anxious, angry or depressed. Telling yourself that you can't stand it is an example of *low frustration tolerance*.

Low frustration tolerance can exist in the areas of achievement: *I can't put in all those hours to succeed in my own business*, in relationships: *it's too hard to go out and meet new friends* and in emotion: *I can't stand how hot this room is*. The fact of the matter is that you *can* stand it. You can stand anything until you're dead. You may *choose* to not tolerate something, by leaving the situation, for example. But that is a different issue than telling yourself that you just can't deal with it, because it's impossible to deal with or tolerate. Telling yourself, *I will not tolerate this* is different from telling yourself, *I cannot tolerate this*. The first statement puts you in control; the second makes you feel helpless. Then the question is moot. If you're still alive, you did stand it, no matter how unpleasant it was. You can stand an adulterous spouse. You may really hate it, but you can stand it. This may seem like a trivial distinction, but think about it. Telling yourself that you really hate something is okay because you're still dealing with it on its own terms. You're not trying to change the world or your ability to cope with it. You're dealing with it realistically, if not optimally. Telling yourself you can't stand it is an untrue, gross exaggeration that can lead to emotional upset. You should be careful how you talk to yourself, even in relatively innocuous situations.

Arbitrary Definitions, Judgments and Excessive Punishments

While there are other things you could tell yourself about the phone call such as, *If my girlfriend loved me, she'd be home when I call or call me back as soon as she does get home*, one other major thing that gets people in trouble is making a final judgment about the offending person (*She's a jerk because she knew I would be calling but wasn't at home and didn't try to return the call right away*) and suggested outcome (*I ought to leave her because of her inconsideration and lack of respect for me*). Labeling people is dehumanizing. It's a distortion and, thus, inaccurate. It's also painful to both parties. There is another good reason why it's not a good idea. If you consistently refer to the person in an intimate relationship with insulting names, you are committing a sort of self-fulfilling prophecy for that person—he will start acting more like a jerk in the future, because that's how he sees himself, at least when he's around you.

When You Judge People You Ultimately Degrade Them

In the movie *Wayne's World*, Garth quotes the famous philosopher, Kierkegaard, by stating, "When you label me you negate me." In labeling our significant others, we strip them of their unique identities and put them in a category. Putting a label on the person closest to you also involves a grade or judgment. We categorize him or her, putting him or her in a nice little nutshell, which is overly simplistic. Why is that so? Well, imagine a basket of fruit with a hundred different varieties in it. Some are ripe, some are green, some are rotten and some are just right. Now, we ask you to judge the basket—what kind of basket of fruit is it? Whatever judgment or grade you put on the basket—ripe, average, good, etc.—is going to be a distortion and consequently inaccurate, because there are just too many exceptions to the label you put on it. The basket is too complex to be categorized accurately. The problem is not with the basket. The problem is in asking you to reduce it to a grade. Now, isn't a person a little bit more complicated than a basket of fruit? How many different traits, attributes and behaviors does the average person possess? Too many to count. When you add them all up, over twenty-four hours a day, for her lifetime, it must be in the zillions. It would be impossible to grade that person accurately using just one label or five labels or even a hundred labels. If you're to be accurate in looking at a person, you must assess *each* of that person's behaviors and features. Judge them all you want, but don't generalize and judge the whole person. That doesn't make sense and it's hurtful.

If a man were to call his significant other a jerk, besides being painful to her if she heard it, and painful to the husband himself—what an idiot he must be to have married a jerk—it is an irrational distortion in thinking. To really be accurate, in order for her to be a jerk, she would have to act like a jerk 100 percent of the time, in all situations. She must never vary in her behavior. The fact of the matter is that no one acts like a jerk all of the time. We all make mistakes but act appropriately at least some of the time. There is a big difference in accuracy and consequently how we feel about a person, between calling her a jerk and telling ourselves that that person is really acting like a jerk right now.

There are few true horrors in the world. Mostly there are just hassles that we can stand. This is not to say that there aren't or haven't been some pretty grim situations, some that might be described as appalling. But, even here, it is important for you to know that no matter how grim the situation, you will always be able to stand it. Likewise, there are no all-good or all-bad people. Mostly, there are just people who fall someplace in the middle of the spectrum. Humans are fallible and make mistakes. Even good people mess up and do stupid things. We have never known a client or patient who didn't make some kind of error or do some wrong thing. By the same token we have never known a client who was totally bad. Even people who chronically do bad things occasionally do good things. What does it make us, then? It makes us human. Rather than judging your own bad behaviors, vow to fix them or minimize them. Work with others to help them reduce their bad behaviors or eliminate them. But always refrain from judging them as human beings or judging yourself as a human being.

If we can't judge ourselves, what remains then? We can choose to accept ourselves and others as human beings and then think about correcting the flaws that cause problems. We can work hard to improve our deficiencies and other faults but not reject ourselves in the process. We can stop judging ourselves. We can stop judging our behaviors. We can stop judging our significant other as well. We can respect their self-worth.

The Downside of Self-Esteem

Self-esteem usually involves a judgment about the whole person based upon some specific trait or behavior: *I have a beautiful physique, therefore I'm a handsome and noble human being*, or, *that person bats .340, is a great baseball player and, therefore, better than other people.* The error occurs when you take one characteristic or several and generalize about the whole person. When this happens, the person can only feel good about himself if he continues to do well or maintains that great physique. How long does this great feeling last? Usually, it's very brief, transient as dew on a petal. To keep feeling good about yourself, you have to continue to do well. The demand to always do well or look good leads to anxiety at some level or another. You may ask yourself, *what if I mess up?* Next thing you know, you are angry and depressed. Your self-esteem is destroyed.

If you stop judging your humanness based on what you do or what you have, you can erase the enormous burden resting on your performance. You can then concentrate on the performance itself, without basing your self-worth on the outcome. We often tell the couples who are our clients that we're going to work very hard to help them get rid of all of their self-esteem. After the amazement in their eyes dissipates, we follow up with the goal of replacing that self-esteem with mutual self-acceptance. If each of you accepts yourself instead and works on the problematic behaviors, you will have moved your relationship satisfaction ahead. Another benefit to accepting yourself—you start accepting the other person as well. Your worth as a human being stays the same; it doesn't go up or down. It's stable, like the temperature on a sunny summer day. Give up self-esteem and all that pop psychology talk and be free. Be content. Be comfortable. Be realistic. Be self-accepting. It's worth the effort.

An Added Bonus: Resolving Historical Anger

Partners often think, *Well I can't change what happened in the past. It happened and I will never stop being angry about it!* This kind of reasoning implies that there is nothing that can be done about changing how you feel about something that already occurred, because it happened a long time ago. However, you can apply the same steps and principles we have shown you in dealing with present circumstances to ones that have happened long ago, by looking for the same kind of demands we've been talking about and applying the four basic steps to your thinking about past events. They work just as well with events that have occurred years ago as those occurring today or tomorrow.

For example, Tony came to our anger group one Monday night last year for the first time. He had a frown on his face, was very quiet and sat down without any eye contact with the rest of the group. When his turn came to speak, he told us that he had been quietly angry with his wife for the last ten years because she hadn't been there for him when his father died. Instead, she had gone to visit her parents.

As we began working with him, he began to see that most of his anger was really the result of his placing an incredibly powerful demand on his wife. It took us a while to help him see that, indeed, what his wife did was not good and that it would have been much better if she had stayed with Tony but that his father's death awoke feelings she couldn't handle at the time about her own first family. Bad things happen and Tony was indeed treated unfairly; but he began to realize that *demanding* that his wife atone for the event ten years later would prove of little benefit to either him or their relationship.

In fact, he began to recognize that there were lots of reasons why his wife did what she did: her father was a chronic alcoholic and she felt rejected by Tony and his mother who shut others out in their time of need. These facts do not excuse her behavior, of course, but they helped Tony see his wife in a more compassionate light and forgive her. He came to the group meeting next week with a new self-confidence and a shy smile on his face. He stated that he hadn't felt this great in years. He felt like a giant weight had been lifted off his shoulders. His and his wife's relationship had improved immeasurably.

A Word about Future Anger

Just as we can resolve our present and past demands with our life partners, we can give up demands about how future events must be or how that person must treat us. We knock that chip off our shoulders the same way: by giving up the demands and replacing them with healthy desires. Going home and thinking, *My husband better be nicer to me today!* sets a person up quickly to be angry once she encounters her husband and he does, in fact, act less than perfectly. We were already primed for the anger by our attitude beforehand our expectations or demands about how things should go. Replace those demands with preferences, just like you have learned to do with past or current situations in your relationship and you will improve your life and make that relationship more satisfying.

Control

One final point should be made. We encounter lots of people—strangers, fellow employees, friends, etc.—daily as we travel to work, labor in our offices or in the field and participate in our various social groups. Then there are our loved ones—these are our primary relationships. With each, we spend various lengths of time and have varying degrees of physical and emotional closeness.

There is a great deal of difference in the degree of emotional involvement that we have with a fellow driver out there on the freeway and with our partners. The type and extent of the interaction we have with others tends to affect our sense of perceived control over that other person. Our sense of *perceived* control over others, in turn, has an impact on the type and intensity of demands that we make on them. As we've discussed before, making unrealistic demands on others seldom, if ever, makes sense. Even the most transient encounter with another human being can, however, occasion the use of a demand.

When we're on the freeway, most of us have made demands on other drivers to not run into us, to give us the right of way when due and to not cut in too closely in front of us. We have very little sense of perceived control over what these other drivers do, however.

As the nature and extent of our closeness to another person increases, the sense of perceived control over that person increases also, as does the quality and intensity of our demands on them. While even the most irrational of persons is likely to concede that she has little control over the thinking or behavior of the freeway driver, her thinking tends to change when it comes to her husband. Because she has known him so long, been involved with him in so many situations and loves him, she therefore thinks that she knows him better and thus can control him better. However, the amount of control we have over another human being remains the same no matter how close we become, whether it's a stranger, lover or spouse. Even though she may in fact know him better, her amount of control doesn't change. She still can't control his thinking, his attitudes, or his behavior. Only he can do that. In fact, we seldom have one hundred percent control over ourselves. Witness the countless numbers of us who do things to ourselves we don't want to, such as eating too much, smoking, drinking too much or exercising too little.

Since we have so little control over our significant others, we had better be careful about the demands we make on them. You may have the opportunity to interact with your partner more persuasively, but you still do not have absolute control over her thinking, or behavior even if it means she must suffer the consequences that you have put in place. Lack of control can be equated with lack of power and the best way to cope with such situations is to focus on what you prefer, rather than demand, of the person closest to you.

Self Empowerment

There is a bonus to giving up the idea of perceived control over our partners. It liberates us to act more spontaneously and happily. It gives us a new sense of freedom and empowers us to act more flexibly and creatively when difficulties arise in relationships. Rather than feeling doomed and hopeless when things don't go our way, we accept the fact that we really have no control over another's thinking or future actions. Our partner is going to act the way they want to act, not the way we want them to act. They'll think what they want to think, not what we want them to think. The only kind of control we really have, then, is to try to persuade them to do differently by reasoning with them or pleading with them or cajoling them. They will either listen to us and agree with us or they will not. If they do things differently from the way we want, the only other option we have is to try to change their behavior by instituting some sort of consequence for it. If they are willing to accept that consequence and act as they please anyway, then we are left with only two alternatives, learning to tolerate their actions or leaving the situation.

Regardless of what course of action we choose to take, we are responsible for our own thoughts and actions. By thinking this way, no matter what others choose to do or not to do, we still have choices that we can make over our own behavior in reaction to our partner's behavior. While we may have little or no control over the behavior of our significant other, we are by no means helpless. We can still do our own self-therapy to master anger. We can still take appropriate and reasonable steps to try to persuade the other person to act differently in the future. We can still apply consequences that we hope are effective in changing their behavior. If we try, however, to force our partners to do what we want, they may do it, but it will be done reluctantly, unwillingly and grudgingly. This works antagonistically to the healthy relationships we are trying to foster. Oftentimes, when partners get the most angry, they are feeling the most powerless and frustrated to do anything about the situation. Each of you can always do *something* constructive instead.

The following are some key points discussed in this chapter that are important for you and your partner to remember.

- We have two basic kinds of thoughts: unrealistic and realistic.

- There are lots of ways to determine if your thought, image or idea is realistic. The main way to tell is to ask yourself whether or not it is factual, whether you can prove it.

- If your thoughts are not rational and realistic, to feel and act better you need to dispute and uproot your unrealistic thoughts and replace them with rational ones.

- The main kinds of irrational thoughts that cause anger are demands of your significant other, yourself and the world.

- Remember that partners are fallible and demanding that they not make mistakes is futile—we all make them (and that includes acting foolishly, stupidly and obnoxiously at times).

- To rid yourself of relationship anger, replace demands with preferences, wishes and desires which make sense, which you can prove (because they exist) and which are manifested in a non-controlling way. Then communicate them to the person who can assist you in getting those desires met.

- The new emotion you are left with will be one that you are comfortable with and can control (such as irritation, annoyance or disappointment), as opposed to anger or rage, which are controllable.

- The goal is not to totally rid yourself or your relationship of anger—that is probably impossible anyway. The aim is to reduce the intensity, quality, duration and frequency of angry episodes and to replace them with constructive communication.

- Once both of you have replaced your unhealthy anger and rage with realistic and healthy feelings and effective communication between the two of you, you will be able to problem solve better, learn better and put new behaviors in place with greater ease, thereby enhancing (rather than tearing apart) your relationship with your loved one.

Partner Homework

1. After you have considered what you're thinking, ask yourself if it is rational and realistic or irrational and unrealistic. If it is unrealistic, why? (Hint: look for the shoulds and demands in your thinking.) Write down the irrational thoughts you are having over a period of two weeks. See if you can find a pattern in the types of irrational thoughts that are typical for you.

2. When you have identified the unrealistic thoughts, dispute them and replace them with realistic ones (preferences), like *I would strongly prefer that she like me, but she doesn't have to* or *I wish that she wouldn't yell at me when she's mad, but it isn't the end of the world if she does and I sure as heck can stand it right now. Now, let me see what I can do to try to help her calm down.*

3. When you do the disputing, do it forcefully and vigorously. Remember, you are fighting very old, entrenched thinking habits. Disputing is really a way of doing your own self-therapy, in a very hardheaded, matter-of-fact way. You are engaging in the process of reasoning and arguing with yourself to get at the real "truth"—the way the universe really operates.

4. See how many other unrealistic thoughts of and about each other you can identify (any catastrophizing? any I-can't-stand-its? judgment of his or her human worth or damning?).

5. If you don't succeed in finding any irrational thoughts when you

first start working on this aspect of your relationship anger (sometimes it takes a little practice, but we guarantee you'll eventually be able to find them), remember that there are still some other things each one of you can do to help yourself in the meantime, such as go get a drink of cold water, perhaps splash some on your face. This will literally cool you off and give you a bit of time to think.

Remember to breathe from your diaphragm. Exhale by pushing your lower abdominal muscles out to completely clear the air from your lungs. Breathe in by pulling these same muscles in. This will oxygenate the lower part of your lungs (where most of the air sacs are located anyway) and greatly help you to relax.

6. Another valuable exercise involves imagery. It is similar to an exercise developed by Albert Ellis called Rational Emotive Imagery. Sit down, close your eyes and visualize a recent anger episode. Recall the event as accurately as you can and get yourself to really feel the anger or rage you felt at the time it occurred. Now, change that feeling to one of disappointment or irritation. Keep at it until you've accomplished that goal. Then ask yourself, "How did I get to this new feeling? What did I tell myself?" Notice two things here: one, you changed your feeling voluntarily; two, you did that by having different mental images or thoughts. See how both thoughts and feelings are interconnected? This is an exercise that you can frequently use when other attempts at modifying your anger don't seem to work well.

7. Don't try to problem solve with your partner without first dealing with your own anger. Take a two-minute time out to regroup, examine your thinking and develop a game plan. This way, you will minimize the damage and keep the relationship problem from escalating.

Chapter 17

Strengths: Characteristics Most Important for Maintaining Relationships

We've discussed a lot of reasons why anger rears its ugly head in relationships and how those reasons fit in with the most common relationship problems: excessive control and poor communication. As we listened to clients' responses about what makes relationships tick, two of the four most common answers fell under the categories of realistic expectations and basic communication skills. The other areas identified were commitment and trust. As you read this next section, think about how anger in your relationship diminishes these qualities.

Realistic Expectations

We've already seen how vulnerable we all are to unrealistic expectations of our partners and relationships and how these expectations set us up to be angry and disappointed. Because this book is about relationships and anger, the focus is on identifying the source of anger—irrational thoughts and expectations—and how this anger is played out between two people. But let's take a moment to look at you without your partner.

It is difficult to have realistic expectations of others if you don't have them for yourself. Too often people enter into relationships expecting others to do something for them that they haven't yet learned to do for themselves—at least not to their satisfaction. Everybody has some need to feel valued, to have some sense of who they are, to feel good about themselves and to know that, even though they may want a relationship, they can also function without one. These, however, are pretty lofty goals—clear identity, self-acceptance, independence. It is possible that they will never really be reached. These goals are even more of a challenge for those with low frustration tolerance and a need for perfection, because they have so little patience for problem solving, whether it's a conflict with their partners or some sort of internal conflict. They would rather take the fast way out and find partners and relationships that give them the value, security or identity that they alone haven't been able to reach to their satisfaction. This is the wrong reason to start a relationship. The problem, they soon find, is that no one can give these traits to them. They have to develop them by themselves.

To have these kinds of expectations of others is another set-up. Partners are likely to feel overwhelmed since it is impossible to make someone else better. And you? Well, once again, you end up angry that your needs, irrational though they are, are not satisfied. The more confused you are about your own identity and value, the more you will demand of your partner. The greater your demands of your partner, the greater the set-up for disappointment. It is important therefore to have some sense of yourself before starting a relationship.

Having clarified your responsibility to yourself, you can now start to develop more reasonable expectations of your partner and your relationship.

• *Gratification*: It is reasonable to expect that your relationship gives you a certain amount of pleasure or satisfaction, what we call gratification. Relationships take a lot of work. The payoff is that some of your essential needs are met, not all of them, but some. If none of your needs are satisfied in your relationship, there is no point in investing in that relationship. You should instead find someone who can contribute to your life in a positive way. The issue of having *all* of your needs met…well, you now know that that's impossible, so enough said.

What is an essential need for you may be different for your partner and others. For example, Joel may feel that companionship and nurturance are priority needs that he wants his partner to provide. Ellen, on the other hand, may identify security, both physical and financial, as a need that she most wants her partner to meet. Joel would also like his partner to be intellectually challenging as well as look like Helen Hunt and Ellen would like her partner to look like Brad Pitt but these are not essential needs for either. These are needs that they can either meet elsewhere, or let go of because more important needs are being addressed. In this case, as long as Ellen is affectionate and available to Joel and Joel is gainfully employed and maintaining a secure home, their relationship has a good chance of surviving.

• *Reciprocity*: It is also reasonable to expect a certain amount of give and take in relationships or reciprocity. Many people don't really understand the notion of reciprocity. They think that it means that things should be equal so that if one gives a certain amount, the other should give the same amount in the same way. True, this is one definition of reciprocity, but if this is the only definition you use in your relationship, you're headed for trouble. As separate individuals, you and your partner are likely to have different assets that contribute to your relationship in different, though equally important ways.

For example, in the traditional, stereotypical American couple of old, one of the husband's primary contributions to the relationship was earning the money to financially support his wife and family; one of the wife's primary contributions was managing the household, including acting as the primary caregiver for the children. Both contributed to the physical support of the relationship and both benefited from each other's contributions, though in very different ways. This is an example of reciprocity in a broader and more functional sense. And though needs and priorities change, the need for reciprocity doesn't.

Basic Communication Skills

Communication is essential in all relationships and, unfortunately, it's a pretty complicated skill. There are a lot of different ways to communicate besides just talking. Body language, tone of voice and facial expression are also important. When couples come to us and complain that they are having communication problems, they're actually not telling us much since communication means so many different things. For instance, one definition would be: sharing information. It simply means saying what's on your mind. The trick is to do this in a way that gets your point across without being insensitive or inconsiderate. This is communication style and one of the ways that it varies is in terms of assertion. For example, you might communicate in a passive way: last night after Suzie's parents left, Max told Suzie that her mother was a barracuda. Suzie was hurt and insulted by Max's criticism of his mother-in-law. Instead of saying something directly to Max, Suzie punished him with the silent treatment for three days.

Communication can also be aggressive, where you say whatever comes to mind without a care for the other's feelings. For instance, in the scenario of Max and Suzie, Suzie may have retaliated and become equally verbally aggressive: "You make me sick! You think your mother is such a prize? Well, let me tell you a thing or two about what I think of her and the way she struts around here…." Or you can communicate in an assertive way, taking responsibility for your own feelings and discussing them in a respectful way. Again, given the last example, Suzie might have assertively responded something like this: "You know, Max, I know that you don't really like my mother and, yeah, that bothers me sometimes. But I also know that everyone can't always get along. I even agree with some of your criticisms of her, but I prefer that you don't call her names. I mean, she is my mother and for that reason alone I would like you to show a certain amount of respect."

Partnership Skills:

• *Listening*

The object of communication between partners is the exchange of information. So you need skills not only for sharing information, but also for listening to each other.

• *Validating Your Significant Other*

Validation is also a type of listening. Simply put, it means to listen to the other partner's opinion without judgment, even when it's different from your own.

• *Tolerating Conflict*

Since you and your partner will not always have the same opinions, there will be some conflict in your relationship. Even though most of us don't like conflict, staying focused on the problem at hand and trying to work out some resolution will yield more positive results than attempting to control the situation or avoiding it all together.

• *Problem Solving*

Addressing the problem together in a constructive way will avoid destructive behaviors such as becoming aggressive and trying to force your way of thinking upon the other person, avoiding the conflict all together only to blow up at the drop of a hat later on or something in between like sulking and stewing without any move to address the problem. You both need skills to resolve relationship problems. Basically these skills include:

> Identifying the problem.
>
> Sharing the problem with your partner: Tell him about the problem using neutral language (in other words, focus on

your feelings and reactions, rather than blaming him).
Listening to your partner's input: Stay focused on the problem to avoid becoming side-tracked or defensive.

Identifying possible solutions together: After defining the
problem and factors that add to the problem, brainstorm to
come up with possible solutions.

Problem solving: Negotiate to decide which solution to try
out first. Some compromise between partners is usually necessary here. Give the solution a trial and change it as needed.

We refer to this process as "I SLIP" because when you skip any of
these steps you're likely to "slip" or fail to resolve the problem at
hand. The following two scenarios where Barb and Tim are trying to
plan their vacation illustrate this point.

Dialogue without Communication

After repeated discussions about going on vacation, Barb decides she
will take the initiative to get some information to plan the trip. Barb
arrives home announcing, "Hey Honey, I picked up some vacation
brochures at the travel agency this afternoon."

Tim barely acknowledges her and does not express any genuine interest.

Barb is not daunted by her disinterested partner and continues, "I picked up brochures on Hawaii. I really want to spend time
relaxing in a tropical paradise." Barb neglects to express any real concern about how and where Tim would like to spend his vacation.

"Didn't you pick up any information on France?" Tim asks,
demonstrating what he is interested in without acknowledging
Barb's effort to get travel information or her desire to go to Hawaii.

Barb replies, "No, but just think about the beach, the tropical fruit, the palm trees and the exotic drinks. It sounds like heaven,
doesn't it? I think…"

"I want to go to the Louvre and see the Mona Lisa, not to

mention the Arc de Triomphe and the Eiffel Tower," Tim interjects, failing to respond to Barb's question in his attempt to assert himself. However, his statement seems more aggressive than assertive.

Barb attempts to persuade Tim and keep her cool at the same time suggesting, "You'll really like relaxing in the sun and surf."

Tim thinks she is telling him what he wants rather than asking him. Becoming defensive, Tim shouts, "Don't tell me what I'll like! It's my vacation and I'll spend it the way I want to!" Like Barb, Tim is focusing on himself and what he wants, ignoring the issue of them trying to plan a vacation as a couple and creating further division.

"Well fine," Barb answers. "You do your thing and I'll do mine!" Barb digs her heels in deeper and, like Tim, fails at problem resolution. There is no attempt at negotiation.

Dialogue with Communication

Arriving home, Barb says to Tim, "Hey Honey, I picked up some vacation brochures at the travel agency this afternoon."

Tim looks at her, "Oh yeah? Did you find any place that looks interesting?"

Barb responds, "Well, I picked up some brochures on several different places since we haven't really discussed where we want to go. But I really want to go to Hawaii and spend time relaxing in a tropical paradise." Although Barb asserts her primary interest, she acknowledges that vacation plans are still unclear and that there is room for Tim's input.

"Hawaii?" Tim says incredulously. "You want to spend your vacation laying around a beach? You're kidding, right?"

"No. I'm really stressed out from work and I would like nothing more than to enjoy the sun and surf, eat pineapple and listen to Don Ho for two weeks," Barb answers, laughing. She could have become defensive with Tim's previous question, but instead, she answers him without getting angry or upset.

"Pineapple and Don Ho, a perfect combination," Tim

laughs. Returning to the topic, Tim asks, "So you really want to see Hawaii, huh?" By restating what he has heard, Tim reduces the chances of miscommunication.

Barb answers, "Yes, I think it would really help me reduce stress."

"Well, to be honest, Hawaii doesn't really appeal to me," Tim tells her. "I kind of had my sights set on Paris. You know, the Mona Lisa, the Arc de Triomphe, the Eiffel Tower." Although Tim clearly states his interests, he leaves room for negotiation by using non-definitive phrases like "doesn't really appeal" and "kind of."

Barb thinks for a moment and says, "Hmmm, well that sounds good too, but I feel like I need to get away from the city for a while, to enjoy the outdoors. I remember that we really had a terrific time in Japan a few years ago, but I was exhausted by the time we got home." Barb demonstrates that she values Tim's interests and has considered a vacation like the one he wants to take, but offers a good reason why she would prefer not to go to Paris at this time.

"Yeah, I was exhausted too, now that you mention it," Tim replies, remembering the hectic trip to Japan. "And I know that you have had a tough year with all the changes at work," he says, empathizing with Barb thereby paving the way for negotiation.

Barb looks at Tim thoughtfully and then suddenly brightens. "I have an idea," she tells him. "How about we go to Hawaii this year, but only take one week so that we will still have enough money and vacation time to go to Paris in a few months?" After considering Tim's and her own interest, Barb's brainstorming allows her to come up with compromise.

"If you'll excuse me from the Don Ho concert, we have a deal!" Tim says, laughing. After an open discussion that was neither defensive nor accusatory, a compromise was reached and the issue resolved.

In the example of "Dialogue without Communication," both Barb and Tim are left with the sense that their partners were not listening to what the other had to say. In fact, neither responded directly to any of the other's questions or statements until, in Tim's case, he became so frustrated by the lack of communication and acknowledgment that he reacted aggressively, shouting, "It's my vacation and I'll spend it the way that I want to!"

Though both Barb and Tim were talking, real communication did not take place. Both partners had preset expectations about where they would spend their vacation and like most couples with problems managing their anger, neither could set aside their wants long enough to hear those of the other. Instead, they both became more controlling and inflexible, hallmarks of the angry partner. This is in stark contrast to the example of Dialogue with Communication where each partner stated their own preferences while also listening to what the other felt about them and leaving room for other options. They also restated what they heard to make sure that they understood each other and listened to each other without interrupting.

There are a lot of factors that affect how you communicate, such as your skills—what you know about good communication—and your temperament—whether you are a passive or aggressive type. Other factors also affect your communication style. For example, how you were raised and what you observed as a child in your family are likely to affect how and what you communicate. People who were taught if you don't have something nice to say, don't say anything at all may have a hard time addressing conflict. Socio-cultural factors are also likely to shape your communication style in such a way that men are generally less talkative than women and freer to express anger and aggression while women tend to talk more in general, especially about feelings. These differences need to be taken into account as you develop expectations of your partner and of people in general. Communication problems are, after all, a common complaint of couples in therapy.

Commitment/Trust

A commitment is an agreement about the terms of a relationship and a pledge to stick to those terms. Committed relationships aren't limited to romantic or sexual relationships. You can have a commitment to a friendship, your child, your company or even to some philosophy. But the terms of commitment differ based on the type of relationship. In love relationships, commitment usually includes some sort of understanding about the terms of sexual intimacy, about the level of priority that relationship has over other relationships and about how much and what you share with each other—money, secrets, desires. In other words, the terms of a commitment are like guidelines. They let you know what you can expect of your lover and what's expected of you. Since much of irrational anger stems from inappropriate thoughts and expectations, having clear and realistic terms like, *I promise not to have sex with others,* versus, *I promise to never look lustfully at another,* can help to reduce disappointment and anger in your relationship.

To zero in on your own feelings, ask yourself: are my expectations reasonable? Do I expect my every need to be anticipated and met? Do I expect to control others? Remember how Marcus expected his girlfriends to meet excessively high standards regarding attractiveness, education and attentiveness? Do you feel the same way about the people you date or with whom you get involved?
When things don't go the way that you think they should, do you become enraged and disappointed or more controlling and passive-aggressive? Both extremes are forms of irrational anger. Another trait to develop is a willingness to change or to be flexible. How demanding are you? To what degree do you think that things should go your way? Do you really think that you always know what's best?

The irrational thoughts that we just discussed are not limited to relationships with your significant other. They are present in all relationships: in friendships, in relationships with children, even with people you don't have any significant relationship with, like strangers. The specifics of the thoughts may change from relationship to relationship, but the nature of the thoughts stays the same—irrational.

Chapter 18

Anger Hot Spots:
How the Two of You
Can Handle Them

As we grow to adulthood, we are subject to a wider variety of experiences with more and more individuals and many of these interactions can be quite complex in nature. These experiences are qualitatively different from the ones we have as infants, children and in our early teenage years. Problems in traffic, for example, are really adult worries. As children, we don't have to cope with the actions of other drivers or vehicles on the streets. We're merely passengers, not car operators. We can blissfully let our parents handle the traffic problems while we sit in the backseat, smiling at their angry reactions to the traffic situations they encounter. We're not involved—yet.

Money is a second area in which adult experiences differ from childhood ones. In childhood, most of the early years do not involve the issue of money at all. And later, when allowances or part-time jobs come into play, the main problem is getting enough money to get the gadgets we want as children. We are not forced to deal with the complexities of tax planning, retirement planning, check writing or handling joint bank accounts with our partners. These areas take the topic of money into new, uncharted territory, where the opportunity for conflict and anger is much larger.

Another area where adult experiences are different from that of childhood is in sexuality. Although we experience myriad sensual and sexual events in infancy and childhood the idea of sex is basically foreign to us. We don't have notions of what sexual parameters we enjoy, what we expect from other partners or what their past histories should be. We don't have preconceived ideas regarding what is moral behavior sexually speaking nor do we have previously developed rules about what kind of sexual behavior is acceptable, allowable or compatible with our own comfort levels. For example, a woman may get very upset to learn that her boyfriend is having sex with someone else. However, a five year-old girl, even if she does have a "boyfriend," doesn't have to worry about such a problem.

As we get older, our range of life experiences, including those in the realm of sexuality, gets larger, more varied and more complicated and, as such, offers opportunities for the development of situations to which we can respond emotionally. Each of those situations can be responded to cognitively in a realistic or unrealistic manner. And if they are responded to with self-generated irrational reactions instead of self-generated rational thoughts, then we may develop a problematic set of beliefs, or philosophy of life, which we take into our future relationships. The more situations that an individual responds to irrationally throughout his life, and the more demanding and controlling he becomes as a result of this philosophy of life, the more likely he is to have difficulties relating well to others. This accumulation of past anger can pervade the entire fabric of a marriage or romantic connection.

Past Anger Brought into
Present Romantic Associations

Whether we realize it at the time or not, we enter into close connections with other people with a whole substructure of highly developed, preconceived ideas of the way things *should* be and the way the other person *should* act. And this cognitive edifice has been erected as the result of thousands of previous interactions and circumstances to which we have been exposed as infants, children and young adults. Past anger is like an invisible anchor that we're dragging around. It weighs us down when we try to make a relationship work. Much of this anger stems from resentments regarding past issues and relationships, along with a lot of frustration and a sense of entitlement.

In addition to anger dragged in from past relationships, some of us can also carry resentments about our present lover's past actions, attitudes and feelings. Sometimes aware of these past resentments and sometimes not, we may tend to react in a disturbed manner to any of life's frustrations and our lovers' mistakes. When involved in a committed relationship, we may have unrealistically high expectations of the other person and of the relationship itself. While on our best behavior in the early stages of the courtship, as the relationship progresses, we may develop a possessive attitude or a sense of ownership and become increasingly demanding and dogmatic. The more possessive we feel, the more demanding we become.

Focusing on the dissipation of anger internally involves each partner getting rid of the weeds in his or her own garden first before trying to improve the other person's yard. In our sessions with angry couples, we help them achieve this by recognizing how to manage their anger in four easy steps.

- First, admit that you are fallible.
- Second, decipher the irrational beliefs and philosophies behind your mistakes, uproot these beliefs and replace them with realistic ones.
- Third, recognize that your expectations regarding your lover and the relationship itself are unrealistic. Replace those expectations with more realistic, appropriate ones.
- Fourth, encourage each other to see that you don't have to fix every problem right on the spot, especially when you find yourselves getting angry with each other.

Often, the best thing a person can do when both partners become angry is take a step back from the situation. It is better to let the other person go uncorrected at that given point in time, than to angrily try to change them and challenge them in ways that make a difficult situation even worse. Let's follow through with some of these ideas with a specific couple, Dave and Linda, in a series of counseling sessions. We'll focus on some of the couple's past issues regarding anger, as well as the resolution of those issues to help build a healthier, more romantic relationship.

Transforming Destructive or Stagnant Relationships into Compatible, Mutually Rewarding Ones

We met with Dave and Linda about a year ago. They came to our office bitterly arguing and on the edge of divorce. Their visit was a last ditch effort to save their marriage. They had been married a little over two years. They agreed to commit to weekly sessions with us for six weeks before terminating therapy. We, in the brief period, contracted to provide them with as efficient an analysis of their marital problems as possible and a series of methods and goals they could work on to improve the state of their marriage.

Gathering data during our first two sessions, we learned that Dave and Linda had quite different backgrounds. Dave came from a working-class family and had held part-time jobs ever since he was nine years old, doing everything from delivering newspapers on a paper route during the school year, to working on farms and packing sheds in the summer to put money away for college. His parents had always watched each dollar spent in a very careful way and nothing was ever bought unless it was paid for in cash. His father didn't know how to write a check or balance a checkbook, as he paid for everything on a cash basis. Dave never took money for granted and always had limited himself to the essentials in life, buying standard economy cars, clothes from discount stores and never any frivolous items. He was raised in a very moralistic family and had firm ideas about what was the right way to do things and what was the wrong way. He was intelligent, college-educated and a very hard worker, with extremely high expectations of himself at his job as an engineer, and on the golf course, his only leisure activity. He kept himself fit and had little sympathy for people who didn't.

Linda met Dave in college. She came from a wealthy family and always seemed to enjoy life and have fun. She did not work before or during college. Her parents paid for everything, including the car she drove. She enjoyed shopping, was carefree and didn't believe in saving money for later when she could enjoy it while she was young. She was attractive, and had had a series of boyfriends, but none of the romances was ever really serious. She liked to take risks, had experimented with drugs recreationally and earned average grades in college. She became attracted to Dave because of his looks, his hard work ethic and his sense of humor. He seemed to be the perfect counterpoint to her own lack of true direction in life.

Explaining

We continued to explore the range and depth of the difficulties in Dave and Linda's marriage. As Dave described his early relationship with Linda, everything seemed ideal. He had been attracted to Linda because she was completely different from anyone with whom he had been previously involved. He could never quite predict how she would feel about something and her behavior frequently surprised him. She added a sense of relief and light-heartedness to his nose-to-the-grindstone approach to life. He found himself loosening up when he was around her and he enjoyed her laid back approach to things.

After the first few months of courtship, however, Dave became increasingly frustrated with Linda's carefree attitude and lack of predictability. While at first her actions had amused him, he now grew tired of her non-studious approach to things, her lack of planning and frequent forgetting of important dates and commitments. He tried to educate her to be a little more methodical in her approach to things, as he was, but it fell on deaf ears. She actually seemed to enjoy doing things *her* way. On reflection, Dave came to the basic conclusion that the major source of his problems with Linda was her approach to money. He resented her early life of ease, but had stuffed that feeling deep in his unconscious mind. He agreed that if he could resolve his feelings about her life prior to meeting him, as well as his attitude about the way she spent their money in the marriage, that things could probably work out.

Linda, like David, had been initially attracted to his differences, his serious nature and mature approach to life. Like his feelings toward her, it had been a short term attraction. After a while she found his attitude tedious. He never seemed to be spontaneous and always seemed to analyze his every move, planning each step of the way in minute detail. He never seemed to be able to make a quick decision. Furthermore, his constant emphasis on how money was to be saved and invested and spent on only necessary things at this point in their lives, seemed unnecessarily frugal to her. She felt that things would work out financially. Dave had an excellent job and was in line for promotion. She couldn't understand his constant worrying about money. It seemed to pervade the entire structure of their marriage. She couldn't even enjoy sex with him anymore, because of her resentment about his attitude concerning money. Much like David's wish for her to change, Linda agreed that if he could loosen up a little about his financial approach to life and cut her a little slack on her spending, that basically they could probably have a pretty decent, even happy, marriage. Everything else could probably be worked out, they both agreed, although they expressed considerable doubt that much progress could be made in the next month.

We pointed out that many brides and grooms are clueless about financial matters in marriage. Discussion of them seems too unromantic during courtship and the subject really doesn't get dealt with properly in terms of shared understanding about goals and commitments. It's therefore not surprising that conflicts are going to arise regarding the issue of how to spend money, what to spend it on and how much to save. In fact, according to a 1995 Roper-Starch survey of 1,117 adults, conflicts about financial issues top the list of items about which couples fight. This certainly seemed to be the case with Dave and Linda. We also told them that according to a recent CitiBank survey, in fifty-seven percent of couples who get divorced, they do so because of money matters. We pointed these things out to Linda and Dave to help them normalize their predicament, to let them know they are far from unique in having the types of problems they're experiencing.

Our next task was to work on the specifics of Dave and Linda's own marriage, and to show them how their faulty attitudes from the past were affecting how well they were coping in the present. Most of these attitudes had to do with thoughts and philosophies that generated considerable anger on both their parts. We showed them that first they must deal with some hidden and not so hidden beliefs that were affecting their joint anger and then we could move on to taking concrete steps to straighten out their financial situation. It was quite a struggle to get them to see how their thoughts affected their attitudes. Finally, we presented to them an *in vivo* experience which convinced them of the importance of thoughts in emotions. We gave them an exercise right in the office: "We want you two to get really mad right here, right now, okay? The only requirement is that you don't *think* about anything while you're doing it—try not to have one thought in your mind, okay? All right, go!" After one minute of intense concentration, they gave up. A light shone in both of their eyes. When they realized that they couldn't just *get angry*, they understood the connection between their anger and their thinking.

Although the specific circumstances and past histories of both Dave and Linda were quite different, the underlying dynamics of their anger problems were essentially the same, as they usually are in cases of irrational anger. We spent most of these sessions helping each of them to see how similar attitudes caused anger in each of them.

Dave carried a heavier anchor of anger into the marriage than Linda did. He had the added onus of a huge link of perfection-ism. Dave had been taught this style of thinking early in his life by his parents, but he also generated a considerable amount of it himself as he grew older. He came to think that the more perfect he was, the more people would like and respect him. Perfection became linked with approval in his eyes. As we worked with him he came to see how his need to be perfect placed an insurmountable burden on him. Holding oneself up to a perfect ideal is an impossible goal. Even if, on occasion, he succeeded in doing something that met his standards of perfection, he wasn't off the hook. The perceived approval was only transient in nature, and he had to continually do things perfectly in order to maintain that approval. When he didn't, he became depressed, since he lost approval in his own eyes. He also became angry with himself for his fallibility. And during the hiatus between accomplishments, he confessed he carried around a large amount of inner anxiety, as he was always *worried* that he wouldn't do well at the next test. We got him to see how his perfectionistic thinking made him anxious, upset and angry most of the time. Therefore, his moments of satisfaction and happiness resulting from his accomplishments were short lived indeed.

We also worked with him on reflecting and monitoring more precisely just how his friends and acquaintances acted when he did something extremely well. Not long afterward, he confided to us that after getting feedback from several friends that they were secretly envious of him when he did well, and although they may have had some grudging respect for him, it tended to distance him from them as they felt insecure and inadequate around him. When we gave him the assignment to make at least a small mistake on his next relatively unimportant encounter, he found to his astonishment, that his friends actually became *friendlier*, warmer and more open with him! When he combined this with the knowledge that all humans, including himself are fallible and, as such, are bound to make mistakes, he started to cut himself and Linda a little more slack and no longer became so angry with Linda when she occasionally erred.

When Linda realized how Dave felt about doing things perfectly and that his very self-worth depended upon it, she began to be more tolerant of his behavior in this regard. Linda began to make a point of showing extra loving behavior to him when in fact he did act more human and make mistakes. She found him very receptive of her approval under these circumstances. As he began relaxing more and more in his behavior around Linda, another key ingredient of his anger, a rigid, intolerant and dogmatic attitude, started to dissipate considerably.

As Linda and Dave began to see that his rigidity and dogmatism were inextricably linked to his need for perfection, they began to experiment with our help in applying more flexibility and different approaches to "hot" issues between them. Dave also began to recognize that there is more than one way to do things. For example, Dave began to see that even though Linda's approach to many things was considerably different from his, she also had some excellent ideas about how to do certain things. As a consequence of the change in Dave's behavior, and our work with her in the therapy sessions, Linda began to see how her own lifestyle tended to promote a rather limited way of looking at things and that the world was a much larger and more complex place than the experiences in her family had led her to expect. She, in turn, became more open to novel ways of looking at things too and didn't reject them outright, just because they were strange, unusual or awkward for her to consider. She learned that she could, in fact, tolerate a little discomfort, and became more patient in trying to reach a better understanding with Dave.

Unrealistic Expectations and Demands

It was a real struggle to get both Dave and Linda to admit that neither was completely right and that they both had very unrealistic expectations of how a marriage should be and how their partner should act. Both had a lot of anger toward the other left over from early arguments in the marriage, mostly concerning finances. Dave had felt that the economics of marriage were basically cut-and-dried and that Linda needed to see how doing things his way was the best way. When she had the *audacity* to see things differently, he became enraged. *How could she do that?* he kept asking himself. *It's clear, from my calculations that this is exactly how much money we need to put away each paycheck if we're going to have the amount of retirement income I've projected for us.* He *expected* Linda to see it the same way he did. When we asked Dave why Linda has to see things exactly the same way he does and where it is written that she must be identical to him, Dave kept coming up with cogent and practical reasons why it would be better if she did see things his way. We responded that we couldn't agree more. To this, Linda gave a look of shock. We continued, asking why, just because it would be better if she did, does that prove that she *has* to see things the same way as he does.

Dave became flustered. Despite all his attempts to prove otherwise, after much mulling and fretting, he was forced to the conclusion that we had a point there. Try as he might, he couldn't prove that Linda *had* to agree with him on his retirement plan and weekly investments. The fourth session turned out to be two hours long. It was emotionally draining for all four of us. Finally, he stated, "You mean that even though my idea is clearly best here, that Linda still doesn't have to see it the same way? That she has the right to look at it differently? To even be wrong about it?"

"Yes," we almost shouted. "You're getting it!" A small smile of understanding crossed Linda's face.

They both began to see that there was room for differences of opinion and that indeed, neither one of them was *mandated* to do things any given way since obviously if that was the case, everyone, including them, would be doing things the same way. This is where the real breakthrough occurred in helping Dave and Linda see that they didn't have to keep hanging onto their previous attitudes. They could change, if they just worked at it. They stated it was harder to do than they thought it would be when they first came to therapy. But it was definitely possible.

We applied the same reasoning to Linda's own laissez faire approach to life and finances and she began to see that not all people looked at finances the same way her parents did and that indeed, people, because of their own experiences, may have drastically different approaches to money matters. At last, Dave and Linda came to appreciate that just because something would be better, it doesn't necessarily *have* to be that way. After all, it would be better if earthquakes didn't happen, but they *do*. As long as they stuck with preferences, instead of rigid demands, they left each other with some negotiating room and a forum for communication was opened for both of them. Preferences were reasonable, realistic and workable in the marriage. Demands were unrealistic, anger-arousing and problematic.

As a consequence, both Dave and Linda started to see that when they were flexible and tolerant, they could in fact *stand* it when the other person disagreed with them and that it wasn't horrible when the other person looked at their financial situation differently. Therefore, they realized, the other person didn't need to be condemned and chastised for his or her approach. As a result of these insights and much practice and dialogue in other "hot spot" areas as well, where we applied the same principles of preferences versus demands, Linda and Dave felt ready to deal with some of the specifics of financial management.

The Last Two Sessions

We began the fifth session with a review of the principles and lessons learned earlier. We went over the notion of unrealistic expectations, not only in life in general, but in relationships as well. We reiterated how perfectionistic tendencies in thinking and attitude lead to irrational demands and rigid, dogmatic attitudes. Once those demands and perfectionistic approaches are brought into line with reality, a more flexible and tolerant attitude is engendered in both parties. Instead of striving for an A+ all the time, we reinforced the notion of shooting for a good solid B. In fact, when this is done, the pressure to perform is greatly reduced and the quality of work often surpasses that B level. Finally, we went over the previous week's homework assignment: Both Linda and Dave had been given the assignment of doing something imperfectly. Then they were to write down arguments for why preferences were preferable to demands in their marriage. Both had done their homework, and came to the session ready to work on the final steps of dealing with their financial impasse.

We aren't financial experts, but we did use this session to offer a few basic tips on money management. We emphasized to Dave and Linda that getting their anger under control before attempting to communicate about money was a necessary and significant first step for them. Next, we suggested that effective communication is essential when discussing such matters. Thus, it was important to set aside a specific time each week devoted entirely to their major anger hot spot: money management. We strongly suggested not trying to talk money matters when Linda was preparing dinner or when Dave was working on his income tax returns. A calm, quiet time should be specifically utilized for discussions of areas between couples which generate anger. Neither Dave nor Linda felt it was necessary to schedule a *specific* time to discuss money—they felt it should be more impromptu, but they reluctantly agreed to give it a try.

In the last session, we urged them to establish a pattern of brainstorming, where no ideas could be dismissed prematurely, no matter how crazy they may seem at first. Then, they needed to decide on a mutually agreeable strategy for money managing, realizing that there was no perfect solution here, just better or worse alternatives. They might consider a joint or separate checking accounts, for example. The idea was to be empirical and flexible, to try something for a while and, if it worked, keep it. If not, consider changing to another strategy.

We also stressed the need to develop a monthly budget to provide an awareness of what they were spending for purchases, savings and investments. This would give them an idea of what their non-discretionary expenses were and what they would have left over for play money. It would be a while, we stressed, before their budgeted expenses got to be good predictors of actual expenses. We suggested the need to build an emergency fund to avoid panic when unpredicted money crises developed. Lastly, we urged them to beware of plastic—try just using cash or checks for the next six months to avoid overextending themselves.

Dave and Linda didn't agree to all of the suggestions and concepts we presented, but they fully committed to working on their anger toward each other by changing their demands to preferences whenever they spotted these distortions in their thinking, and to concentrate on a monthly budget. They understood that there is no magic in therapy, only a lot of hard work and practice and that improvement doesn't necessarily come easily. They returned for a follow-up visit three months later, reporting much progress in managing their anger and in developing a financial plan they both could live with. We had them keep an informal log of their anger episodes which revealed that their anger never totally disappeared, but it went from about twenty flare-ups a week to approximately two a month. When they told us this, they said, "We both can live with that."

There were very important lessons learned by Dave and Linda and hopefully by you and your partner. First of all, you should understand that anger can be generated not only from present situations and conflicts, but also from memories of past events, and that irrationally rethinking old problems can bring about a present state of anger. Therefore, before attempting to resolve any current conflicts in your life and relationship, it is important to deal with this anger first. Doing so helps you to avoid making a bad situation even worse. Making yourself aware of how this past anger is brought out in the present will also help you to identify and deal with it in your own life. The major causes of bringing past anger into the present are unrealistic expectations, demanding instead of preferring attitudes and perfectionistic tendencies. Once you uproot these, the sense of self-righteous rigidity gives way to a flexible and compromising approach to conflict resolution. Remember, to really build these cognitive changes into your personality, you must institute new behaviors based on a rational approach and then practice these behaviors.

Partner Homework

1. Figure out what the anger hot spots of your relationship are.
    Each partner should make a list on their own, then compare the
    lists and combine them into one overall list.

2. Plan to do at least one thing imperfectly each week—see how
    you feel when you do. Share your experiences with your partner.

3. Each partner should write a list of "shoulds" you may have about
    each other—examine them together to see if they're realistic.

4. Both partners should consider which areas in their relationship
    must be compromised to satisfy them.

5. Both partners should consider and discuss what changes they
    would be willing to make to accommodate the other's needs in
    areas that are especially important for each of them.

Chapter 19

Managing Anger
through Discharge Techniques:
Is It Enough?

*"You cannot change the outer event...so you must change
the inner experience. This is the road to mastery in living."*
—Neale Donald Walsh

Simply put, discharge techniques are behavioral strategies that help us reduce the energy associated with anger. By now, it is clear that anger can take many forms, obvious and subtle. Certain forms of anger, especially rage, are often accompanied by a surge of energy caused by an adrenaline rush. This energy is a large part of what makes some anger so uncomfortable. The physical symptoms of such a rush include accelerated heart rate and breathing and sometimes feeling flushed or shaky. The cognitive effect is getting stuck on a problem and being unable to change focus to something else. Because of these obvious symptoms, traditional anger control methods have focused on behavioral strategies to discharge anger, that is, ways to reduce the energy associated with the rush, thereby reducing uncomfortable symptoms. The underlying theory of discharge techniques is that if we reduce the energy associated with anger, we are less likely to explode in anger, and less likely to escalate the anger.

Band-Aid vs. Real Change

Now you're probably thinking, *If the root of anger is irrational thoughts, how are these superficial changes going to help me master my anger?* The fact of the matter is that their value is limited because they focus on symptom relief, rather than the core issue of irrational thoughts. Hence, these techniques alone usually fail. When we focus on symptoms only, we merely learn to *act* less angrily. The irrational thoughts that fuel anger persist so we still *feel* angry. Eventually, those feelings win out over symptom relief and soon we're headed down that familiar path called anger.

This is not to say that discharging anger doesn't count for something. It does. It helps us to calm down and to feel less overwhelmed. Discharging anger provides us with an opportunity to evaluate and correct irrational thoughts at the core of our anger. So while these techniques are rarely useful by themselves, they may be valuable when used in conjunction with skills that combat irrational cognitive patterns. The following analogy applies here: treating a broken leg with pain killers isn't enough; you must set the bone. The same is true with anger: symptom relief is not sufficient; in order to master anger we must treat the source—our irrational thoughts.

Tess, 31 years old, came to the clinic complaining about weight problems. She reported that since settling into marriage with Hank, 23 years old, she had been rapidly gaining weight. Marriage had been pretty good, though she was stressed about Hank's difficulty holding a steady job. Still, Tess loved him and figured that eventually he'd find the right position.

Tess's therapy focused on her frustration with Hank's sporadic employment, while sessions with a nutritionist focused on diet for weight loss. It didn't take long to recognize that as Tess lost weight, she became more frustrated and, eventually, openly angry with Hank. She found herself yelling at him, calling him names and blaming him for all of their problems, not just the financial ones.

Tess used food to stifle both her anger and underlying irrational thoughts such as: *Marriage will make Hank more responsible* (inappropriate expectation); *Hank is lazy* (judgment); *He's supposed to be taking care of me* (demand); *I can't stand feeling like I'm supporting him* (low frustration tolerance). When the discharge technique of eating was removed, Tess's anger surfaced.

Tess did not like the person that she was becoming and, in fact, told her therapist that she would rather gain all the weight back than allow herself to destroy her marriage. Tess's therapist had just begun to focus on Tess's irrational cognitive patterns when Tess discovered aerobics. Though she hadn't made any changes in her thought patterns, she had noticed that she wasn't as angry all the time. She felt as though she had a new lease on life. Whenever she felt angry at Hank, she just took off for the next aerobics class. It felt good to do something for herself. So good, as a matter of fact, that Tess was ready to drop out of therapy until we began to question what motivated Tess to go to aerobics: doing something good for herself or being away from Hank. The fact that Tess even had to think about the answer to that question helped her to see how angry she still was and how much trouble her young marriage was in.

Healthy Ways to Discharge Anger

While there are a lot of techniques to discharge anger, some emphasize mental activities as outlets, while others emphasize physical outlets. All tend to fall into one of two categories: *self-soothing techniques* and *distraction techniques*.

Self-Soothing Techniques

Self-soothing techniques are simply activities that we engage in to help ourselves feel better when we are angry or otherwise distressed.

Usually, they are physical acts that reduce uncomfortable symptoms of anger. They are important skills to have since the circumstances of life are often frustrating, and their solutions rarely immediate. To be in a healthy relationship, to cope with the discomfort of some forms of anger, we all need to be able to comfort ourselves to some extent. Most self-soothing techniques directly focus on decreasing the physical symptoms of anger's adrenaline rush. The danger, of course, is using these techniques at the expense of addressing the real issue.

• *Exercise*

How many times have you gone out for a jog or a bike ride when you were feeling really angry? If you've tried this, you have probably found that you felt better after a bit of exercise. You see, aerobic exercise, like biking and swimming, helps you to discharge the excess energy associated with anger. But even better than that, this type of exercise actually helps your body to produce endorphins, chemicals that improve mood.

• *Time Out*

Removing ourselves from situations that stimulate our irrational thoughts also allows us to discharge anger. We can reduce the discomfort of anger when we change environments, from stressful to peaceful. The most commonly espoused time out technique is walking away when we are in a situation that is making us angry. We simply leave before we get too hot and bothered. This technique is especially useful for people who become violent under such circumstances. Leaving the situation is a good start, otherwise someone could end up getting hurt.

• *Blowing Off Steam*

Have you ever screamed into a pillow or beat your bed or savagely waxed your car or floors when furious? Well, these are all examples of blowing off steam. These techniques are similar to exercise in that you discharge the physical energy of anger on these tasks. The only difference is that these tasks are usually more direct expressions of anger than, for example, jogging.

Distraction Techniques

Distraction techniques focus on mental, rather than physical, outlets for discharging anger. The idea behind these techniques is to get your mind off of your problem long enough for you to get a grip. This means discharging excess mental energy so that you can think rationally again and appropriately deal with the problem. The assumption, of course, is that we all think rationally when we are not burdened by mental effects of the adrenaline rush.

There are a lot of different distraction techniques that people use. Some play a computer game, others bury themselves in their work. One very popular distraction technique is counting. How many times have you heard people say, "When you're angry, count to ten before you say or do anything?" Counting is the mental counterpart to walking away. It mentally takes you out of situations that stimulate irrational thoughts by focusing your attention on a mental task. This presumably gives you some time to re-think the situation, as well as your options for coping with it.

• *Meditation*

Meditation is a mental exercise where we focus on something specific like breathing, or a certain image to calm ourselves. Beyond the mental distraction, meditation, like exercise, can affect our body's chemistry, helping to reduce symptoms of anger, thereby boosting its efficacy as a discharge technique.

Other Potential Discharge Techniques

Yoga
Tai Chi
Deep Breathing
Prayer

Hobbies and Sports
- Arts and crafts
- Gardening
- Cooking
- Going to the batting cage
- Rollerblading
- Going to the driving range

Chores
- Cleaning the house
- Washing the car

Reading

Journal writing

Talking with a friend

Listening to calming music

Watching a silly or engrossing movie

Take a moment to list some of your favorite discharge techniques.

Do Not:

Operate any heavy or potentially dangerous machinery
- Cars
- Power tools

Engage with weapons
- Guns (avoid the shooting range)
- No knife-play
- No wood chopping

Discharge techniques can bring you temporary relief and perhaps even reduce incidents of rage to allow you time to think before acting irrationally. Beyond that, they alone will not improve how you manage anger with your partner, nor will they significantly improve your relationship since the goal of each and every one of them is symptom relief, not conflict resolution. As such, without skills for combating irrational thoughts at the core of anger, discharge techniques increase the likelihood that conflicts are pushed to the background, only to resurface later.

Unhealthy Avenues for Discharging Anger

The appropriate way to use discharge techniques is as a stop-gap between irrational thoughts and angry behavior. Just as there are healthy ways to discharge anger, there are also unhealthy ways.

- *Medicate the Anger*

Let's face it, we live in a culture that demands a fast, simple solution for even the most complex issues. Our approach to anger is no different. So, many people find themselves using drugs or alcohol to help them "mellow out" when they feel angry. Using alcohol and certain drugs alters our brain chemistry and, in doing so, discharges anger chemically by inhibiting the adrenaline rush. Some people have a drink to relax and relieve symptoms, others take a Valium and still others use street drugs like marijuana. But anger is a cue that something is wrong. When we chemically discharge this cue, we are less likely to address the immediate problem and, therefore, more likely to be confronted by it again. Beyond this, anger is a part of being human. If drugs or medication is the way that we cope with this very human experience, we will end up using these things frequently. In other words, we'll probably end up addicted to something.

- *Feed the Anger*

If you're like most people, food is very comforting. It soothes us, helps us feel good and distracts us from daily stressors. It is not surprising then that when uncomfortable feelings of anger crop up, many head for the refrigerator, recognizing that the rush of anger can be discharged by devouring a gallon of ice cream, just as it can be by sprinting a mile. Again, since there is no such thing as an anger-free life, those who use food as a means to discharge anger often end up with another problem—excess pounds.

• *Excessive Exercise*

The adrenaline rush is almost always a part of overt anger and is one of the things that makes people so uncomfortable with anger. It didn't take long for people to figure out that if they discharged some of that energy, they would feel better—less explosive, less irritable, less frustrated. Maybe you do this yourself when you're angry: pump iron, go for a run, or beat pillows with you fists. *What could be wrong with this technique?* you ask. After all, exercise is good for you, right? Well yeah, but just as with food, alcohol and drugs, you can become addicted to exercise too, since it also changes your body's chemistry by increasing endorphins. Furthermore, too much exercise can have a bad impact on your body, potentially leading to excessive injuries.

In addition to the fact that exercise has an addictive quality, research shows that certain types of exercise can actually increase aggression. Experiments have been conducted where people are told to punch a life-sized doll when frustrated. Over time, it was found that the subjects in the experiment not only hit the doll more often but they also threw harder punches! So, certain types of aggressive exercise may actually increase anger and hostility.

Avoidance: The Downside of Discharge Techniques

Clearly, discharging anger helps us to feel better whether we do it in constructive ways, like throwing ourselves into our work, or destructive ways, like using drugs. Anything that helps us feel better carries with it the risk of overuse. At best, discharge techniques are useful as a stop-gap; at worst they are mechanisms of avoidance. Too often we find that our clients who use discharge techniques do so at the expense of working with their partners to resolve conflict. Any time we use discharge techniques without the intention of following up with the problem at hand, we are practicing avoidance. The fantasy here is that if we can distance ourselves from problems long enough, the problems will disappear.

Returning to the example of Tess and Hank, Tess began to see that she had traded one discharge technique of overeating for another—exercise. More importantly, she saw that she was using exercise to avoid her anger and marital problems. Once she understood that she was using discharge techniques as a substitute for developing anger mastery skills, Tess got serious about her therapy. She started a journal to help her develop insight into: key irrational thoughts, unconscious triggers and ways in which she acted out her anger. After some clarity in these areas, Tess was able to develop more neutral, rational thoughts to combat the irrational ones. She even invited Hank into some sessions to focus on both clarifying her triggers and problem solving around them.

Through journaling, Tess came to recognize that while Hank was significantly younger than her previous boyfriends, she had the same expectations of him: he should be settled in a career, educationally equipped to successfully climb the job ladder and able and willing to be the sole provider so that she could get on with starting a family. She had forgotten that his youthful good looks, high energy, sexual prowess and carefree live-and-let-live attitude were what attracted her to him in the first place—all qualities that were diametrically opposed to her demands of him as her lifelong mate.

By addressing her irrational cognitive patterns, Tess was able to develop more reasonable expectations of Hank, reduce her demands of him and gain his help in negotiating a life plan that came closer to accommodating the priorities of both. Although they started out on a bumpy road, Tess's anger mastery skills will go a long way in smoothing the path ahead.

It's easy to see how these discharge techniques can be used to take the edge off of some forms of anger. And if, in fact, you are able to count to ten, or go for a vigorous bike ride and then get back to resolving the problem at hand by negotiating rather than controlling the situation, you are constructively utilizing discharge techniques.

What this tells us is that you have the skills to manage your anger and resolve problems; you just need a moment to calm yourself before you can apply your skills and our advice to you is to keep on doing what you're doing. This is the value of discharge techniques: buying time so that you can figure out how to best apply your anger mastery skills. However, if you lack such skills, discharge alone will not help you to see the distortions in your thinking, develop other ways to approach the problem, or lend you communication skills to work with your partner.

Myths of Discharge Techniques

•   *Calm Means Rational*
One of the major problems with discharge techniques is the inherent assumption that a calm person is a rational one. Not true! Tess was quite calm once she replaced food with aerobics. Yet, both her irrational thoughts about the way that Hank should be, and the destructive effects of her anger persisted. We have to learn to think differently in order to wipe out irrational anger. What makes anger irrational isn't just the behavior, but the underlying thoughts that incite anger. We may be able to count to calmness, but we can't count our way to rational thinking, self-awareness or good communications skills—all of which are necessary to stamp out destructive anger.

•   *Discharge Techniques Are Universal*
Until now, discharge tips and techniques have been touted as *the* means of anger management. Yet, these techniques offer only temporary symptom relief that can only be successfully applied to certain types of anger, those types that are associated with the hot rush of anger. As noted earlier, the idea is that by discharging anger, we reduce the energy of anger, the symptoms of anger, thereby avoiding explosions of anger. But simply avoiding the explosion is not mastering anger, for the source—irrational thoughts—still exists and the

problem persists. Besides, many forms of anger are not rageful at all. Some are quiet and, therefore, not associated with adrenaline rushes and related symptoms. These quieter forms, however, are just as deadly to our relationships, manifesting themselves as passive-aggression, avoidance and distancing. Given the absence of the rush, techniques for discharging anger contribute little to coping with these types of anger.

The Final Word on Discharge Techniques

Although discharge techniques can be helpful in coping with the rush or rage, they are inadequate for mastery, as they focus on surface change only, rather than the core problem of irrational thinking. For years, the only weapons we had against anger were discharge techniques. They were better than nothing; they helped to stave off rage. We know now, however, that the primary source of anger is irrational thoughts. This, then, is the place to focus our energy. While it is unlikely that we can eliminate anger from our lives entirely, we can greatly reduce its frequency and destruction by better learning how to control the source, not just the symptoms.

There were many important points discussed in this chapter that you should understand, remember and put into practical use. First, remember that a number of quick-fix techniques have been developed over the years to help discharge anger, including self-soothing techniques and distraction techniques. And, although they can be helpful in reducing the symptoms of some types of anger, the use of such techniques is associated with risks of potential conflict avoidance and failure to acquire the skills necessary to reduce the incidence of anger.

Also, to truly understand why discharge techniques do not work well to remedy the problem of irrational anger, you must remember what irrational anger is. Irrational anger is more than just angry behavior. It's a way of life, based on a philosophy that includes distorted thoughts like unrealistic expectations about ourselves and others and fantasies of control that are deeply rooted in our cognitive patterns, like critical judgment and intolerance. Because irrational anger is not just a behavior, discharge techniques, which ignore underlying thoughts and feelings, are often insufficient for managing it. However, discharge techniques are not a complete waste of your time. Combining them with anger mastery skills can be quite valuable. The former may help us to manage uncomfortable feelings associated with anger quickly so that we can concentrate on applying what we learned about true anger management.

Partner Homework

1. Determine which of the discharge techniques you use most frequently.

2. How does this behavior affect your relationship with your partner in the short run? Does it calm you down or help smooth over conflict?

3. How does discharging anger affect your relationship in the long run? Does it postpone arguments, reduce open communication or allow you to avoid confrontation? Ask your significant other for help on this, if necessary.

4. What information or skills have you learned thus far that you can use instead of or in addition to discharge techniques. How would this be better for you and your relationships?

Chapter 20

Anger Between Partners: Is It All Bad?

Anger is Only One Letter Short of Danger

Most of us recognize that there were times in the past when our anger at our life partner not only got our blood pressure up but made us both miserable in the process. We wish we knew then what we know now. We can all relate to such frustration. But the important thing we hope you've learned from this book is effective ways for you both to manage anger and recognize and change your irrational thoughts and beliefs, rather than relying on superficial quick fixes.

The Destructive Aspects of Relationship Anger

Psychologically Harmful Effects of Anger

One thing is clear—being angry with each other just doesn't feel good. Couples may get angry and vent some steam or be righteously indignant for brief periods of time, but couples don't enjoy being angry for very long. It is physically and psychologically draining and occupies an amount of the couple's attention and concentration that they could have devoted to other more important issues. Most couples don't want to be obsessed and focused only on their anger.

One of the consequences of directing anger at your partner is that it forces you to reject the whole person who has done the injustice to you, rather than the behavior itself. Focusing on the issues at hand, rather than making sweeping attacks that escalate a situation, is more conducive to problem solving. Anger can thus lead to reduced self-control and increase the possibility of acting out. It is damaging to couple communication and to your relationship.

For example, you just caught your wife laughing with an attractive colleague of yours at a cocktail party. You go over to her in a quiet rage, draw her aside from the others, and accuse her of being unfaithful to you. Your imagination wreaks havoc on your mind. You envision her sneaking away for sexual trysts with this man and not having any respect for you or the relationship. You call her names and tell her you are sorry that you married her. She is stunned by your behavior, starts to cry and leaves the party to go home alone. You have taken a glance at a situation she was involved in at the party, drawn several conclusions from it, gotten incredibly angry and said mean, hurtful things to your wife while in this emotional state. Your behavior and speech strongly imply a severe condemnation of her both as a wife and as a person who led you to judge her harshly, rejecting her in the process. When you reject the entire person, there is not much room left for negotiation or acceptance. Even if you and your wife realize you are in crisis and you seek therapy, it's going to take a great deal of work, patience and communication to get your relationship back on track. Had you focused on the danger signs of your anger earlier, resolving the anger would have been a far more attainable goal and you could have maintained a decent, loving relationship with your significant other in the process.

Another consequence of anger, stemming from such irrational thoughts, is that it makes the other person defensive or angry and therefore more difficult to deal with. This in turn escalates the original problem into a situation that is even harder to correct. Partners who have acted out their anger tend later on to get depressed or anxious about their outburst of anger. They regret having had the explosion and worry about the short and long-term effects of their emotional explosion. Partners even get angry about being angry. Displaying anger also tends to stir up bad reactions from the other person involved. A partner with whom you have just had a serious fight is likely to react negatively to you. Anger can compound the problem and deflect your attention away from the real underlying issues, creating additional ones. By getting angry, you think you are dealing with the problem, when in reality it just sidetracks you from it and doesn't solve the underlying conflict between the two of you.

Many people report that they feel totally out of control when they have an episode of angry fury. In relationships and life in general, people do not like to feel out of control. Each partner wants to perceive themselves as being in charge of their own destiny, directing themselves toward fulfillment. When both partners are furious, those goals and objectives are no longer in focus. This feeling of being out of control often leads a couple to inadvertently overreact to the source of their anger, hitting, screaming or taking some other very dramatic action. They use a sledgehammer when they need a fly swatter.

Physically Harmful Effects of Anger

Beyond the emotional issues, there are health problems associated with anger. One of the things that happens to the body when we are angry is that a powerful hormone, adrenaline, and other stress hormones are released in the body. This hormone and the limbic system in the body are primarily responsible for the "fight or flight" response. This response, as well as most other emotional responses, has survival value. It enables the body to engage in extreme kinds of activities. The anger triggers the autonomic nervous system and sends blood pressure soaring, pulse and respiration rates go sky high and the blood supply gets diverted to the skeletal muscles, while the pupils of the eyes dilate. All of these biochemical responses prepare the body to engage in powerful muscular activity—such as hard running or mortal combat. One other side effect of all this bio-chemical activity is that it tends to promote the formation of blood clots. As Dr. Bill Elliott, an internist at Kaiser-Novato in California, states: "Adrenaline can be a very dangerous drug. Seconds after act-ing on an angry impulse, adrenaline pours into the blood stream. Its first effect is to raise the pulse rate; soon after the blood pressure increases. Blood vessels in the skin and muscles dilate… clotting cells in the blood stream become activated allowing the blood to clot more readily, in case you are about to bleed. All these effects can damage blood vessels."

While the effects of short-term anger may have life-preserv-ing value in what they allow the body to do, if these reactions are occurring in the body all the time, like when you're chronically angry, you can be in danger not only in your relationships but with your health as well.

Attention first was widely directed to the relationship between psychological factors and medical status in 1969, when two California cardiologists, Dr. Meyer Friedman and Dr. Ray Rosenman, presented evidence suggesting a relationship between what they called a "Type A" personality and heart disease. There were many facets they included in this Type A personality: a hard-driving nature, competi-tiveness, hostility, tenseness, aggressiveness and impatience. Such patients, they found, were more likely to have angina or chest pain and heart attacks. The Framingham Heart Study, an important, large-scale longitudinal study on the East Coast, found support for this correla-tion also. Moreover, they found evidence that this relationship was equally hazardous for women as well as men. Several subsequent stud-ies have failed to confirm the initial interesting findings, however.

Recently, Dr. Redmond Williams at Duke University, a leading behavioral medicine research center, seemed to find a relationship between hostility and heart disease. He found, for example, that youths who had been identified as having hostile personalities when they were nineteen years old had significantly higher levels of total cholesterol and lower levels of beneficial HDL cholesterol at age forty-two and thus were at higher risk for heart attacks. In *Anger Kills*, a book by Dr. Williams and his wife Virginia, they concluded that a group of men who scored high on a measurement of hostility at age twenty-five had a mortality rate of twenty percent by age fifty. This was five times the rate for those who scored low on the hostility scale. They found basically the same pattern for women. Dr. Charles Spielberger of the University of South Florida has also concluded that anger is probably the deadliest component of heart-attack-prone "Type A" personalities.

It should be noted, though, that other researchers have failed to find this link. Dr. Dianne Helmer, at the University of California at Berkeley, failed to find a significant link between hostility, as measured by certain psychological tests, and heart disease. As Dr. Leonard Syme of the University of California at Berkeley points out, part of the problem that we are dealing with here is the fact that it "may well be the lack of control over the situations that cause anger, rather than the hostility itself" which affects the negative long-term health consequences of anger. Such differences are difficult to interpret, due to the methodological design of the studies, subject differences and statistical techniques. However, the evidence at best seems to imply the definite possibility that anger is not medically good for you and that the most conservative action, given the present state of knowledge, would be to take steps to reduce anger.

Violent Effects of Anger

Finally, at the extreme end of the anger spectrum lies the issue of violence. Violence in domestic abuse is one of the major arenas gaining increasing attention in the media today. Although violence may manifest itself anywhere, as indicated by the frequent occurrences of phenomena like road rage, anger is very destructive in relationships. It is probably fair to conclude that anger is the number one destroyer of relationships, particularly when you consider its pervasiveness and various behavioral manifestations across a wide variety of circumstances. According to the Family Violence Prevention Fund, four million American women were physically abused by their husbands or boyfriends last year. Two-thirds of the attacks on women in general are committed by a person they know—usually a husband or boyfriend. A woman is abused every nine seconds in this country and more than one in three Americans have witnessed an incident of domestic violence. Nearly nine out of ten Americans say that spousal abuse is a serious problem facing many families. This concern cuts across race, gender and age lines. This organization found that women are more often the victims of domestic violence than they are victims of burglary, muggings or all other forms of physical crime combined.

Moreover, the *New York Times* in July 1994 stated that "violent youths are four times more likely than nonviolent youths to come from homes where mothers were beaten by fathers." It is very difficult to solve interpersonal problems when either person is angry. It is virtually impossible to solve these kinds of problems in any type of constructive way when violence occurs.

Anger tends to sabotage our intimate relationships and other personal goals. We don't problem solve very well when we're angry and being angry causes us to be unhappy or to suffer other emotional distress, like depression and anxiety. There is a lot of physiological wear and tear on us when we are chronically angry. It isn't good for our hearts and it leaves us drained emotionally. It also has a poor modelling effect for others around us, especially the person closest to us.

Anger as Manipulation

Anger can also be used *as a way to* manipulate or intimidate a significant other. If my husband comes home two hours later than he promised, my display of temper may cause him to change his behavior in the future. This may not work, however. And even if it does, the detrimental effect it has on the relationship is probably too high a price to pay. In a similar manner, if I feel threatened by whether or not I can perform adequately with my sexual partner, getting angry with that person offers a convenient excuse to refrain from sexual intimacy. It serves as an opportune red herring of the moment by distracting us from the real issue.

The Benefits of Anger in Relationships

The Flashing Red Light

There are some advantages to anger in relationships. It lets us know that something is wrong. It serves as a warning signal, a red flag. If we never reacted with the initial anger about and toward our partners, it is very unlikely that we would have the motivation to go about changing the situation itself. If my companion is nice to everyone and neglects me, my anger may lead me to do something about it. It brings the event to the center of my attention. I can choose to ignore it or I can talk to my partner about it. I can work harder to help ensure proper attention from him the next time around. Or I can leave the relationship. Without the original feeling of anger, it is unlikely that I would do anything about the unfair treatment.

Anger also has a definite survival value for us. *It energizes the body* biochemically and mobilizes us for immediate, powerful action, the "flight or fight" response discussed earlier. This biological derivation and function of anger is a very important concept to remember.

Anger can also serve to protect us from a significant other by keeping him or her at a distance. It helps keep our more vulnerable feelings, such as hurt, from reaching the surface of awareness. It serves to distract us from other emotions, such as fear and anxiety, that can have an even more negative impact on us. If I react angrily when my sweetheart calls me a name in front of a bunch of people, I serve warning that I am not a wimp, I gear myself for possible further action to deal with the other person and I push down my feelings of being hurt when rejected. My partner, meanwhile, is alerted that I am ready for a confrontation and am not approachable in any kind of psychologically accepting way, at least for that moment.

Anger as Revelation

The expression of anger has informational value as well. It tells others in our presence a lot about our values and beliefs. If someone tells an off-color story or one that is racially biased, then a sense of outrage, disgust or an angry outburst can serve the purpose of communicating a sense of injustice, dislike or non-acceptance. The idea may be expressed verbally, by facial expression or by body posture. The result is that the teller of the story learns about some of the ideals of the receiver by their reaction to the story.

Anger as Release

Anger feels good sometimes. To be completely uninhibited and to spontaneously act in a free fashion can have a paradoxically relaxing effect on us and can provide a certain amount of catharsis. Of course this not holding back can be very costly to ourselves and to our significant other in terms of its consequences. To act furiously in haste allows you to repent at leisure. For example, a person who strikes out and harms his partner is likely to spend some time in jail reflecting on his actions.

Resolution vs. Exacerbation

Resolving anger is necessary for effective problem solving and thinking creatively about ways to get along well with our life partners. If we can do this, we are more likely to achieve the goal of a mutually satisfying relationship. If we can't do this, we can hardly arrive at the compromises and negotiations with the other person in our life. Venting anger usually exacerbates situations. Resolving anger tends to allow solutions in our interpersonal conflicts to occur. It gets us out of the blaming mentality with each other and into the solution mode in our primary relationship.

The problem is that when most couples come for help with their anger, they want help in changing the *other* person whom they perceive to be the cause of their distress. They seldom look inside themselves for a way out of their dilemma. Self-change, not other-change, is the key.

Anger as Taboo

Mental Health Ignores Anger

Though we can see some benefits of anger, in modern culture anger is mostly seen as an ugly, selfish, destructive emotion that is not only uncomfortable for the couples who are our clients but sometimes for professionals, too. This is evidenced by our own profession's attempts to avoid anger. Mental health professionals, more often than not, do not see anger itself as the main problem when a couple goes to them for help. They see it as an offshoot of some deeper problem that needs to be dealt with; they don't recognize the true nature of anger as one of our most powerful emotions in its own right.

Couples often recognize the disturbing nature of their anger long before their therapists do. Sometimes the couples work harder on improving themselves and their relationships and dealing with their anger than do the professionals who are meanwhile exploring the inner meaning of that anger. We all know that human behavior changes slowly one step at a time even when we're really motivated to change it. To have the professionals that clients rely on not even recognize that anger is a major problem only compounds the difficulty in resolving the important therapeutic issues involved. Anger is every bit as legitimate an entity in each partner's psychic makeup as are depression and anxiety. For a couple to change something in themselves, they need two things: they have to want to change and they need a plan.

Anger cuts across so many different problems in our lives and it isn't even mentioned in psychological books or journals.

Generally speaking, professionals are not even taught to talk in terms of anger. The concept of anger itself appears not to be professional enough to merit attention on its own. It is rarely mentioned in graduate psychological texts and the *bible* of the mental health profession, the Diagnostic and Statistical Manual of Mental Disorders, Fourth Edition (DSM IV), doesn't even mention it by name! The DSM IV is a reference publication that contains a comprehensive listing of thousands of psychiatric conditions by which people are troubled, but not anger. As Dr. Raymond DiGiuseppe of the department of psychology at St. John's University concludes from a study he and his colleagues did: "We found [psychologists] don't even have a DSM category to use, even though they claim to see many more anger clients than anxiety clients." Incredibly, the DSM finds a way of talking about anger without ever mentioning the word itself. Parenthetically, it should be noted that anger is not the only important human emotion that this manual neglects. Shame, guilt, and hurt are all commonly experienced by us yet fail to merit mention in their own rights in the DSM IV.

Why Couples Come to Therapy

Generally, when couples come to the therapist's office for help, they come there because, first, their relationship is troubled and unsatisfying and second, they are in some kind of emotional pain. One or both partners is depressed or anxious. They also come in because they are angry—angry at each other and often their bosses, in-laws, traffic and the world at large.

Of course, these categories may be somewhat related in complex manners. The interaction between a person's behavior, emotions, thinking and self-concept is fairly apparent. Any attempt to change one of the factors in this interaction will have an effect on the others.

You can imagine the difficulties we first had when confronted with couples who in a very real sense had problems with anger and yet we couldn't draw help from our training, colleagues, the DSM IV or other books in working with them. Nevertheless, we did the best we could, often trying to make educated guesses and insights as to the appropriate way to help these couples. We had some success using the traditional approaches to therapy, yet we wanted more tools at our disposal. Our goal was to find a technique that quickly and efficiently helped couples get better as well as feel better. The goal was to work like a surgeon, quickly finding the problem and precisely treating it in a way the clients could use to get and feel better almost immediately. What we needed was a conceptualization of the couple's problem that made psychological sense, was accurate and helped the two people efficiently and expediently.

Couples seldom see anger as the underlying problem when they come to our office. Upon arrival, what he or she believes to be their problem may or may not be reflected in any of the standard traditional diagnoses. The clients may be coming to therapy for help in getting their sex life back, but one or the other may be unaware that it is his anger that drove his partner away in the first place. Our job is to help find out what went wrong and to fix the real problem the couple has, which, often, is their anger.

Anger and Hurt

Another point should be made about anger. It often is just the surface feeling of something much deeper—the feeling of being hurt. This is especially true for men. In our culture, it is difficult for men to be open about their hurt feelings. This feeling of being hurt results from attitudes and thinking, often just below the surface level of awareness that are similar to but different from those involved with anger. They are tied to each other in subtle and complex ways that are discernible upon closer examination. Men are also looked upon as weak if they display feelings of vulnerability or sensitivity. Anger, on the other hand, while distasteful to observe, is accepted from men more readily by other men than the hurt that is often beneath it. This is probably the case, in many instances, for women too—although there appears to be a greater acceptance of emotional vulnerability from women in our society than from men.

As we have already noted, angry people tend to have several things in common with each other. They tend to be impatient, perfectionistic, judgmental and have keen senses of humor. They often use anger to defend themselves psychologically, motivate themselves to accomplish things and control others through intimidation. Wouldn't it be neat if there were a key principle that could be used which would cover most, if not all, of the situations in which you find yourself angry? Then, it would be just a matter of applying that principle to the situation at hand.

The Myths of Anger

It's Better to Suppress Anger Than to Vent It

As with anything that is considered a taboo and not to be discussed, many myths have developed around anger. There are many studies that are challenging the old notion that if you hold anger in you will burst. In fact, Dr. Bill Elliott points out that it may not be the anger itself, but the expression of it that leads to problems. Certainly, if your spouse only thinks you're angry when you're silent, the situation is different than when you start screaming at her and remove all doubt from her mind.

Dr. Mara Julius of the University of Michigan found in her study that women who suppressed their anger in confrontations with their spouses had twice the mortality risk of other women, when other factors such as high blood pressure and smoking were considered. On the other hand, in a study at the University of Tennessee of eighty-seven middle-aged women, researchers found that women who vented their anger outwardly rather than suppressing it were the ones whose health was most adversely affected.

As Dr. Jerry Deffenbacher at Colorado State University points out, the research on whether it is better to vent or suppress anger is equivocal at present: while expressing it may provide some temporary relief, it may also serve as a venue to get angry the next time even more quickly and more intensely. According to Dr. Spielberger, what may really count, regardless of whether the anger is vented or suppressed, is how often the intense anger and rage are experienced. Maybe we'll find out that if you vent the anger less often, you may actually *experience* it less often. Some research suggests that venting anger in aggressive ways actually serves to increase aggressive behavior.

Anger Is the Right Response to Injustice

People have ideas that they've learned from others about which emotions are appropriate in given situations. Many people expect us to get angry when a person treats us unfairly and then react strongly if they see us handling it differently and more calmly. Anger does not allow us to think the most clearly and problem solve most efficiently and effectively. Actually, a state of calm, objective detachment probably would allow us to function best in circumstances like these. Although calmness might be an ideal mental state, probably a more achievable, practicable goal would be a state of irritation or annoyance. The angry emotional reaction that is scripted for us by others may be very dysfunctional for us in an intimate situation where we've been treated unfairly, regardless of whether or not others think we should react that way.

Men Get Angry More Often Than Women

Dr. Deffenbacher found that 75% of the cases of anger were in reaction to other people, 25% to objects. Dr. DiGiuseppe found that the number one cause of anger in relationships was a sense of injustice suffered by the angry person—the person was treated unfairly and was infuriated by their feelings about that.

Dr. Ann Frodi at Nazareth College in New York believes that while men are more likely to express their anger outwardly, women tend to internalize it. She believes that this is one reason why women tend to be more depressed than their male counterparts in such situations. In *Men, Women and Aggression*, Dr. Anne Campbell finds that there is little difference in either the intensity or frequency of anger experiences between men and women. They both tend to have them about six times per week on average. She states that a big difference is that women tend to cry, while men tend to move more readily to violence when angry. Note that there is not a direct cause here between anger and violence. If there were, we would all be violent when sufficiently angry. Research clearly implies that this is not the case. Hofstra University's Howard Kassinove, Ph.D., reminds us that perhaps the focus has been too much on the aggression associated with anger, rather than the anger itself.

Anger Can Be Entirely Eliminated

We are, as Dr. Albert Ellis has said, biologically scripted to think irrationally. Since irrational anger is mostly a product of this type of thinking and since the limbic system is an intrinsic part of us, the anger within us is never going to go totally away. This is not even a realistic goal of ours as therapists and authors. Our goal is to have you as a couple and as individuals experience anger less frequently, less intensely and for shorter periods of time than you have in the past. When you can manage to change the quality of that anger to a gentler, more appropriate emotion (such as disappointment, sadness, irritation or annoyance) your relationship will improve. You both can now handle most, if not all, situations in a much more capable and efficient fashion. Congratulations!

Chapter 21

How to Do It:
Applying the Skills You
Learned to Your Own Relationship

Riding the Bike: Applying What You Know

You'll find that the more you use anger management steps, the easier they'll become and the more comfortable you'll be managing your anger constructively. You'll also find yourselves not only *feeling* better, but *getting* better, much sooner than you had ever hoped.

The Faces of Relationship Anger

Remember, one of the key steps to dealing with relationship anger quickly and effectively is to catch it early before it gets out of hand and escalates. Waiting until either you or both of you is in a rage state is much less efficacious. Concentrate on *early recognition*. (Refer back to chapter two for a more in-depth look at the many faces of anger, from the subtle to the overt.) There are two aspects involved in recognizing anger in relationships: identifying the early signs of your own anger and watching for the telltale signs of anger in your partner. The key to catching your own anger quickly is to learn to be keenly attuned to your own internal physical state: your heart beating a little faster, your face warming up and becoming flushed, your breathing quickening and your muscles tightening. Pay attention to how you're talking: is your voice getting louder and speech rate faster?

When Your Partner Is Angry: A Cardinal Rule To Remember— Remain Quiet!

The main thing you want to focus on in building a solid, satisfying relationship is dealing with your own anger. It's also helpful, however to be aware of when your partner is getting angrier. Pay attention to his or her speech rate and voice volume—are they escalating? Watch your partner's eyes—do they seem angry? Are you and your partner interrupting each other? Be sensitive to the content of the conversation as well. If the content is touchy or the subject is one with a history of angry or combative responses, be extra alert.

If you see your partner is losing his composure, but you're still pretty much in control: Don't say anything. Let your partner "vent." Let him have the floor. Don't try to stop him or reason with him. Let him keep talking, with minimal input on your part until he is finished. Pay attention to what your partner is saying, maintain eye contact and a respectful attitude, nod when appropriate, and remember, *remain quiet* and *listen.*

When your partner has calmed down or stopped ranting for a bit, your main message is to let them know you're aware that they are very upset right now, and that you want to work with them to straighten out your disagreement. You don't have to solve the problem instantaneously. Also, don't try to resolve the argument by bringing other issues into the conversation. The main thing you want to let your partner know at this point is that you heard what he said, you understand that he's upset and you want to work with him to address the problem. And resolve to do it. But don't attempt to do it at just that moment. The key is to not try to force yourself on your partner when he or she is upset. Arrange for a time when you can both approach the problem fresh.

The Second Cardinal Rule To Apply When Anger Arises: Take A "Time Out"

When arranging a time to discuss the problem at hand, make sure the designated area is free of distractions. This is a time when you should give each other your undivided attention. The goal at this follow-up meeting is not to resolve the problem between you and your partner. It is to hear your partner out when "cool," to brainstorm and to work on joint communication in order to clear up any misunderstandings or distortions that are in evidence. You can be assured that if your partner is in a rage or irrationally angry, there is a distortion somewhere. Your job is to be a collaborative and helpful detective, working with your partner to find out what and where it is.

Whether or not you resolve the situation at this follow-up meeting is not the crucial thing. The important thing is to communicate that you are committed to keep working on it until both of you are relatively satisfied. That may take some time. With a deep-seated problem, it may take years. Don't be in a hurry and don't be impatient about solving it. Given time, effort and joint resolve, you both can work out the vast majority of difficulties. After you've had the follow-up meeting, do something pleasant with your partner. Reward yourselves by going to dinner, a movie, anything you both enjoy. Couples who enjoy each other better tolerate the frustrations that any relationship is bound to experience. Another important point is that, virtually all problems can be resolved if *both* parties don't go crazy at the same time!

Why We Get Angry: Characteristics That Predispose You to Anger

Review your own personality and behaviors to see if you exhibit many of the common characteristics of angry people. If so, you will initially have to work a little harder on your own anger issues first but you can do it. Do you tend to be impatient? Do you find that you get frustrated easily? Do you possess a strong sense of what is right and wrong? Are you demanding of yourself and others? Do you need to be perfect? Do you have a keen sense of humor?

If so, then you may be prone to getting angry more easily than others who do not possess these characteristics. It's ironic, that the very same features that can make you the life of the party, and an interesting and exciting person to be around, can be your Achilles' heel in your primary relationship. Keep in mind too, that these features, while attractive at a distance or in a casual social context, tend to be exacerbated the closer you become to another person. That is, the closer the relationship you have with a romantic partner, the greater your sense of commitment and of perceived control over that other partner becomes. You subconsciously lose some of your sense of appreciation of the fact that human beings are created independently, and have wills and thoughts of their own. No matter how intimate you are, you cannot control another person's thoughts or actions. You can influence them, but you can't control or dominate them. Just as they can't control or dominate you.

Hot Thoughts: The Warning Flags of Irrational and Unrealistic Thinking That Cause Anger

Once you both have reviewed the faces of anger in your relationship, courses of action to take when your partner gets angry and characteristics that predispose you to anger, analyze what triggers your own angry responses. We want you to turn to this section the next time you and your partner have unresolved issues and are feeling angry or rageful. Dog-ear it or bookmark it. You must deal with your anger before you try to fix the relationship. If you don't, you'll likely make a difficult situation even worse and further disrupt the relationship with your loved one as a result of your anger, over and above what the original situation did. You won't think, problem solve, brainstorm, communicate or negotiate as well angry as when you're calm, cool and rational. Those are the reasons we ask you to tune the engine of your mind before racing it. Here's what to do if steps like remaining quiet and taking a time-out have not lessened your or your partner's anger.

• *Examine Your Thoughts*

When you are angry, we want you to get into the habit of going *internal*. We want you to ask yourself, "What am I thinking right now? What's going on in my head? What am I telling myself?" (Reread chapter three on the ABCs of Anger.) Realize that you may not be immediately aware of *thinking* anything, at least when you first try this. But the more you practice it, the better and quicker you'll be at identifying the thoughts going on inside your head.

Write the thoughts down. Put them on paper so you can examine them more objectively. Remember, some kind of *thinking* is always there when you're feeling emotional or angry. Always. They may be "subconscious" at first, but the more you get in the habit of focusing inward, the more quickly you'll be able to identify what your thoughts are.

Remember, you can't have an emotion without thinking *something*. Try it out again: try to get angry without thinking something—you can't do it. Even if you're not first aware of the thoughts, go back and ask yourself what it could be that's making you angry. Remember, you can have dozens of thoughts within a few seconds. They happen very quickly. Remember, too, that your *thoughts* don't necessarily reflect *reality*. They may but they may not. Your first hint that they don't is if you're feeling very angry and having "hot" thoughts instead of "cool" ones. Recall, also, that the times when you're fatigued or hungry or in physical pain of some sort will predispose you to think irrationally and therefore you'll have to work a little harder at those times to be accurate in your thinking about whatever the situation is that's contributing to your anger.

Review the idea that your thoughts are merely hypotheses to be tested by reality, by empirical data. They are cognitive "maps" of reality, not reality itself. As such, maps can be more or less accurate.

The more accurate your map is, the greater the chance that you won't get lost in a city of anger. Whatever motives you may be finding for your husband's "bad" behavior may or may not be accurate. You need to test them out. When you get angry before testing them out, you're wasting energy and making huge assumptions that may not only make the situation worse, they may be totally false, no matter *how strongly* you believe them to be true. Just because your thinking is intense or even white hot doesn't make it accurate! There is always more than one way to look at or think about things. Your way is not the only way. It may not even be the most accurate way.

- *Debate Your Thoughts: Fact Or Fiction?*

Once you've discovered that it's not the event (A, or what your wife did) that's making you angry but your thinking (B, your beliefs *about* what she did) that's critical here, you can continue with your self-therapy. If your thinking is rational and realistic, your attitude will be well in control. You may be irritated, annoyed, disappointed, or sad, but you won't be angry, upset, rageful or homicidal (as you might be if your thinking is highly unrealistic and irrational).

Do you recall the tests to determine whether your thoughts are accurate (factual) or fiction (mythical)? You can use any or all of the tests we've talked about in chapter fifteen (whether your thinking is logical, whether it promotes your survival or enhances your relationship, whether it leads to emotional well-being or long as well as short-term goals or whether it's factual). We recommend that you use this last goal, factuality, in determining whether your thinking is accurate or not. Remember, while you're in the midst of your anger episode, you are basically taking a time out here to regroup and do your own self-therapy. You may have to actually leave the situation while you're examining your thinking, in order to be effective at it. (After you practice more and more, you'll be able to do it while you're in the upsetting situation itself, but right now, at first, it's best to physically leave the situation so you can concentrate better.)

The second step of your self-therapy with anger is how you learn whether your thinking is factual and therefore, accurate or not (the first step being realizing that you're having some very strong hot thoughts about whatever is going on with your lover or spouse). The easiest way to find out is to ask yourself: "Can I prove what I'm telling myself?" Or, "Where is it written in the universe that (such and such) is true?" If you can't prove it, then, no matter how much or how strongly you believe what you're thinking, you'd better reframe it to something you can prove. Once you've done that, your new feeling state (C, or emotional or behavioral consequence) will be much more manageable, productive and conducive to dealing with the problem and enhancing the romance in your relationship. And if you can't prove or come up with hard data to back up your thought(s), you'd better stick to thoughts or attitudes that you *can* prove. Let's look at this more closely.

- *Find and Fight Your Demands—*
  The Key To Unlocking The Door To Romance

Remember that *the* major type of irrational or unrealistic thinking that's going to make you angry is a demanding, rigid, dogmatic and controlling attitude. We're still in step two here. After you've written down all of your thoughts, *look for the should*, as any good rational emotional behavioral therapist would have you do. If you search long and hard enough among your thoughts, trying to sort out which are real and which are not, those you can prove and those you can't, you'll find the one that's really causing the trouble! *The* major type of unrealistic thought in your thinking is the demands you're making on the situation itself, on your partner, or on yourself. Once you find the demand or "should" or "ought to" or "must" in the situation, you're ninety percent of the way home. Find your demand and try to "prove" it. If you can't, despite your best efforts, replace it with a preference, desire or strong wish. You *can* prove that!

- *Give Up Demands For Preferences*

While you may try to "prove" your demand, we're virtually certain that you cannot. The only thing you'll be able to prove is that it would be *better* if your wife did such and such or that it would be *preferable* that

marriage wasn't so hard or that it would be *nice* if your husband was-
n't screaming at you right now. As long as you stick with this reality,
you will feel in control, relatively comfortable and emotionally on top
of the situation, ready to tackle it in a constructive way. If you go
beyond the real world and into the magical universe of fantasy, you'll
find yourself getting upset and angry, virtually every time. "Because it
would be nice if my wife set better limits with the kids, therefore she
has to." Is that a demand? You bet it is. Is it provable? No. You can't
prove that just because you'd like her to be a better disciplinarian, that
therefore she *must* be that way. You can't prove that your wife *has* to
be the way you want her to be, right?

    Okay, you can use the above examples and apply it to virtu-
ally every situation you're angry about. Look at what you're thinking, find the demand(s) you're making and then see if it's rational or
not by seeing if you can prove it. When you find that you can't,
replace the demands with preferences. Notice the change in your
feeling state. See how much more calm and collected you are.
Preferences are always cool thoughts. Demands are always hot.

• *Challenge Other Unrealistic Thoughts*

Review all the other types of thoughts that you have too. Is it true
that you can't *stand* your husband doing what he's doing? If you're
still alive, then you are indeed *standing* it. Is it *horrible* and *awful*
what your loved one is doing to you or merely a hassle and big pain
in the neck? If it's horrible, then by definition, it can't get much
worse since almost nothing is worse than horrible. Well, can it get
worse? Of course it can. How do you feel when you tell yourself it's
horrible? How do you feel when you tell yourself it's bad, and you'd
like to change it, but you can stand it in the meantime? See the difference? Finally, should your lover roast in hell because she had sex
with another man? Is that the worst thing she could do? Does she
have no redeeming qualities at all? Or is she human and therefore
fallible, and prone to make mistakes, sometimes huge ones? Do you
know any perfect humans?

Post Anger Techniques

By reviewing the above steps in each anger-arousing situation, you will get better and better at being your own therapist and calming yourself down while you defuse your anger. Once you've defused it, you can finish working on the original problem by doing several of the following things.

1. Work on Your Communications:
Opening the Door With a Rational Key

Once your anger is under control, you're ready to work on the problem that you got yourself upset about. By diffusing your anger, you unlocked the door. Now you can open it with effective communications. Review the chapter in this book on ways to enhance your communication ability. Learn to listen more and talk less. Learn to repeat back to your partner what you heard him say, to see if you *really* got it right. A lot of times we think we heard what our spouse said but we were only half listening. And you're not going to be listening well when you're angry. Once you've done your ABCs of anger therapy, go back and really listen to what your loved one is saying this time. Remember that the difficulty may lie in both of you: you may only be half listening and she may not be expressing herself as clearly or as precisely as she could. By going over the details of the upsetting situation in a careful and slow way, you can clear up many distortions and misunderstandings.

Learn to brainstorm, laying all of your options and cards on the table, without prejudging them. Learn to be as scientific and objective as you can when problem solving. The more flexible and reasonable *you* are, the more likely it is that your partner will be too. The more rigid and dogmatic you are, the more likely that is to induce the same behavior in your mate. If you reject outright any or all ideas she may bring up in the brainstorming session, you have closed down communications. Learn to postpone judgment and hold your tongue, while giving your mind a chance to review in a more leisurely manner what she's presented. Your goal should be to include all ideas, no matter how seemingly outrageous at first, as possibilities and then you can narrow them down later.

2. Negotiate

After you've defused your anger, communicated and brainstormed, you're ready to negotiate. The art of maintaining romantic relationships involves the ability to negotiate in loving and caring ways, without prejudging the other person. It consists in knowing that you can allow your partner to have her own way at times. You can allow her to make mistakes and learn at *her* own pace, not yours. It means that you can take your time to iron out difficult situations and don't need to panic just because a very difficult circumstance occurs. It involves realizing that you can't *control* your romantic partner's thoughts, beliefs or attitudes. They are going to do and think what *they* want to do, not what you demand they do. If you try to force your will on them, they will become resentful, angry and distant. Do you like it when you're told you *have* to do something, rather than being asked to do it? These are the kinds of demands that lead to unromantic partnerships.

3. Be Willing to Continue to Work on Your Anger: A Travel Guide

Remember to set regularly scheduled discussion times to begin the process of resolving differences of opinion and goals. You are disputing and uprooting age-old habits and ways of looking at things that you learned from irrational statements made by others in your life or that were generated by your own belief system. Diffusing your anger is not just a one-time process. It takes hard work and practice, over and over again. Recall what we said earlier: the bad news is that you can't blame other people for your own emotional state; the good news is that since you're the one upsetting yourself, you can learn to stop upsetting yourself and get yourself back into control again and defuse your anger by examining your thinking repeatedly. The more you practice disputing your unrealistic thoughts and replacing them with realistic preferences, the easier it gets and the quicker you'll be able to do it. The goal of this book is not to have you totally get rid of your anger. Remember, we're biologically scripted to be irrational and angry at times. The goal is to help you be angry less often, for a shorter duration and to change the quality of your anger from white hot intensity to that of cool, well-controlled disappointment or annoyance. You can handle annoyance and disappointment much better than anger and rage.

Remember to focus on a problem solving, rather than a blaming orientation when conflict and arguments arise. Remember that conflict is inherent in any relationship where both people have brains, as they will occasionally view things differently, and act differently. Monitor your behavior so that you refuse to name-call or engage in abusive behaviors. Stay cued in to traditional triggers that have been a problem in the past. Remember that you probably have anchors of past anger from your own and your shared pasts that can weigh you down and distort the current situation.

The goal of this book is to help you defuse your own anger first, before concentrating on your partner's anger. Remember, undefused anger is *the* major cause of dysfunctional and failed relationships and you, not your partner, are responsible for your own anger.If you make improvements, chances are great that your partner will too. We strongly believe that if you're having fun together and enjoy each other's company because of shared values and interests, then largely eliminating anger from your relationship will keep the romance alive and sparkling. It's not the specific problems that would destroy your relationship, it's your *anger* about those problems. More importantly, it is unrealistic thoughts and a demanding attitude that lead to anger. When you replace demands with preferences, the anger can be more easily defused and problem solving can occur. Even if you don't resolve all of your differences, if you resolve the anger, you'll probably make it and be quite happy. That's our firm belief and our extended promise to you.

Chapter 22

Beyond Self-help for Couples: When Reading a Book May Not Be Enough

We wrote this book for couples who are having problems with anger that are destroying the most important relationships in their lives. Our basic presumption is that neither of you has a history of other conditions which would complicate your attempt to apply the principles contained in this book to your own relationship problems with anger. Sometimes, however, this is not the case. We should point out that there are various conditions and specific characteristics which could complicate your ability to fully utilize the material contained in this book. If these factors exist in your life, you will most likely need more help than is available here. Self-help books are meant to be helpful, but if used inappropriately, they can do more harm than good. In this book, we presume your major problem area is anger. If you have other significant issues going on at the same time, we suggest you must first deal with these before tackling your anger. Let's discuss some of these issues now.

Chemical Dependency

One thing that can really complicate things in your primary relationship and the rest of your life is drug and alcohol use. While the use of prescription drugs can also be a problem, what we are referring to here is the abuse or addictive use of alcohol and street drugs. This includes beer, wine, hard liquor, methamphetamines (e.g. speed), cocaine, marijuana, opiates such as heroin and the psychedelics (e.g., LSD, PCP, mescaline, etc.). There are many other types of drugs out there on the street, but these are some of the most common ones that we find with which people have problems. Dependency on alcohol and drugs creates a type of coping style and personality change that interferes with a person's normal approach to life. He begins to lie, manipulate, cheat and engage in other behaviors that lead others to view him as unreliable and untrustworthy. Until these issues are dealt with, it is very difficult to change the nature of his primary relationship just by working on his anger alone. Moreover, alcohol and drugs rob the brain of its ability to deal with things rationally and thus the main tool that a person uses to deal with his anger is taken away. Alcohol and street drugs act as disinhibitors of behavior and allow initial impulses and emotions to go unchecked by our higher thinking processes. The person is in the boat but has no oars to get him where he wants to go.

Major Psychiatric Disorders

Other kinds of significant psychological problems, such as psychosis, major depression, severe anxiety and PTSD (post traumatic stress disorder), to name a few, will also limit a partner's ability to use this book most effectively. Persons with severe or chronic psychiatric disturbances should have these problems addressed before they undertake reading a self-help book in order to obtain maximum benefit from that book. Once again, this book assumes the absence of other significant mental disturbances. Oftentimes, psychotropic medication can be enormously helpful in allowing the person to focus on her anger issues or giving her the energy to do so. Individual psychotherapy from a competent therapist with the appropriate credentials should also be an important part of the treatment.

Troublesome Early History

A person who comes from an extremely dysfunctional family or who has a history of neglect, abandonment or sexual or physical abuse (either from a family member or a non-relative) would do well to consult with a competent therapist for individual therapy prior to utilizing self-help books such as this to remedy relationship problems. People who have experienced the kinds of behaviors mentioned here are often traumatized to the point that they don't respond well to new input, either verbal or written, until they have worked through the issues generated by these stresses. Individual therapy for any given significant emotional or psychological problem is always the first treatment of choice in such cases. Other, more focused treatment techniques, including self-help books (bibliotherapy), can then be considered.

Physical Abusers and Violent Individuals

Finally, partners involved in relationships where physical violence exists obviously need in-depth help and support. When conflict and anger between a couple have reached this stage, a book such as this can only be of limited help. Working with competent therapists and professional groups with training in this area is the treatment of choice. Other skills (such as providing a safe environment for both the abuser and victim) need to be learned prior to working on the tools spelled out in this book. A book such as this, used in conjunction with or shortly after the initial safety issues and behavioral modification techniques have been applied, can be very useful in restructuring a relationship.

A Final Word

While we have tried to be explicit, informative and helpful, a book, no matter how well written, has some inherent limitations. A major one is the lack of feedback from the reader to the author(s). We can tell you and your partner things, but you can't respond to let us know how you feel or ask questions when needed as you might in a two-on-two therapy context. Barring this drawback, however, a great deal can be gained from this book when you apply the material together and in addition use your own common sense. If need be, consult a professional therapist who shares a similar enlightened cognitive framework for couples such as we present here.

We frequently present anger workshops and you might consult your local sources for a workshop that's going to be in your area soon. If you have any questions about the material or self-help steps presented in this book, wish to provide us feedback or wish to be on our mailing list regarding upcoming anger management workshops, please contact us at one of the following:

Anger Management
P.O. Box 1971
Danville, CA 94526-6971
e-mail: lorelmar@wenet.net
website: http://www.wenet.com/~lorelmar

We look forward to hearing from you!